A Requiem for Evolution

Pierre W. Beausejour

ISBN 978-1-0980-2487-1 (paperback)
ISBN 978-1-0980-2488-8 (digital)

Copyright © 2021 by Pierre W. Beausejour

All rights reserved. No part of this publication may be reproduced, distributed, or transmitted in any form or by any means, including photocopying, recording, or other electronic or mechanical methods without the prior written permission of the publisher. For permission requests, solicit the publisher via the address below.

Christian Faith Publishing, Inc.
832 Park Avenue
Meadville, PA 16335
www.christianfaithpublishing.com

Printed in the United States of America

Author's Notes

Welcome, ladies and gentlemen, to *A Requiem for Evolution*. This is no ordinary book as you will quickly ascertain. A manual that seeks to present irrefutable proof for the existence of God (chapter 3) is no ordinary feat.

An attempt to present to the world a cogent outline of God's thoughts and motives in creating the universe and in allowing the manifestation of evil in His perfect world order (chapter 9) will provide to the reader a fresh and new perspective for a more rational raison d'être of the present world order.

Salvation of fallen mankind, the central focus of the biblical revelation, remains a subject very much alien to the masses and terribly misunderstood by the vast majority of Christians. As such, this book (chapter 10) offers a comprehensive delineation of the most important topic in the Holy Writ.

Do you suffer from HEXAKOSIOIHEXEKONTAHEXAPHOBIA? When was Jesus Christ born? How old was He when He was crucified? Who is the Antichrist? What is Heaven Like? Is Hell real? This volume (chapter 8) offers quite a few insightful tidbits vis-à-vis those important albeit difficult questions.

Is the Bible really the word of God? Are the biblical verses the words of God in the words of men, or simply the words of men? What sets the Bible apart from any ordinary book? The Holy Scriptures relate that its words are not only sacred and true but living. Is that really so (chapter 4)?

How can anyone study the Bible? Is the clergy the only entity with the mental and spiritual fortitude to understand the Holy Scriptures? Quite interestingly, the Bible (chapter 5) makes itself accessible to anyone who is born again, and quite impenetrable to the most intelligent unregenerate mortal. Why is that the case?

Patterns seem to appear everywhere in this world. The people we know, the things we see, hear, touch, taste, and eat seem to embody and exhibit patterns that are fairly consistent. What are some of the patterns of the Holy Scriptures (chapter 7)?

The universe consists of three dimensions: time, space and matter. The Bible is replete with epic historical time references whose accuracy speaks volume vis-à-vis its truthfulness. Are the biblical time markers reliable (chapter 6)?

Evolution the great is fallen…and is fallen indeed. The soliloquies of President John F. Kennedy, William Paley, Richard Dawkins, Nazia, Eugenica, Collectiva and Darwin render the requiem for the fair lady a most solemn occasion (chapter 2). The whole world watches in utter amazement as one of the most celebrated women of all time is eulogized and is finally laid to rest.

The list of the invited guests to the requiem for Evolution (chapter 1) runs the gamut of the crème de la crème of the most influential individuals who have ever set foot on planet earth. In fact, it corresponds to the author's suggestive ranking of the top one thousand most influential individuals who have ever called planet earth home. A sample of the most important people in this world's history rises in unison to carry the darling of the world's elites, the sweetheart of the intellectuals, and the beloved of the rich and powerful to her final resting place: R.I.P., Evolution!

Who do you think are the top 100 most important people of all time? Does your list match the author's (Please, use the "MY TOP 100 INDIVIDUALS OF ALL TIME" form at the end of the book and start ranking your personal list, then post your list on social media, and email it to the author at the following e-mail address: Piwb101@aol.com)?

Learning history really entails studying the men and women whose lives have helped change in a meaningful way the trajectory of the significant events of this world.

Even though He tops the list of the guests of honor, Jesus was not requested to participate in the festivities, and was not even seen in the pews of the Saint-Patrick Cathedral in New York City.

Acknowledgements

To God be the glory, great things He has done!
> To the late Dr. D. James Kennedy whose broadcasts inspired this book.
> To Dr. Ross whose constant naggings remind me to continue with this project.
> To Fred, my Jewish neighbor, who has shown a great deal of interest in the work of a gentile.

Dedication

To my wonderful mother Alaudee (and her best friend Claudette), my faithful father Jean, my brothers Paul (wife Evangeline) and Machli (wife Tessa) (Thanks Machli so much for all the corrections and suggestions!), my sister Eunice (husband Rodin), my cousin Paul Max, my nephews Machli Jr., Leo, Francisque, my nieces Vahlerie & Victoria (Mother Rashell) and Rodnicka, my sisters-in-law Maline, the late Astride and Eol, my brothers-in-law Paul-Andre, Alex & the late Serge, and my aunt Flavie.

The Outline

Chapter 1: The Invited Guests
Chapter 2: The Requiem for Evolution
Chapter 3: The Living God
Chapter 4: His Living Words
Chapter 5: How to Study the Bible: A Poor Man's Biblical Hermeneutics
Chapter 6: A View of Time through the Prism of Biblical Chronology and Modern Dating
Chapter 7: The Patterns of the Biblical Timetable
Chapter 8: An Attempt at Correcting Various Misunderstood Biblical Concepts
- The Fear of the Number 666
- The 70 WEEKS or 70 SEVENS of Daniel 9
- When Was Jesus Born?
- How Many Years did Jesus Spend on the Earth?
- Raising a Few Questions on the Antichrist
- A Pithy Look at Heaven
- A Bird's Eye View of Hell
Chapter 9: All to the Praise and Glory of God
Chapter 10: The Bible Unveils God's Salvation Program for Mankind

Chapter 1

The Invited Guests

1. Jesus Christ
2. Adam
3. Eve
4. Mary (mother of Jesus)
5. Abraham
6. David
7. Moses
8. Elijah
9. John the Baptist
10. Paul the Apostle
11. Enoch
12. Samuel
13. Daniel
14. Isaiah
15. Elisha
16. Noah
17. Joseph (husband of Mary)
18. Muhammad
19. Buddha
20. Confucius
21. Isaac
22. Jacob
23. Solomon
24. Christopher Columbus
25. Isaac Newton
26. Albert Einstein
27. James Clerk Maxwell
28. Michael Faraday
29. Aristotle
30. Leonardo da Vinci
31. Plato

32. Socrates
33. Leonhard Euler
34. Gottfried Leibniz
35. Benjamin Franklin
36. Thomas Edison
37. Guglielmo Marconi
38. Ts'ai Lun
39. Charles Babbage
40. Bill Gates
41. Steve Jobs
42. Johannes Gutenberg
43. James Watt
44. Henry Ford
45. Alexander Graham Bell
46. Nikolaus August Otto
47. Orville Wright and Wilbur Wright
48. James Watson and Francis Crick
49. Alexander Fleming
50. Mark Zuckerberg
51. Edwin Hubble
52. Larry Page and Sergey Brin
53. Jimmy Wales and Larry Sanger
54. Chad Hurley, Steve Chen, Jawed Karim
55. Antonie van Leeuwenhoek
56. William T. G. Morton
57. Joseph Lister
58. Louis Pasteur
59. Marie Curie
60. Wilhelm Conrad Röntgen
61. Otto Hahn
62. Nikola Tesla
63. Edward Jenner
64. Gregor Mendel
65. Galileo Galilei
66. Louis Daguerre
67. Raymond Tomlinson
68. Nicolaus Copernicus
69. Johannes Kepler
70. Charles Darwin
71. Antoine Laurent Lavoisier
72. John Dalton

73. Amerigo Vespucci
74. Tim Berners Lee
75. Max Planck
76. Werner Heisenberg
77. Ernest Rutherford
78. Euclid
79. Rene Descartes
80. Alan Turing
81. Carl Friedrich Gauss
82. Ezekiel
83. Jeremiah
84. Peleg
85. Constantine the Great
86. Julius Caesar
87. St. Augustine
88. Martin Luther
89. John Calvin
90. George Washington
91. Abraham Lincoln
92. Karl Marx
93. Genghis Khan
94. Alexander the Great
95. Thomas Jefferson
96. Alexander Hamilton
97. Shih Huang Ti
98. Napoleon Bonaparte
99. Sui Wen Ti
100. Mao Zedong
101. Cyrus
102. Peter the Great
103. Asoka
104. Lenin
105. Locke
106. Oliver Cromwell
107. Simon Bolivar
108. Adolf Hitler
109. Adam Smith
110. Ezra
111. Nehemiah
112. Joseph (of Jacob)
113. Esther

114. Martin Luther King Jr.
115. Hezekiah
116. Jehoshaphat
117. Uzziah
118. Job
119. John the Apostle
120. Peter the Apostle
121. James (brother of Jesus)
122. James (brother of John)
123. Jude (brother of Jesus)
124. Billy Graham
125. Jonah
126. Ruth
127. Joshua
128. Zechariah
129. Malachi
130. Hosea
131. Joel
132. Amos
133. Obadiah
134. Micah
135. Nahum
136. Habakkuk
137. Zephaniah
138. Haggai
139. Luke
140. Matthew
141. Mark
142. Silas
143. Asa
144. Jotham
145. Josiah
146. Queen Isabella I
147. Charlemagne
148. Louis XIV
149. William Harvey
150. Charles Lyell
151. Donald J. Trump
152. Homer
153. Menes
154. Enrico Fermi

155. Edward de Vere (William Shakespeare)
156. Ludwig van Beethoven
157. Johann Sebastian Bach
158. Wolfgang Amadeus Mozart
159. Sampson
160. Michelangelo
161. Barnabas
162. Umar Ibn Al-Kattab
163. Charles Ranlett Flint
164. William C. Durant
165. James Monroe
166. Walter Chrysler
167. William Boeing
168. Charles Coffin, Elihu Thomson, Edwin Houston
169. Warren Buffett
170. John Stith Pemberton
171. Caleb Bradham
172. St. Thomas Aquinas
173. D. James Kennedy
174. R. C. Sproul
175. Jonathan Edwards
176. Stephen Meyer
177. Ronald Wilson Reagan
178. Jerry Falwell
179. Jimmy Swaggart
180. Immanuel Kant
181. Oprah Winfrey
182. Henry Wells and William Fargo
183. Sam Walton
184. Jeff Bezos
185. Bernard Kroger
186. Bernard Marcus, Arthur Blank, and Pat Farrah
187. Carl Buchan
188. Amadeo Giannini
189. Sandford I. Weill and John S. Reed
190. Marcus Goldman
191. George Dayton
192. Arthur L. Williams Jr.
193. Cornelius Vander Starr
194. James E. Casey
195. Frederick W. Smith

196. Walt Disney
197. Richard M. Schulze
198. Henry Sturgis Morgan and Harold Stanley
199. Eddy Hartenstein
200. Steve Ross
201. Rowland Hussey Macy
202. Jerry Yang and David Filo
203. Evan Williams, Noah Glass, Jack Dorsey, and Biz Stone
204. Pierre Omidyar
205. Craig Newmark
206. Reid Hoffman, Konstantine Guericke, Jean-Luc Vaillant, Allen Blue
207. Kevin Systrom and Mike Krieger
208. Reed Hastings and Marc Randolph
209. James Sinegal and Jeffrey Brotman
210. Franklin D. Roosevelt
211. Saint Clement of Rome
212. Saint Justinian the Great
213. David Berlinski
214. Saint Ignatius
215. Saint Polycarp
216. Saint Irenaeus
217. Papias
218. Justin Martyr
219. Tatian
220. Theophilus
221. Athenagoras
222. Origen
223. Hippolytus of Rome
224. Vladimir Putin
225. Jerome
226. Novatian
227. Dionysius the Great
228. Domitius Afer
229. William Lane Craig
230. Eusebius of Caesarea
231. Gregory of Nazianzus
232. Basil the Great
233. John Chrysostom
234. Augustus Caesar
235. John F. Kennedy
236. Saint Athanasius of Alexandria

237. Tertullian
238. Saint Cyprian of Carthage
239. Saint Ambrose of Milan
240. Saint Bernard
241. Queen Elizabeth
242. Pope St. Gregory VII
243. Pope Innocent III
244. Pope Julius II
245. Pope Paul III
246. Pope Pius IX
247. Niels Bohr
248. Francis Bacon
249. Sigmund Freud
250. Claude Bernard
251. Franz Boas
252. Linus Pauling
253. Rudolf Virchow
254. Jack Ma
255. Paul Dirac
256. Andreas Vesalius
257. Tycho Brahe
258. Comte de Buffon
259. Ludwig Boltzmann
260. William Herschel
261. Pierre-Simon Laplace
262. Joseph J. Thomson
263. Max Born
264. Justus Liebig
265. Arthur Eddington
266. Marcello Malpighi
267. Christiaan Huygens
268. Albrecht von Haller
269. August Kekule
270. Robert Koch
271. Murray Gell-Mann
272. Emil Fischer
273. Dmitri Mendeleev
274. Sheldon Glashow
275. XI Jinping
276. John von Neumann
277. Richard Feynman

278. Alfred Wegener
279. Stephen Hawking
280. Max von Laue
281. Gustav Kirchhoff
282. Hans Bethe
283. Heike Kamerlingh Onnes
284. Thomas Hunt Morgan
285. Hermann von Helmholtz
286. Paul Ehrlich
287. Ernst Mayr
288. Charles Sherrington
289. Theodosius Dobzhansky
290. Max Delbruck
291. Jean-Baptiste Lamarck
292. William Bayliss
293. Noam Chomsky
294. Frederick Sanger
295. Lucretius
296. Louis Victor de Broglie
297. Carl Linnaeus
298. Jean Piaget
299. George Gaylord Simpson
300. Claude Levi-Strauss
301. Lynn Margulis
302. Karl Landsteiner
303. Konrad Lorenz
304. Edward O. Wilson
305. Frederick Gowland Hopkins
306. Gertrude Belle Elion
307. Hans Selye
308. J. Robert Oppenheimer
309. Edward Teller
310. Willard Libby
311. Ernst Haeckel
312. Jonas Salk
313. Emil Kraepelin
314. Trofim Lysenko
315. Francis Galton
316. Alfred Binet
317. Alfred Kinsey
318. B. F. Skinner

319. Wilhelm Wundt
320. Archimedes
321. Joseph Stalin
322. William the Conqueror
323. Elvis Presley
324. Mencius
325. Lao Tzu
326. Thomas Malthus
327. Niccolo Machiavelli
328. Robert Kennedy
329. Gregory Goodwin Pincus
330. Mani
331. Harold Camping
332. Charles Martel
333. Harper Lee
334. F. Scott Fitzgerald
335. Mark Twain
336. J. D. Salinger
337. John Steinbeck
338. Ray Bradbury
339. Ernest Hemingway
340. William Faulkner
341. Maya Angelou
342. Nathaniel Hawthorne
343. Margaret Mitchell
344. Arthur Miller
345. Herman Melville
346. Emily Dickinson
347. Robert Frost
348. Stephen King
349. Alice Walker
350. L. Frank Baum
351. Tennessee Williams
352. William Safire
353. Eugene O'Neill
354. T. S. Eliot
355. James Fenimore Cooper
356. Edith Wharton
357. Robert Penn Warren
358. Carson McCullers
359. Dan Brown

360. Jean de La Fontaine
361. Moliere
362. Voltaire
363. Victor Hugo
364. Rousseau
365. Marcel Proust
366. Honore de Balzac
367. Zoroaster
368. Winston Churchill
369. Mikhail Gorbachev
370. J. Edgar Hoover
371. Alfred Hitchcock
372. Patrick Henry
373. Jeremy Bentham
374. Nicolas Sadi Carnot
375. Frederic Chopin
376. Betty Friedan
377. Henry VIII
378. James Hutton
379. Muhammad Ali
380. John Hancock
381. Ferdinand Magellan
382. Maria Montessori
383. Blaise Pascal
384. Pythagoras
385. Erwin Schrodinger
386. Francisco Pizarro
387. Hernandez Cortes
388. Babe Ruth
389. Charles H. Townes
390. Robert Watson-Watt
391. Aesop
392. Aristarchus of Samos
393. Antoine Henri Becquerel
394. Robert C. W. Ettinger
395. Gottlieb Daimler
396. John Maynard Keynes
397. John Bardeen and Walter Houser Brattain
398. Samuel Morse
399. Ivan Pavlov
400. Moshe Dayan

401. William B. Shockley
402. William Henry Talbot
403. Harry S. Truman
404. Mary Wollstonecraft
405. Howard H. Aiken
406. Richard Arkwright
407. Otto von Bismark
408. Bill Gaither
409. Dante Alighieri
410. George Fox
411. Mahatma Gandhi
412. Theodor Herzl
413. Cleopatra
414. Georg W. F. Hegel
415. Meijo Tenno
416. Pablo Picasso
417. Galen
418. Alessandro Volta
419. Frank Lloyd Wright
420. Susan B. Anthony
421. Neil Armstrong
422. Suleyman The Magnificent
423. Karl von Clausewitz
424. Hippocrates
425. Joan of Arc
426. Pericles
427. Gottfried W. von Leibniz
428. Marco Polo
429. Greg Bahnsen
430. Charles Lindbergh
431. Selman A. Waksman
432. Louis de Broglie
433. Rudolf Clausius
434. Democritus
435. Franz Schubert
436. Thomas Hobbes
437. Jim and Carol Cymbala
438. Etienne Lenoir
439. Montesquieu
440. Gerard K. O'Neill
441. Ptolemy

442. Sophocles
443. Euripides
444. Aeschylus
445. Vladimir Zworykin
446. Osman Ali Khan
447. Lorenzo de' Medici
448. Heshen
449. Jakob Fugger
450. Marcus Licinius Crassus
451. By the Grace of God, Nicholas II, Emperor
452. Rothschild
453. Croesus
454. John D. Rockefeller
455. Cornelius Vanderbilt
456. Andrew Carnegie
457. John Jacob Astor IV
458. Carlos Slim
459. Tadashi Yanai
460. Li Ka-Shing
461. Clint Eastwood
462. Mark, Megan, Josh, Melodee, Chris, Brian
463. Al Pacino
464. King Alfred the Great
465. Sargon of Akkad
466. Mustafa Kemal Atatürk
467. Tiglath-Pileser III
468. Henry IV
469. Nabopolassar
470. Johannes
471. Thutmose III
472. Hatshepsut
473. Paul Newman
474. Rajendra Chola I
475. Marlon Brando
476. Ptolemy I Soter
477. Robert de Niro
478. Margaret I
479. John II Komnenos
480. Charles Wesley
481. Cnut the Great
482. Scipio Africanus

A REQUIEM FOR EVOLUTION

483. Jane Addams
484. Aspasia of Miletus
485. Nancy Astor
486. Nelson Mandela
487. Aung San Suu Kyi
488. Jane Austen
489. Ella Baker
490. Sirima Bandaranaike
491. Clara Barton
492. Simone de Beauvoir
493. Aphra Behn
494. Shirley Temple
495. Elizabeth Blackwell
496. Eric Heiden
497. Rosa Bonheur
498. Pearl S. Buck
499. Catherine the Great
500. Catherine of Alexandria
501. Michael Jackson
502. Cleopatra, Egyptian
503. Glenn Frey, Don Henley, Bernie Leadon, and Randy Meisner
504. Phillips, Craig, Dean
505. Amelia Earhart
506. Marian Wright Edelman
507. Eleanor of Aquitane
508. Beatrix Jones Farrand
509. Anne Frank
510. Rosalind Elsie Franklin
511. Alfred the Great
512. Elizabeth Gurney Fry
513. Margaret Fuller
514. Indira Gandhi
515. Sarah and Angelina Grimke
516. Caroline Lucretia Herschel
517. Judith E. Heumann
518. Dorothy Mary Crowfoot Hodgkin
519. Ariel Hollinshead
520. Mary Phelps Jacob
521. Helen Keller
522. Mia Hamm
523. Elisabeth Kubler-Ross

524. Susette LaFlesche Tibbles
525. Maya Lin
526. Juliette Gordon Low
527. Anne Sullivan Macy
528. Wilma Mankiller
529. Barbara McClintock
530. Catherine de' Medici
531. Lise Meitner
532. Rigoberta Menchu Tum
533. Leonidas I
534. Mother Teresa
535. Murasaki Shikibu
536. Florence Nightingale
537. Georgia O'Keeffe
538. Vijaya Lakshmi Pandit
539. Emmeline Pankhurst
540. Rosa Parks
541. Eva Peron
542. Christine de Pizan
543. Pocahontas
544. Queen Anne
545. Queen Victoria
546. Jeannette Rankin
547. Sally Ride
548. Alexandra Romanov
549. Eleanor Roosevelt
550. Sacagawea
551. Margaret Sanger
552. Gloria Steinem
553. Lucy Stone
554. Harriet Beecher Stowe
555. Harriet Russell Strong
556. Bertha von Suttner
557. Emma Tenayuca
558. Valentina Tereshkova
559. Margaret Thatcher
560. Alexandrine Tinne
561. Sojourner Truth
562. Harriet Tubman
563. Phyllis Wheatley
564. Woody Allen

565. Albert Schweitzer
566. Raoul Wallenberg
567. Leonardo DiCaprio
568. Tom Cruise
569. Vasco de Gama
570. Cheops
571. Hammurabi
572. Dwight L. Moody
573. George Whitefield
574. Kemal Ataturk
575. Anwar el-Sadat
576. Homer
577. Arturo Toscanini
578. George Gershwin
579. Louis Armstrong
580. George Muller
581. Virgil
582. Joyce Meyer
583. Fred Astaire
584. Charles Dickens
585. Anne Frank
586. Johnny Carson
587. Rembrandt
588. Christopher Wren
589. Katsushika Hokusai
590. Joseph Mallord
591. Vincent van Gogh
592. Nostradamus
593. Oscar Wilde
594. Menachem Begin
595. Charlie Chaplin
596. Jean Renoir
597. Sergei Eisenstein
598. Orson Welles
599. Steven Spielberg
600. Walter Cronkite
601. Frédéric Chopin
602. Roger Ailes
603. Dustin Hoffman
604. Benito Mussolini
605. Tom Hanks

606. T. D. Jakes
607. Roald Amundsen
608. Rabindranath Tagore
609. Yuri Gagarin
610. Kalidasa
611. Methuselah
612. Nimrod
613. Adi Shankar
614. Morgan Freeman
615. Jawaharlal Nehru
616. Saladin
617. John Bunyan
618. John Knox
619. John Smith
620. Gordon Moore
621. John Wesley
622. Muhammad Ibn Abd Al Wahhab
623. James Springer White
624. George Frederick Handel
625. Charles Taze Russell
626. Sri Aurobindo
627. Charles Fox Parham
628. Louis Braille
629. L. Ron Hubbard
630. John Hagee
631. C. I. Scofield
632. Carl Friedrich Keil
633. John Paul II
634. John Lennon, Paul McCartney, George Harrison, Ringo Starr
635. Mick Jagger and Keith Richards
636. Lee "Scratch" Perry
637. Curtis Lee Mayfield
638. Sean Connery
639. Charles W. Missler
640. Robin Williams
641. Clark Gable
642. Kirk Douglas
643. Booker T. Washington
644. Kevin Spacey
645. Eric Hilliard Nelson
646. Carlos Santana

647. Cary Grant
648. Miles Dewey Davis III
649. Gram Parsons
650. Dr. Dre
651. Jack Nicholson
652. James Taylor
653. Gregory Peck
654. Humphrey Bogart
655. Robert Duval
656. Elvis Costello
657. Harrison Ford
658. Brad Pitt
659. Sidney Poitier
660. Lee Van Cleef
661. Malcolm and Angus Young
662. Hank Williams
663. Robert Plant, Jimmy Page, John Paul Jones, and John Bonham
664. Will Smith
665. Frank Zappa
666. Laozi
667. Carl Perkins
668. Jackie Wilson
669. Don Moen
670. Van Morrison
671. Al Green
672. Taylor Swift
673. Etta James
674. Tina Turner
675. Joni Mitchell
676. Louis Thomas Jordan
677. Diana Ross
678. Werner Gitt
679. Brian, Dennis, Carl Wilson, Mike Love, and Al Jardine
680. Matthew Henry
681. Willie Nelson
682. Eric Clapton
683. Freddie Mercury, Brian May, Roger Taylor, and John Deacon
684. Howlin' Wolf
685. Craig Venter
686. Baby Face
687. Jerry Lee Lewis

688. Patti Smith
689. Janis Joplin
690. Richard Dawkins
691. Barret, Mason, Waters, Gilmour, and Wright
692. C. S. Lewis
693. Oswald Chambers
694. Mike Brant
695. Simon and Garfunkel
696. David Bowie
697. Steven Weinberg
698. Roy Orbison
699. Watchman Nee
700. Bart, James, Robby, Nathan
701. Neil Young
702. Nana Mouskouri
703. Smokey Robinson
704. Johnny Cash
705. Sting
706. Andrae Crouch
707. Prince
708. Rick Warren
709. Roone Arledge
710. Charles Krauthammer
711. Ramones
712. Celine Dion
713. Tchaikovsky
714. Bono, the Edge, Adam Clayton, and Larry Mullen
715. Walt Whitman
716. Otis Redding
717. Bo Diddley
718. Elton John
719. Marvin Gaye
720. Igor Stravinsky
721. Stevie Wonder
722. Mary Magdalene
723. Buddy Holly
724. Justin Timberlake
725. BB King
726. Bob Marley
727. Ray Charles
728. Aretha Franklin

729. Witness Lee
730. James Brown
731. Jimi Hendrix
732. Chuck Berry
733. Bob Dylan
734. Michael Jordan
735. Tiger Woods
736. Matt Redman
737. Chris Tomlin
738. Wayne Gretzky
739. James Naismith
740. A. W. Tozer
741. Joseph Haydn
742. William Paley
743. Jesse Owens
744. Jim Thorpe
745. Joel Osteen
746. Jack Nicklaus
747. Babe Didrikson
748. Joe Louis
749. Carl Lewis
750. Gordon Clark
751. Hank Aaron
752. Jackie Robinson
753. Ted Williams
754. Earvin "Magic" Johnson
755. Bill Russell
756. Martina Navratilova
757. Ty Cobb
758. Gordie Howe
759. Joe DiMaggio
760. Jackie Joyner
761. Sugar Ray Robinson
762. Chanakya
763. Antonio Vivaldi
764. Karl Barth
765. Red Grange
766. Arnold Palmer
767. Charles-Valentin Alkan
768. John Vernon McGee
769. Johnny Unitas

770. Mark Spitz
771. Lou Gehrig
772. Jerry West
773. Oscar Robertson
774. Mickey Mantle
775. Ben Hogan
776. Walter Payton
777. Lawrence Taylor
778. Wilma Rudolph
779. Sandy Koufax
780. Julius Erving
781. Bobby Jones
782. Persi Diaconis
783. John Foxe
784. Jimmy Page
785. Charles Townes
786. Amy Grant
787. Chris Evert
788. Rocky Marciano
789. Jack Dempsey
790. Bryan Trottier
791. Mario Lemieux
792. Pete Rose
793. Willie Shoemaker
794. Hakeem Olajuwon
795. Eddie van Halen
796. Axl Rose, Slash
797. Stan Musial
798. Bon Jovi
799. Jeremy Camp
800. Horace
801. Althea Gibson
802. G. K. Chesterton
803. Bob Gibson
804. Guru Nanak
805. Bonnie Blair
806. Dick Butkus
807. Roberto Clemente
808. Andrea Bocelli
809. Josh Gibson
810. Mike Bossy

811. Dan Marino
812. Ovid
813. Cy Young
814. Bob Mathias
815. Randy Johnson
816. Alan Guth
817. Denis Potvin
818. Vladimir Horowitz
819. Honus Wagner
820. Chandragupta Maurya
821. Aryabhata
822. Barbara Walters
823. Henry Armstrong
824. Mark Levin
825. Muddy Waters
826. Bob Hope
827. Bob Beamon
828. Bing Crosby
829. William Randolph Hearst
830. Michael Johnson
831. Rush Limbaugh
832. Glenn Beck
833. Jane Goodall
834. Bill O'Reilly
835. Jack Johnson
836. David Hume
837. Michael Phelps
838. Pele
839. William Carey
840. Luciano Pavarotti
841. John Piper
842. Usain Bolt
843. Jean, Alaudee, Paul, Eunice, Machli
844. Sergei Rachmaninoff
845. John Williams
846. Shania Twain
847. Jim Brown
848. Jerry Rice
849. LeBron James
850. Wilt Chamberlain
851. Joe Montana

852. Peyton Manning
853. Howard Hughes
854. Cotton Mather
855. Michael W. Smith
856. TobyMac
857. Adi Shankara
858. John Leland
859. Shaquille O'Neal
860. Twila Paris
861. Dante Alighieri
862. Steven Curtis Chapman
863. Herodotus
864. Nero
865. Awakum
866. Malcolm X
867. Al-Waleed bin Talal
868. Thales
869. Mary Baker Eddy
870. Cicero
871. Sophocles
872. Vincent van Gogh
873. Mary Pickford
874. Bette Davis
875. Martyn Lloyd-Jones
876. St. Leo the Great
877. St. Gregory the Great
878. Immanuel Kant
879. Gale Sayers
880. Barry Sanders
881. Allan Sandage
882. Larry Bird
883. Willie Mays
884. Brett Favre
885. Jackie Kennedy
886. Garth Brooks
887. Hippocrates
888. Nefertiti
889. Swami Vivekananda
890. Epicurus
891. René Descartes
892. Marcus Aurelius

893. Alfred Stieglitz
894. Tim McGraw
895. Barry Bonds
896. Donald Knuth
897. Saladin
898. Tom Brady
899. Sugar Ray Leonard
900. Albert Pujols
901. Nadia Comaneci
902. Chanakya
903. Kareem Abdul Jabar
904. Mikhail Baryshnikov
905. John Wycliffe
906. Heraclitus
907. Serena Williams
908. Christopher Stallone
909. Denzel Washington
910. Rocky Marciano
911. Friedrich Nietzsche
912. Sun Tzu
913. Mariano Rivera
914. Brad Paisley
915. Steffi Graf
916. Derek Jeter
917. Arminius
918. Mac Powell, Mark Lee, David Carr
919. John Elway
920. Archibald Alexander Hodge
921. Rod Laver
922. Manny Pacquiao
923. Maradona
924. Xerxes of Persia
925. Sachin Tendulkar
926. Kenny Rogers
927. Bobby Orr
928. Leo Tolstoy
929. Felix Mendelssohn
930. Nolan Ryan
931. Franz Liszt
932. Leif Ericson
933. Bruce Lee

934. George Best
935. Paavo Nurmi
936. Thomas Nast
937. Valentino Rossi
938. Dale Earnhardt
939. Tom Landry
940. John McEnroe
941. Henry Hudson
942. Frank Sinatra
943. Thomas Eakins
944. John Muir
945. Giovanni da Verrazzano
946. Kit Carson
947. Roger Penrose
948. Robert E. Lee
949. John Brown
950. Frederick Douglass
951. John James Audubon
952. Vince McMahon
953. W. E. B. du Bois
954. Roger Staubach
955. Elizabeth Cady Stanton
956. Ulysses S. Grant
957. Andrew Jackson
958. Martha Washington
959. Simon Cowell
960. CeCe Winans
961. Aaron Burr
962. Dean Kamen
963. John Wooden
964. Pat Summitt
965. Geno Auriemma
966. Dean Smith
967. Terry Bradshaw
968. Reggie Jackson
969. Johan Cruyff
970. George Steinbrenner
971. John Dillinger
972. Lucky Luciano
973. Taylor Swift
974. Andy Warhol

975. Frederick Law Olmsted
976. James Abbott McNeill Whistler
977. Jackson Pollock
978. Beyoncé
979. Jean-Jacques Dessalines
980. Donnie McClurkin
981. Toussaint Louverture
982. Ansel Adams
983. Joseph Smith Jr.
984. Brigham Young
985. Henri Christophe
986. Dalai Lama
987. Deng Xiaoping
988. Grover Cleveland
989. Ali, founder of Sufism
990. King Arthur
991. Richard Wagner
992. Robert E. Lee
993. Tchaikovsky
994. George III of the United Kingdom
995. Jerry Seinfeld
996. Shigeru Miyamoto
997. Heston Blumenthal
998. Jonathan Ive
999. Madonna
1000. Edward De Bono

Chapter 2

The Requiem for Evolution

There is no wisdom nor understanding nor counsel against the Lord. (Proverbs 21:30)

Welcoming Address
President John F. Kennedy

President Lincoln, President Washington, President Roosevelt, President Reagan, President Madison, President Jefferson, President Trump, outstanding citizens of the world, welcome!

    We have not come here today simply to mourn the passing of a celebrity; but we are gathered in this momentous occasion in this magnificent cathedral in this marvelous city in this the greatest country on earth to celebrate the enormous contributions that Evolution has brought to our marvelous country and to the entire civilized world.

We live in a new world. For man holds now in his feeble hands the power to eliminate all types of human misery and, through nuclear warfare, all forms of human manifestation on this planet we all call home. And yet the same freedoms for which our ancestors gave their lives are still being exhibited in every part of the globe—the freedom to worship according to one's belief and one's conscience, to pursue life in its fullest extent, liberty in its ultimate expression, and the pursuit of happiness in its clearest exhibition.

We who are present in this solemn assembly must remember vividly that we are the heirs of the Evolution Revolution. As a result, let the word go forth from this sublime edifice to mankind everywhere that the baton has been passed to a new class of world citizens—born in the postwar era, united by our modern means of communication and transportation, strengthened by warfare, vindicated by the fall of the Berlin Wall, victorious over the Cold War and unwilling to see the fruits of the labors of our forebears misappropriated, and ready ourselves to lay down our own lives for the preservation of the liberties we have inherited and hold so dear.

Let all the people of the world, whether they like us or not, be reminded once and for all that we will offer any sacrifice, withstand any misfortune, meet any challenge, climb any mountain, and travel to the remotest parts of the world to make sure that all the people of the world can enjoy the same freedoms we have enjoyed in this country for over two centuries.

This much you can depend upon—and much much more!

Thank you very much.

The Universal Prayer
Pope Clement XI

Lord, I believe in you: increase my faith.
I trust in you: strengthen my trust.
I love you: let me love you more and more.
I am sorry for my sins: deepen my sorrows.

I worship you as my first beginning,
I long for you as my last end,
I praise you as my constant helper,
And call on you as my loving protector.

Guide me by your wisdom,
Correct me with your justice,
Comfort me with your mercy,
Protect me with your power.

PIERRE W. BEAUSEJOUR

I offer you, Lord, my thoughts: to be fixed on you;
My words: to have you for their theme;
My actions: to reflect my love for you;
My sufferings: to be endured for your greater glory.

I want to do what you ask of me:
In the way you ask,
For as long as you ask,
Because you ask it.

Lord, enlighten my understanding,
Strengthen my will,
Purify my heart,
And make me holy.

Help me to repent of my past sins,
And to resist temptation in the future.
Help me to rise above my human weaknesses
And to grow stronger as a Christian.

Let me love you, my Lord and my God,
And see myself as I really am:
A pilgrim in this world,
A Christian called to respect and love
All whose lives I touch,
Those under my authority,
My friends and my enemies.

Help me to conquer anger with gentleness,
Greed with generosity,
Apathy by fervor.
Help me to forget myself,
And reach out towards others.

Make me prudent in planning,
Courageous in taking risks.
Make me patient in suffering, unassuming in prosperity.

Keep me, Lord, attentive at prayer,
Temperate in food and drink,
Diligent in my work,
Firm in my good intentions.

Let my conscience be clear,
My conduct without fault,
My speech blameless,
My life well-ordered.
Put me on guard against my human weaknesses.
Let me cherish your love for me,
Keep your law,
And come at last to your salvation.

Teach me to realize that this world is passing,
That my true future is the happiness of heaven,
That life on earth is short,
And the life to come eternal.

Help me to prepare for death,
With a proper fear of judgment,
But a greater trust in your goodness.
Lead me safely through death,
To the endless joy of heaven.

Grant this through Christ our Lord.
Amen!

Introducing Remarks
William Paley

Evolution is dead … is dead! Tell it to Oprah, tell it to Obama. The only begotten daughter, whom Darwin spoke into existence out of nothing while the sons of men sang for joy, has breathed her last breath.

Ladies and gentlemen, I anticipated all of that when I wrote my book *Natural Theology*, in which I used the watchmaker analogy to make a teleological argument for a creator. I remarked then the following insightful observation:

> There cannot be design without a designer; contrivance without a contriver; order without choice; arrangement, without anything capable of arranging.

I still believe now what I related in my book that "arrangement, disposition of parts, relation to a use, imply the presence of intelligence and mind."

Having read Aristotle's *On Generation and Corruption* and Cicero's *De Natura Deorum*, I felt confident in my critique of the "infinite monkey *theorem*" and disheartened by the philosophical implications of the chaos theory with its butterfly effect.

My acquaintance for many years, David Hume, after a "quick glance" at my *Natural Theology* manuscript, sent me a nice letter and two of his books, *Dialogues Concerning Natural Religion* and *An Inquiry Concerning Human Understanding*, in order to dissuade me from publishing my masterpiece.

Well, I still remain unconvinced of his much heralded classical design critique; after all, while it may be true that order and purpose do not come only from design—any of the well-known biologists in attendance at this requiem can attest that the formation of crystals and snowflakes proves that point fairly well—the discovery of millions of molecular machines operating, within a normal cell, with breathtaking speed, harmony, and sophistication in a factory-style production of multicellular organisms, provides a death blow to the critical design argument.

Ladies and gentlemen, there is not one single scientist, philosopher, or naturalist present at this ceremony or anywhere in the world that can offer a coherent, valid, and naturalistic argument vis-à-vis the development of the software in the DNA. Where does the information telling the cell the types of proteins necessary for the production of cellular tissues in the development of complex organisms come from? Who put it there?

Bill Gates, the founder of Microsoft, is quoted as saying that the "DNA is like a computer program but far, far more advanced than any software created." Ladies and gentlemen, the presence within living things of so sophisticated a software program as the DNA, which commands and controls the scheduling and the formation of all the proteins responsible for all living things, warrants categorically the a priori intervention of an intelligence agent.

I tried very hard to convince Darwin, my fellow Britt, of the negative consequences of his experiment on his return trip from the Galapagos Islands without success. He related to me that his friend Lyell had given him a copy of his manuscript, *Principles of Geology*, which made him approach the Origins studies from a uniformitarian perspective.

While it remains true from a purely naturalistic standpoint that the present consists of a clear reflection of a bygone past, we have not factored in our imperfect origin assumptions the manifestation of any major global catastrophe. In fact, Dr. William Ryan and Dr. Walter Pitman from Columbia University recently provided in their wonderful book, *Noah's Flood*, scientific proofs concerning a flood affecting the contours of the Mediterranean. We need to include such data in making the case for our fundamental assumptions in dating the earth and in calculating the half-life of the elements.

My condolences go to my friend Darwin and to all the family and friends of the deceased. Thank you very much!

A REQUIEM FOR EVOLUTION

Kyrie Eleison
St. Augustine

Lord, have mercy, for we are part of your great creation.
Christ, have mercy, for you came to make us one great nation.
Lord, have mercy, you bled and died to grant us dominion.
Lord, have mercy, our adversary has caused us to err.
Christ, have mercy, the Father has made us your glad coheirs.
Lord, have mercy, bring renewal to the created pair.
Lord, have mercy, all your creation tells one great story.
Christ, have mercy, the earth needs to see some of your glory.
Lord, have mercy, create again and make this world hoary.

Dies Irae (Day of Judgment)
(The Greatest of Hymns)
Luciano Pavarotti

Day of wrath! O day of mourning!
See fulfilled the prophets' warning!
Heaven and earth in ashes burning!

Oh, what fear man's bosom rendeth,
when from heaven the Judge descendeth,
on whose sentence all dependeth.

Wondrous sound the trumpet flingeth;
trough earth's sepulchers it ringeth;
all before the throne it bringeth.

Death is struck, and nature quaking,
all creation is awakening,
to its judge an answer making.

Lo! the book, exactly worded,
Wherein all hath been recorded:
thence shall judgment be awarded.

When the Judge His seat attaineth,
and each hidden deed arraigneth,
nothing unavenged remaineth.

PIERRE W. BEAUSEJOUR

What shall I, frail man, be pleading?
Who for me be interceding,
when the just be mercy needing?

King of majesty tremendous,
who does free salvation send us.
Fount of pity, then befriend us!
Think, good Jesus, my salvation
Cost thy wondrous incarnation;
Leave me not to reprobation!

Faint and weary, thou hast sought me,
on the cross of suffering brought me
Shall such grace be vainly brought me?

Righteous Judge! For sin's pollution
grant thy gift of absolution,
ere the day of retribution.

Guilty now, I pour my moaning,
all my shame with anguish owning;
spare, O God, thy suppliant groaning!

Thou, the sinful woman savedst;
Thou the dying thief forgavest;
And to me a hope vouchsafest.

Worthless are my prayers and sighing,
yet, good Lord, in grace complying,
rescue me from fires undying!

With thy favored sheep O place me;
nor among the goats abase me;
but to thy right hand upraise me.

While the wicked are confounded,
doomed to flames of woe unbounded
call me with thy saints surrounded.

Low, I kneel with heart submission,
See, like ashes, my contrition;
Help me in my last condition.
Ah! That day of tears and mourning!

From the dust of earth returning
man for judgment must prepare him;
spare, O God, in mercy spare him!

Lord, all pitying, Jesus blest,
grant them thy eternal rest.
Amen.

Keynote Speech
Richard Dawkins

Thank you very much! Thank you! Thank you very much! How do you tap Pavarotti? He is simply the best. I wonder why he was never knighted; he should have applied for British citizenship a long time ago!

I felt my heart cringe while listening to Mr. Paley's remarks. What utter nonsense! Evolution is not dead! In fact, Evolution has left a legacy that will live forever. Though the beautiful lady we have known and adored appears—and I choose this word very carefully—absent in body, she is forevermore present with us in spirit and in truth.

That beautiful musical rendition, "The Elephant March from Aida," is the musical piece I've reserved for my funeral ceremony; and—I am certain that you can quickly understand my drift here—it is majestic! I am…I will…I will not experience anything: I will not be there! I will not be part of that marvelous experience. However, if I could be found anywhere at all, I would feel victorious and justified for all the achievements of my personal existence on this lovely, remarkable planet that we, *Homo sapiens*, call Mother Earth; and having been granted the chance—and again let me remind you that I choose all my words very carefully—to comprehend the rationale of my appearance on this wonderful planet.

By the way, I want to apologize with all the powers granted to me by the Queen for my peculiar English accent. And like all of you, I was mesmerized yesterday by the animal presentation at the American Museum of Natural History. Our colleagues Robert Full and Frans Lanting did a marvelous job in exhibiting the sheer magnificence of all the species at their disposition. My only reservation about their demonstration entails the moment when Jeffrey Katzenberg reported that the mustangs consisted, and I quote, "the most splendid creatures that God put on this earth." Now, quite naturally, we all believe that he chose the wrong words to express his sentiment—but in our present world of political correctness, we can be guilty of being too careful.

I'm a natural scientist and a biologist to be exact; and the overarching axiom of our field of inquiry—Darwin's theory of evolution by natural selection—is universally regarded as absolute truth by all the professional venues everywhere in our present world. In the places where academia does not have a foothold, it's considered as sacrilege. Even in America, outside the realms of our academic circles, it elicits so much fear and hostility that one can conclude that all the natural scientists in North America are involved in an epic warfare.

The war has so many repercussions that lawsuits are being filed in one state after another; and, of course, I was forced to join the cavalry. If you are much obliged to learn my disposition concerning Darwinism, I'm afraid you're going to have to buy all my books on the subject; and let me relate here that at the present moment, you still can't find my books on the shelves of many bookstores in this country.

All the present lawsuits entail creationism masqueraded as a scientific endeavor. The present form is called Intelligent Design, or ID. Don't be deceived! There's nothing scientific about ID. It's just creationism under a pseudo name rechristened—and I choose the word quite purposefully here—for strategic and sociopolitical ramification. The claims of so-called ID scientists entail the same old and faulty arguments that have been rebuffed over and over from the days of Darwin up to our present time.

There exists an effective and efficient evolution lobby organizing the war for science, and I constantly do my very best to help; but they seem to get quizzical when people of my ilk dare to relate that we are avowed atheists, as well as national scientists, and as well as evolutionists. We are known as the party poopers. You all can plainly see why.

Creationists, in search of a systematic scientific argument for their faulty theories, feel justified in developing and popularizing fear against all those who are skeptical of religion and open to atheism as a better logical alternative. They sincerely believe that if their children are taught evolution in biology and national science classes, they'll upgrade to crime, drugs, and sexual perversion.

As a matter of fact, enlightened theologians and Bible students—from the pope down to the lowest Christian intellectuals—are adamant in their respect for the truth of evolution. In his remarkable book, *Finding Darwin's God*, Kenneth Miller presented the most effective attacks on Intelligent Design that I have seen, and it's all the more interesting because it's the work of a truly devout Christian. An intellectual of the ilk of Kenneth Miller could be considered as a "messenger from God" because he extinguishes the perverted lie that evolutionism is equal to atheism. A person like me, on the other hand, is considered as a party pooper.

But here I want to say something nice about creationists. It's not a thing I often do, so listen carefully. I think they're right about one thing—I think they're right that evolution is fundamentally hostile to religion. I've already said that many individual evolutionists, like the pope, are also religious, but I think they're deluding themselves. I believe a true understanding of Darwinism is deeply hostile to religion.

Now it may sound as though I'm about to preach atheism, and I want to reassure you that that's not what I'm going to do. In an audience as sophisticated as you are, that would be preaching to the choir. No! What I want to thrust upon you instead is what I call MILITANT ATHEISM; and, for special effects, I deliberately opt to capitalize all the letters here!

But I don't want to sound pessimistic today in my little discourse with you. If I were a Christian, I would be very weary of the real power of the science of evolution—and indeed of science in general—to elicit the sympathy of the elites and masses of the world simply because it is atheistic.

Now, the most pressing concern of any theory of biological design is to explicate the enormous mathematical improbability of living things. Sophistication entails another term for that notion. The most common creationist arguments—please, notice that there is only one truly good one!—reduce to this one: The species are too sophisticated to have evolved or come about by chance; as such, they all must have been designed.

This argument quite naturally begs the question. Any designer susceptible of creating something really complex must be even more complex himself. And that's even before he has to focus on such important matters as saving the lost, forgiving our sins, blessing our marriages, listening to our prayers, receiving our tithes and offerings, favoring our side in a war, disapproving of our sex lives, and so on. Complexity is the overarching hurdle that any theory of biology has to overcome. And you can't jump over it by extrapolating an agent that is even more sophisticated, thereby making the hurdle even higher.

Darwin's natural selection is incredibly beautiful because it brings a panacea to the problem of explicating sophistication and incredible complexity in terms of simple principles. Actually, it makes its point by relying on a perfect incline of common sense. But may I relate here again that the beauty of Darwinism is hostile to Christianity in particular and religion in general simply because it is so beautiful, so exquisite, and so strong. It elicits the idea of an elegant skyscraper. The "God argument" is not simply a bad argument, it is also impossible to get the ball rolling.

So going back to strategy and the evolution movement, may I argue here that "being a party pooper" may just happen to be the best course of action. My approach to attacking creationism is—unlike the evolution lobby—to attack religion as a whole. And I'm going to make my point by quoting my great dear friend, the late Douglas Adams, who should have been invited to this great gathering.

He begins a speech he was giving in Cambridge a few days before he died. He tries to explicate the dynamics of science through the hypothesis testing method, framed to be vulnerable to disproof. And then he continues, and I quote:

> Religion doesn't seem to work like that. It has certain ideas at the heart of it which we call sacred or holy. What it means is—here is an idea or emotion that you are not allowed to say anything bad about. You're just not. Why not? Because you're not. Why should it be that it's perfectly legitimate to support the Republicans or Democrats, this model of economics versus that, Macintosh instead of windows, but to have an opinion about how the universe began, about who created the universe—no, that's holy. So we're used to not challenging religious ideas. And it's very interesting how much of a furor Richard creates when he does it. He meant me, not that one. Everybody gets absolutely frantic about it. Because you're not allowed to say these things. Yet when you look at it rationally, there

is no reason why those ideas shouldn't be as open to debate as any other. Except that we've agreed somehow between us that they shouldn't be.

In my view, not only is science destructive to religion, religion is also destructive to science. It makes the perfect case that people can benefit with meaningless, mystical gobbledygook, and alienates them to the marvelous and truthful explications that can be grasped with simple logic. It preaches the acceptance of faith, myths, revelation, and authority instead of the embrace of experimentation and evidence.

Now as a guest editor I have written in *The Quarterly Review of Biology*, a standard scientific journal, a very interesting article entitled "Did an Asteroid Kill the Dinosaurs?" And in that article, I presented concrete evidence for that theory. Let me outline for you my drift: "Iridium layer at K/T boundary and potassium argon dated crater in Yucatan indicate that an asteroid killed the dinosaurs." Now, that's a perfectly valid scientific argument.

Now let's suppose I would have written: "The top scientist at the Royal Society has been vouchsafed a revelation that a powerful asteroid killed the dinosaurs." Let me grant you another example: "It has been privately revealed to professor Dawkins that a mighty asteroid killed the dinosaurs." Or how about that one: "Professor Einstein's great faith in the Deity revealed to him that an asteroid killed the dinosaurs." Finally, here is one for the ages: "Professor Watson has formulated an official dogma binding on all biologists of the world that an asteroid killed the dinosaurs." Do you think that science can make progress with such utter nonsense? Of course not!

That would be unbelievable, quite naturally. But let's now imagine that a prominent reporter would ask George Bush Sr. whether he believed that atheists can be considered as good citizens and great American patriots as well. Now, that actually happened! Mr. Bush's reply exposes the utter stupidity in the heart of Christian believers:

> No, I don't know that atheists should be considered citizens. Nor should they be considered patriots. This is one nation, under God.

Bush's outright bigotry was not an isolated incident, exhibited under the intense pressures of a political campaign and later rebuffed. He repeated later in spite of enormous criticism from the press: He really believed that. He felt that his biased assertion did not threaten his election to the presidency. Au contraire, in the United States, politicians of all stripes proclaim that they are "born again" as a positive campaign strategy. And Democrats and Republicans preach "One Nation, Under God." What would the American Founding Fathers have said?

In actual life, what is an atheist? An atheist is simply someone who views Yahweh in the same prism that any practicing Christian views Baal, or Ashtoreth, or Molech, or Chemosh, or the golden calf. Let me relate to you what has been stated by many before me: "We are all atheists about most of the gods that humanity has ever believed in. Some of us just go one GOD further." And here, I humbly use capital *G*, capital *O*, and capital *D*, just to be religiously and politically correct!

Furthermore, no matter how we relate to atheism, it's the sound point of view that a thoughtful individual is allowed to formalize without being criticized and ostracized as an unelectable and unpatriotic noncitizen. Also, it's an overwhelmingly acceptable fact that to present someone as an atheist is equivalent to categorize him as Hitler or Beelzebub. And that is the unfortunate consequence of labeling atheists as some odd and crazy people intent of destroying the fabric of our modern societies. In that realm, I empathize with Natalie Angier, who wrote a rather melancholic article in the *New Yorker* asserting the loneliness she has experienced as an atheist. She clearly feels part of a chastised minority.

But as a matter of fact, how do American atheists fare numerically against some of our most important social groups? The latest polls reveal some incredible results. The Christians, quite naturally, make up the largest portion of the population with approximately 160 million. But who do you think make up the next largest group? Practically outpolling the Jews, with 2.8 million, the Muslims with 1.1 million, the Hindus, the Buddhists, and all the other sects put together? The next largest group, ladies and gentlemen, with over 30 million, is the one identified as "nonreligious," or "secular."

You can't fathom why any ambitious politicians in search of votes would rather pander to the Jewish Lobby—the nation of Israel owes its very subsistence to the American Jewish Lobby—at the expense of the "nonreligious," or "secular," vote, which they deem insignificant. This popular "secular" and "nonreligious" vote, if properly organized, is at least nine times as popular as the Jewish vote. Why has not this far more numerous minority not made its mark in the political world by exercising its political muscle? No one knows.

Well, we are not talking simply about quantity here; what do we have to say vis-à-vis quality? Have researchers found any correlation, positive or negative, between being intelligent and being religious?

The research data that I have mentioned here, the Eris survey, didn't differentiate its variables by socioeconomic class or religion or education or IQ or anything else; however, a recent study by Paul G. Bell in the *Mensa* magazine adds plenty of wind to our sail. Mensa, as all of you are plainly aware, entails an international group for very intelligent people. Mensa has carried forty-three studies since 1927 on the correlation between intelligence and level of education with religious belief. We proudly announce that all but four of those studies reveal an inverse correlation.

In other words, the higher the intelligence or level of education of an individual, the less she or he is prone to be religious. Well, I have not examined personally those studies to proclaim to you the ultimate truth; however, I would like to challenge all the scientists in this marvelous audience to study this matter carefully and publish their results so that science can once and for all identify religious people as lacking intellectual discernment.

But let me strut in front of you some very encouraging news. In 1998, Larson and Witham surveyed the top American scientists—those who have been elected to the prestigious National Academy of the Sciences; and incredibly among this elite group, belief in a creator or a personal god fell to a whopping 7 percent! Almost 20 percent are agnostic, and the remainder could be categorized as atheists. The numbers are equally drastic for the belief in eternal life. Amidst natural scientists, the numbers are even more pathetic: 5.5 percent only believe in God. Physical scientists stand at a dismal 7.5 percent.

I do believe the same figures would be obtained for scholars in other fields of study such as philosophy or history or sociology or medicine.

So we've ascended to the summit of the ridiculous and the absurd where we behold a bizarre confrontation between the American electorate and the American intellectual class; and the latter holding an epistemological view of nature and the universe that is so disgusting to the former that any politician seeking office would not dare articulate. If I'm correct, we have in the United States, the greatest country in the world, a deplorable situation where the highest positions are off limit to the intellectual class, the class best qualified to hold them.

The elite intellectuals, unless and until they are ready to conceal to the masses their true beliefs, are barred from holding office in the greatest country in the world. That, ladies and gentlemen, entails a very disturbing proposition.

Well, I have not decided to be a United States citizen, and I pray that my comments may not be deemed inappropriate; but, as you all can ascertain, something drastic must be done. And I've already described precisely the steps that will lead us to victory; however, those steps cost a lot of money, and as such, all of us must pinch in.

We need the gospel of atheism to be preached with power in all the centers of power of America so that the American people will finally see the truth. This must be similar in style to the great campaign that the homosexual lobby organized a few years ago.

In the final analysis, when all the members of the American intelligentsia start exhibiting their true colors to the American people, they will start destroying the boldfaced lie that atheists are weirdoes, wackos, and radicals intent of destroying the moral fabric of the country. Moreover, they will start to show the world that atheists are the role models that their children should emulate, the types of models an advertising agency could utilize to market successfully a service or product. You all here, ladies and gentlemen, or almost all of you, represent those kinds of people.

I envision a snowball impact, a multiplying effect where every name enlisted in our campaign for atheism brings in tens, hundreds, or even thousands of names; and today, I am starting such a campaign. Every one of you should pick up a card at the door of this great cathedral and fill out your name, phone number, and e-mail address and register for the enlightenment of the American people and the people of the world.

I gather that the word *atheist* itself carries negative connotations; but it's only a matter of time: very soon, the word *atheist* will be akin to the word *Christian* or *Jewish* or *Muslim* or *Buddhist*. We shall prevail, for the truth is on our side. Very soon that word will no longer be a stumbling block for people wishing to come out of the closet. So at the present time, what other words might be a good substitute for the word *atheist*? What other word can we use now to pave the way, or smooth the path, or oil the wheels, or sugar the pill?

Our great high priest Darwin himself, who by the way is in our midst today, opted for the word *agnostic* as a gesture of honor to his very good buddy Huxley, who invented the term.

Our beloved prophet and priest once uttered the following:

> I have never been an atheist, in the same sense of denying the existence of a god. I think that generally an agnostic would be the most correct description of my state of mind.

And as he might tell you himself in his speech following mine, Darwin even became uncharacteristically suspicious of Edward Aveling, a militant atheist who tried his best to convert him, to sanction the dedication of his book on atheism.

Let me now relate to you a very important story which Darwin might be unwilling to promote. That story has remarkably given fodder to the absolute lie that Karl Marx wished to dedicate *Das Kapital* to Darwin, which is of course a big lie: he never tried to. It was as a matter of fact Edward Aveling! Karl Marx's daughter was Edward Aveling's mistress, and after both Darwin and Marx passed away, Marx's research papers became entangled with Aveling's papers; and now the famous letter from Darwin attesting "My dear sir, thank you very much but I don't want you to dedicate your book to me" was mistakenly believed to be addressed to Karl Marx. And all of that provided fodder to the famous myth which you are familiar with. You can see clearly that Karl Marx did not really try to dedicate *Das Kapital* to Darwin.

Now, let me explain to you the story about the "tooth fairy agnostic." A dear friend of mine, a brilliant Jewish man, who by reasons of serendipity and cultural identity if not theology, observes the Sabbath, was very fond of identifying himself as a "tooth fairy agnostic." Well, my friend refused to describe himself as an atheist: He believed it impossible to prove a negative. But the term *agnostic* suits him rather well, because it implies that God's existence was equally plausible as His nonexistence. So my dear friend settled for agnostic about the tooth fairy.

Our friend Bertrand Russell made the same assertion vis-à-vis using a hypothetical teapot in orbit about Mars, but that in a way implies the equal likelihood of its existence with its nonexistence.

The list of items that we wish to be agnostic about is not limited at tooth fairies and teapots: it's infinite! If you opt to believe one in particular or all of them, like the unicorns, or the tooth fairies, or the teapots—or here we go Yahweh!—the burden is on you to prove your point. The burden cannot fall on us to prove a negative. We who claim to be atheists, we are also "a-fairy-ists" and "a-teapotists." But we do not care to pontificate our belief. And that is the reason my Jewish friend used "tooth fairy agnostic" as a description for what the rest of the world would label atheist.

Notwithstanding, if we desire to bring to our camp anonymous atheists who wish to remain as such, we need to find a much better label than "tooth fairy" or "teapot agnostic." So what do you think of the term *humanist*? It falls under the umbrella of all the well-publicized associations, periodicals, and journals and all the organizations that are currently in place.

My main reservation entails its apparent anthropocentrism. Let's recall the main lesson we've learned from Darwin is that the human species is but only one among millions of cousins, some very close, others very distant. And there are many more possibilities, like "naturalist," but that term tends to confuse people, because it stands in contrast to the term *supernaturalist*, thereby granting underserved legitimacy to myths, mysticism, and spiritual gobbledygook.

I think the very best alternative for the term *atheist* is simply *nontheist*. It lacks the strong allusion that there is definitely no God, and it could theoretically be well accepted by "teapot" or "tooth fairy agnostics." It's completely compatible with the "god" of the physicists, the one everybody can like and respect. Now when we atheists use the word *god*, we imply a metaphorical illustration for that profound and portion of physics which we don't yet comprehend. *Nontheist* seems to be politically correct, and more importantly, unlike *atheist*, it doesn't elicit the same phobic, hysterical responses.

Now let me repeat myself, if I were a Christian or even religious, I'd be very much at enmity with the concept of evolution. I'd go further—I would hate and fear science in general. And that is because the scientific worldview is so much more systematically beautiful, exciting, majestic, and poetic; it's more filled with sheer wonder than anything in the poverty-stricken arsenals of the religious imagination.

As my hero Carl Sagan aptly describes it:

> How is it that hardly any major religion has looked at science and concluded, "This is better than we thought! The Universe is much bigger than our prophets said, grander, more subtle, more elegant?" Instead they say, "No, no, no! My god is a little god, and I want him to stay that way." A religion, old or new, that stressed the magnificence of the Universe as revealed by modern science might be able to draw forth reserves of reverence and awe hardly tapped by the conventional faiths.

Now, this is a supremely elite audience, and I would therefore suspect that about 10 percent of you to be religious. Many of you most likely subscribe to our politically correct notion that we should respect religion. But I would also expect that a fair number of those secretly loathe religion as much as I do. If you happen to be one of those—and of course many of you may not happen to be—but if you are one of them, I'm with all the fiber of my being asking you to quit being cute and polite—come out of the closet and say so!

And if you are in possession of a small fortune, come and join us in our crusade to rid the world of religion. The religious institutions in the United States are tremendously financed by powerful entities that operate as nonprofit organizations without any liabilities from the Internal Revenue Service. Dare we mention the Templeton Foundation and the Discovery Institute, two faith-based organizations masquerading as scientific endeavors? We need an anti–Discovery Institute to step forward. If you start buying my books as well as Stephen Hawking's books, I can create my own anti–Discovery Institute and start organizing the effort against the powerful religious lobby.

Finally, people always ask, "How did September the 11th change you?" Well, here's how it changed thusly: Well, I stopped being so damn politically and religiously correct!

Thank you very much!

Eugenica

Ladies and gentlemen, I thank you very much for your presence at this ceremony celebrating my mother's life and accomplishments. As you all know, the world owes a debt of gratitude to my mother for all the progress we see around us today.

The survival of the fittest is nature's way to select the best and most adaptable genes in living organisms in the universe, thereby eliminating the weakest and less desirable genes from the general pool.

I hold in total contempt all those who have called me the product of science racism or pseudo-science; after all, my modus operandi is the application to the human pool of genes what nature does to the pool of animal and plant genes.

My dear father, Sir Francis Galton, was perfectly right in all his assertions in his famous book, *Heredity Genius*. I assume you all here do agree that a man's natural abilities are derived by inheritance, under exactly the same limitations as are the form and physical features of the whole organic world.

Consequently, it is easy—notwithstanding those limitations—to obtain by careful selection a permanent breed of dogs or horses gifted with peculiar powers of running, or doing anything else, so it would be quite practicable to produce a highly gifted race of men by judicious marriages during several consecutive generations.

And I want to pay tribute to a lady that has stood by me through thick and thin, Margaret Sanger. Margaret, I sincerely love you! Misunderstood by many, Margaret is arguably the world's pre-eminent feminist. I love the title of her monthly periodical, "The Woman Rebel," with its cunning slogan, "No gods and no masters." Wow, that should be the cry of every enlightened woman in the world!

I want to thank Margaret for having the foresight to coin these two wonderful words: *birth control*. I also want to congratulate her for establishing a Planned Parenthood center in so many minority neighborhoods. By arguing that "the undeniable feeble-minded should indeed, not only be discouraged but prevented from propagating their heirs," Margaret has masterfully made her case for my raison d'être; and for that, I will forevermore be grateful.

Thank you very much!

Nazia

Welcome! Welcome, ladies and gentlemen. Nearly two hundred thousand people die all over the world every single day! Now, who is responsible for that? Do we hold Mother Nature in contempt for that? We must all realize that death—as much as life—is part of the natural selection of the fittest.

Why am I continually held responsible for the biggest lie in the history of the world? The purported death of six million Jews entails the greatest fabrication that the Zionist Zealots have manufactured to play their victim cards in the influential centers of the world. No…no…no! Please, do not boo me! Am I also at fault for the death of the seventy million people who died during World War II? Why am I always blamed for the gassing of six hundred thousand gypsies and two hundred thousand physically and mentally handicapped?

Ladies and gentlemen, it is time to stop being politically correct and start being scientifically convicted of the important role of Mother Nature in weeding out the weak, feeble, and retarded races in favor of the strong and smart Aryan race.

Let me be frank with you all: The blond and blue-eyed Aryans, with their elongated toes and picture-perfect sitting posture, are the most advanced and physically attractive *Homo sapiens* roaming the earth today. Please, look carefully around you for this amazing and most despicable fact: An Asian girl, with a husband or boyfriend from a different race, will most likely pick a blond, blue-eyed white man as a mate. When was the last time you saw an Asian woman going out with a non-Asian man with black hair? No…no…no…ask Yoko Ono, that weirdo who destroyed the Beatles, the greatest rock and roll band in the history of the world! Better yet, check out the Columbia University research on racial preferences in dating. Thank you! Thank you! Thank you!

Please, please, please…could you all say with me three times loud and clear the following three words: Gentlemen prefer blondes! Gentlemen prefer blondes! Gentlemen prefer blondes! Wow! That makes me feel so much better! Blondes have more fun always!

I often wonder why my mother shortened her name to Eva when she met my father, Adolf: Evolution seems to carry a lot more weight for me. I still believe today that Dad was the one who coerced her into adopting the shorter moniker. Dad, am I right?

My dad remains one of the greatest men who ever lived! Misunderstood, ridiculed, and hated by many, he believed that speeding the physical and mental development of the human race is the greatest gift one can contribute to the world.

Thank you very much, ladies and gentlemen, for coming today!

Collectiva

Hello, everyone! Thank you very much for coming today. One word I want you all to carry with you in memory of my mother is the word *struggle*. My sisters have already underlined very eloquently nature's struggle in producing and reproducing the very best and fittest species. The racial struggles that my sister Naz pointed out—although politically incorrect—are nonetheless true scientific occurrences.

I want at this time to focus on a very important topic that my mother cared a great deal for: the natural class struggles taking place in most of our societies today. The imperialist powers headed by the United States have brought upon the world a destructive capitalistic system where a few rich individuals, families, and countries continue to exploit the rest of the world's goods, services, and resources unopposed.

It is now the right time that the workers of the world unite and rise up to bring about a new world order, a classless and stateless world, an "open society"—if I may quote one of my heroes, the philanthropic George Soros, who daily finances our struggles around the world—where the bourgeoisie no longer abuses the proletariat, where geopolitical decisions are made on behalf of every country and society, where private property belongs to everyone, where the global means of production belongs to every human living on our planet, where social justice maintains the rights of every individual, where the same outcomes are guaranteed to every citizen of the world, where every human on the planed is granted by the one world government his or her proper rights to decent housing, health care, education, employment, fair income, and equitable social security benefits.

As you all can plainly see, the capitalist model has failed, and it is again the right time for the workers of all the nations of the world to bring about a caliphate…a revolution that would overthrow by any means necessary the evil and polluting corporations of the rich industrial countries, cease control of the world's wealth, and empower the one world government with the power and authority to redistribute fairly and equally the stolen fortunes of the citizens of the world to the people of the world.

Thank you very much!

Darwin

Thank you very much…thank you…thank you very much…thank you…thank you. Thank you! Thank you! Thank you!

Ladies and gentlemen, I am honored today at your presence, and I shall forevermore be grateful for your support in my moment of sorrow.

Dear honored guests, death, arguably the most painful element of the natural selection process, has visited my family four times. As many of you already know, two of my children died in their infancy, and my beloved Annie passed away at the tender age of ten!

When Eva, my preferred name for my beloved deceased daughter, passed on, I was taken aback at the tremendous amount of sorrow that my wife Emma and I shared: The first three died unexpectedly of course. Eva's slow degeneration, however, made us feel paralyzed at our powerlessness to reverse the slow, gradual, and natural extinction of life.

Ladies and gentlemen, the success that my other children have achieved in their careers has convinced me that marrying my cousin was not the cause of the untimely passing of the first three; and the strong support and love that Emma has always provided to my children and myself constitute the two most important reasons I am standing before you today.

Ladies and gentlemen, life is indeed the product of chance and natural selection. As you may not know, my dad was the major reason I got into medical school at the University of Edinburgh. Well, I flunked medical school! Well…I really did…really. Natural history was the field of study that really aroused—and I use that word quite intentionally—my interest.

Greatly disappointed in my performance in school, and concerned that my love for shooting and riding would most likely overcome my loathing of studying, my dad got me enrolled at Cambridge, with the intent of converting a drifter into a parson, a priest in the Anglican Church.

My low grades would not allow me to register for the honor programs at Cambridge, and I was obliged to apply for one of the simpler degree programs. I am forevermore thankful to botanist Professor Henslow…John Stevens Henslow, for making me a firm believer in my tremendous intellectual capacity. My love for natural history was rekindled, and my grades improved to the point that I became the tenth best student in my class.

For most of my adolescence and early adulthood, I carried a heavy weight on my shoulders. As most of you may know, Erasmus Darwin, my paternal grandfather, is a famous scientist, poet, inventor…an intellectual heavyweight in the first order: I never felt that I could measure up. That is why I escaped to the world of athleticism as a clever excuse to deny my intellectual heritage.

I read countless of times his masterpiece, Zoonomy; and I memorized the part where Grandpa miraculously articulated:

> Would it not be too bold to imagine that in the great length of time since the earth began to exist…that all warm-blooded animals have arisen from one living filament, which The Great First Cause [God's Creation] endowed with…the power of acquiring new parts…and thus possessing the faculty of continuing to improve by its own inherent activity, and of delivering down those improvements by generation to its posterity [descendants], world without end?!

Ladies and gentlemen, do you all see now why the apple does not fall far from the tree? Thank you! Thank you! My magnum opus—as you all know I am the proud writer of *On the Origen of Species*—was not written to replace the Bible, as is reported to me by quite a few individuals: I had to top Grandpa! As a matter of fact, I was in a tight race with my good friend, Sir Alfred Russell Wallace, for the publication of my theory of evolution through natural selection.

I could not believe his letter to me expressing my theory in content albeit not in the exact terms: Wow! I was shocked to be sick. My good friend forced me to abandon the long, detailed, and meticulous book I was writing on the subject for a hurried "abstract" version that took me ten long and painful months to produce. I could never live with myself if I was not the first to introduce the theory of evolution to the world, an idea I pondered for nearly a quarter of a century.

I am again grateful and thankful to Professor Henslow for inciting and arranging my participation in Captain Robert FitzRoy's famous South American boat expedition on the HMS *Beagle*.

Chance—what my lovely Christian wife, Emma, would call divine providence—has always played an important part in my life. To keep a young and seasick lad busy and interested, Captain handed to me one of the greatest books I have ever read…one of the most important books in the history of the world, Lyell's *Principles of Geology*. Charles Lyell's three volumes displaying his uniformitarian theories—the present is a key to the past, and the forces in operation today across the surface of the earth help immeasurably in the understanding of the earth's recent and distant changes—constitute a must for any aspiring young scientist; and I credit Lyell as the central figure in my evolutionary theory. Thanks for your applause! Thank you very much.

My wife is fond of saying to me that Saint Peter—and not Lyell—was the originator of the Uniformitarian Principle. She likes to quote to me 2 Peter 3:4:

> Where is the promise of his coming? For since the fathers fell asleep, all things continue as they were from the beginning of the creation.

I would laugh quite often, agreeing with her in my heart even when I absolutely knew that she was totally wrong. Thank you! Thank you very much! Even though I believe she was wrong, do you really believe that she was erroneous?

My friend and great supporter Thomas Huxley—I've never known who was the first person to call him my bulldog—my friend and hero Lyell, my great buddy Hooker, and I, we were what I consider now the scientific rat pack of the time. No…no…no…we did not party, mess around, and burned the midnight candle like Sinatra and his crew; but we sure did pretty much everything else! Boy! Do I often reminisce about those lovely days!

Not privy to the incredible sophistication of the transmission electron microscope—Wow! Their 3-D pictures of the cell are awesome!—we all thought that animal and plant cells were simply "homogeneous and structure-less globules of protoplasm," akin to your Jell-O. Based on that erroneous cellular viewpoint, I wrote the most regrettable words of my life, and I quote from my masterpiece:

> If it could be demonstrated that any complex organ existed, which could not have been formed by numerous, successive, slight modifications, my theory would absolutely break down.

And I understand that many young scientists, after examining some of the trillions of amazing molecular machines that operate within the cell, are awestruck at the incredible level of cellular sophistication. I like reading this passage which I think summarizes their findings from the book *Darwin's Black Box*, written by this bright and elegant young American biochemist:

> The cumulative results show with piercing clarity that life is based on machines—machines made up molecules! Molecular machines haul cargo from one place in the cell to another along "highways" made of other molecules, while still others act as cables, ropes, and pulleys to hold the cell in shape. Machines turn cellular switches on and off, sometimes killing the cell or causing it to grow. Solar-powered machines capture the energy of photons and store it in chemicals. Electrical machines allow current to flow through nerves. Manufacturing machines build other molecular machines, as well as themselves. Cells swim using machines, copy themselves with machinery, ingest food with machinery. In short, highly sophisticated molecular machines control every cellular process. Thus the details of life are highly calibrated, and the machinery of life enormously complex.

Wow! That flies in the face of everything my rat pack and I believed and preached with fervor for many, many years! Machines…built…to specifications…and…operating…with precise…calibration? What…what about the undirected process of natural selection? Who…excuse me…what principle is at work here? And I myself have examined some molecular machines with design and performance features unlike anything anyone has ever seen. The challenge for us today is to come up with a natural, reasonable, and believable step-by-step explanation and demonstration of the successive evolutionary stages of those nanomachines. No one, I repeat, no one so far has done that. I have cast the first stone: who will throw the next?

Ladies and gentlemen, the evolution of the engineering features of cellular machinery, although at present inadequately explained by modern biology, does not trouble me as much as the codes…the codes…the codes…the information in the DNA. Some of the young computer scientists at Cambridge have told me that the packaging and the design of the genetic information in the cell are built to accommodate the challenges of communication using more advanced engineering principles than those in operation today in our most technologically advanced communication and computing businesses, laboratories, research centers, or government operations.

Finally, what troubles my friends and I the most…what gives me shivers while lying in bed at night is the embarrassing specter of all the missing links that still have not been discovered in the fossil records! Moreover, where did all the major animal phyla that suddenly appeared during the Cambrian Explosion come from? That, ladies and gentlemen, represents as great a devastating blow to my theory as anything else. To quote my fellow Brit, Sir Winston Churchill, this is the real "riddle, wrapped in a mystery, inside an enigma."

At the risk of repeating myself, I wish to reemphasize to you the fear that I have kept secret from the first day that I wrote my famous masterpiece: the Cambrian Explosion again! Wow! Those pathetic words have given me countless nightmares! Where do all those organisms come from…all of a sudden? What about common descent?

We all thought that within a few years of my publication of *The Descent of Man* that most—if not all—of the pieces of the puzzle would have been found by now. Most of the intermediate forms between the major species should have already been identified and catalogued. Nothing of the sort has materialized! Instead, the fossil record seems to indicate that a universe of new species suddenly appears out of nowhere!

Ladies and gentlemen, the scientific institutions of the world have failed to appropriate the amount of money necessary to find the missing links of all those organisms. For that, I hold all the governments of the world responsible for spending too much on global warming and not enough on fossil research. Thank you very much! Thank you very much!

Ladies and gentlemen, I find very fascinating a number of comments articulated by this young lad, Stephen Meyer, a very promising American scientist in his book *Signature in the Cell*. I recall this young philosopher insinuating that the time required for chance to have arranged the amino acids in the earth into the various organisms we find today on our planet is far greater than the time this universe has existed! He presents statistical data that appear to support this far-fetched idea. I would challenge you all—we Brits are very much in love with the vernacular of the American South—to investigate this matter thoroughly and report to me afterward.

Well, was I wrong to have conducted my little evolutionary experiment? I do not think so! I have no regret about writing and publishing *On the Origin of the Species*. I had to set my footprints as a thinker in the mold of Isaac Newton, Charles Lyell, and John Herschel come hell or what may!

I should have held the publication of *The Descent of Man*, had I then known what the biochemical world is now revealing about cellular structures, information, and machinery. My wife, that dear Christian lady, warned me ad infinitum not to proceed any further in that important endeavor; however, I could not wait any longer: I had a score to settle with Christianity. I could not...nor will I ever forgive a god who claims to hear and answer prayer while my beautiful daughter Annie died in my arms at the tender age of ten!

The numerous cries of mercy and agony of my wife, a pious and virtuous Christian woman, were ignored and went unanswered! The whole tragedy confirmed my previous suspicion that religion was mere superstition. What kind of rational being would send living beings and children to an eternity of suffering in a lake of fire?

I had my mind made up when I turned forty; and at forty-two when my daughter died, I became hostile, secretly at first in order not to disappoint my wife, my family, my colleagues, and the readers of my publications, and then overtly when my legacy could not be threatened by family, friend, or foe.

Am I responsible for eugenics, Nazism, the Holocaust, racism, World War I, World War II, Communism, and the secularism of the world? I do not think so! History is marred with the violent actions of crazed men; and Christianity is fairly a recent player in the history of the world and the history of world religion.

Am I an atheist? No...no...no! My good friend Huxley coined the word that accurately describes my belief: agnostic. I do not believe that the existence of God is unknowable, but rather unknown and inconsequential.

As a scientist, I worship Mother Nature through the sacraments of observation and experimentation at the altar of sound and logical reasoning. Anything else is hearsay...superstition...religion... and not science.

Thank you, ladies and gentlemen!

The Steve Martin Song

Steve Martin, Johnny Carson, Frank Sinatra, Bing Cosby, and Bob Hope.
Atheists don't have no songs
Christians have their hymns and pages,
Hava Nagila's for the Jews,
Baptists have the rock of ages,
Atheists just sing the blues.
Romantics play Claire de Lune,
Born-agains sing He is risen,
But no one ever wrote a tune,
For godless existentialism.
For atheists, there is no good news,
They'll never sing a song of faith.
In their songs they have a rule
The "He" is always lower case,
The "He" is always lower case.

Some folks sing a Bach cantata,
Lutherans get Christmas trees,
Atheist songs add up to nada,
But they do have Sundays free.
Pentecostalists sing, they sing to heaven,
Coptics have the books of scrolls,
Numerologists can count to seven,
Atheists have rock and roll.
For atheists, there's no good news,
They'll never sing a song of faith.
In their songs, they have a rule,
The "He" is always lowercase,
The "He" is always lowercase.
Atheists, atheists, atheists, they have no songs.
Catholics dress up for Mass,
Watch football in their underpants,
Watch football in their underpants.
Atheists, atheists, atheists don't have no songs.

Gradual (Psalm 136) with the Assembly Responding, "For His Mercy Endures Forever."
Saint Gregory the Great

Oh, give thanks to the Lord, for He is good!
For His mercy endures forever.
Oh, give thanks the God of gods!
For His mercy endures forever.
Oh, give thanks to the Lord of lords!
For His mercy endures forever:
To Him who alone does great wonders,
For His mercy endures forever;
To Him who by wisdom made the heavens,
For His mercy endures forever;
To Him who laid out the earth above the waters,
For His mercy endures forever;
To Him who made great lights,
For His mercy endures forever—
To rule the sun by day,
For His mercy endures forever;
The moon and stars to rule by night,
For His mercy endures forever.

A REQUIEM FOR EVOLUTION

To Him who stuck Egypt in their firstborn,
For His mercy endures forever;
And brought Israel from among them,
For His mercy endures forever;
With a strong hand, and with an outstretched arm,
For His mercy endures forever;
To Him who divided the Red Sea in two,
For His mercy endures forever;
And made Israel pass through the midst of it,
For His mercy endures forever;
But overthrew Pharaoh and his army in the Red Sea,
For His mercy endures forever;
To Him who led His people through the wilderness,
For His mercy endures forever;
To Him who struck down great kings,
For His mercy endures forever;
And slew famous kings,
For His mercy endures forever—
Sihon, king of the Amorites,
For His mercy endures forever;
And Og, king of Bashan,
For His mercy endures forever—
And gave their land as a heritage,
For His mercy endures forever;
A heritage to Israel His servant,
For His mercy endures forever.
Who remembered us in our lowly state,
For His mercy endures forever;
And rescued us from our enemies,
For His mercy endures forever;
Who gives flood to all flesh,
For His mercy endures forever.
Oh, give thanks to the God of heaven!
For His mercy endures forever.

PIERRE W. BEAUSEJOUR

Offertory
Vladimir Horowitz in His Interpretation of Tchaikovsky's First Piano Concerto
and
Beethoven's Fifty (Emperor) Piano Concerto
Agnus Dei
Michael W. Smith

Alleluia
Alleluia
For the Lord God Almighty reigns
Alleluia
Alleluia
For the Lord God Almighty reigns
Alleluia
Holy
Holy are You Lord God Almighty
Worthy is the Lamb
Worthy is the Lamb
You are holy
Holy are You Lord God Almighty
Worthy is the Lamb
Worthy is the Lamb
Amen

Libera Me
Andrea Bocceli and Luciano Pavarotti

Libera me, Domine, de morte aeterna
(Deliver, O Lord, from eternal death)
in die illa tremenda
(that awful day)
quando coeli movendi sunt et terra,
(when the heavens and the earth shall be shaken)
dum veneris judicare saeculum per ignem.
(And you shall come to judge the world by fire)
Tremens factus sum ego et timeo,
(I am seized with fear and trembling)
dum discussio venerit atque venture ira:
(until the trial is at hand and the wrath to com:)
quando coeli movendi sunt et terra.
(when the heavens and earth shall be shaken)

Closing Prayer
Reverend Billy Graham

Heavenly Father, we come before You today to ask Your forgiveness and to seek Your direction and guidance. We know Your Word says, "Woe to those who call evil good," but that's exactly what we have done. We have lost our spiritual equilibrium and reversed our values. We confess that.
We have ridiculed the absolute truth of Your Word and call it pluralism.
We have worshipped other gods and called it multiculturalism.
We have endorsed perversion and called it alternative lifestyle.
We have exploited the poor and called it the lottery.
We have rewarded laziness and called it welfare.
We have killed the unborn and called it choice.
We have shot abortionists and called it justifiable.
We have neglected to discipline our children and called it building self-esteem.
We have abused power and called it politics.
We have coveted our neighbor's possessions and called it ambition.
We have polluted the air with profanity and pornography and called it freedom of expression.
We have ridiculed the time-honored values of our forefathers and called it enlightenment.
Search us, O God, and know our heart today; cleanse us from every sin and set us free.
Guide and bless these men and women who have been sent to direct us to the center of
Your will; and I ask it in the name of Your Son, the Living Savior, Jesus Christ. Amen.

Benediction
Reverend Martin Luther King Junior

As the Savior so taught:
Go now and overcome!
Overcome racial hatred with love and understanding.
Overcome sexism with mutual honor and respect.
Overcome social inequities,
with fair and equal educational and employment opportunities.
Overcome mean-heartedness with a kind word for a good deed.
Overcome war!
Overcome poverty!
Overcome hunger!
Overcome thirst!
Overcome suffering!
Overcome discrimination in all its forms!
Overcome religious bigotry!

PIERRE W. BEAUSEJOUR

Overcome greed and selfishness,
by sharing the love of Jesus Christ with the least of these!
Ladies and gentlemen,
Go now and overcome! Go now and overcome! Go now and overcome!

Chapter 3

The Living God

In the Beginning God created the heavens and the earth. (Genesis 1:1)

We read from the Holy Scriptures the following account:

> And in Lystra a certain man without strength in his feet was sitting, a cripple from his mother's womb, who had never walked. This man heard Paul speaking. Paul, observing him intently and seeing that he had faith to be healed, said with a loud voice, "Stand up straight on your feet!" And he leaped and walked. Now when the people saw what Paul had done, they raised their voices, saying in the

Lacaonian language, "The gods have come down to us in the likeness of men!" And Barnabas they called Zeus, and Paul, Hermes, because he was the chief speaker. Then the priest of Zeus, whose temple was in front of their city, brought oxen and garlands to the gates, intending to sacrifice with the multitudes.

But when the apostles Barnabas and Paul heard this, they tore their clothes and ran in among the multitude, crying and saying, "Men, why are you doing these things? We also are men with the same nature as you, and preach to you that you should turn from these useless things to the living God, who made the heaven, the earth, the sea, and all things that are in them, who in bygone generations allowed all nations to walk in their own ways. Nevertheless He did not leave Himself without witness, in that He did good, gave us rain from heaven and fruitful seasons, filling our hearts with food and gladness." And with these sayings they could scarcely restrain the multitudes from sacrificing to them.

Who is this "Living God" that mankind is commanded to turn to? What is He like? Throughout the pages of the Bible, men from every nation on the face of the earth are adjured to turn from "useless things" to the Living God who "made the heavens, the earth, the sea and all that are in them." This Living God has revealed in the sacred pages of the Holy Scriptures four direct and distinct aspects of Himself.

First, *God is Spirit* (John 4:24), and they that approach Him *must* do so in spirit and in truth. God cannot be apprehended by the mind, the emotions, or the will of the most erudite human being. The God of the universe created the heavens, laid the foundation of the earth, and "formed the spirit of man within him" (Zechariah 12:1) in order to establish relationship with mankind and elicit worship from the crown jewel of His creation (John 4:23, 1 John 1:3, Exodus 34:14). We must learn to serve God in spirit (Romans 1:9, 7:6), worship God, our Creator, in spirit (John 4:24), sing and pray with our spirit (1 Corinthians 14:1–5): the spirit of man is then his primary channel of communication with the Living God. The fall (Genesis 3) has deadened the spirit of man (Ephesians 2:1, 5) and severed his fellowship and communion with his Maker. With a dead spirit, mankind is deprived of his sole faculty capable of interacting with God, who is Spirit. The Spirit of God must take the initiative to quicken or regenerate or make alive the spirit of man (Ephesians 2:1, 5), thereby giving him a new birth (John 3:3) and remaking him into a totally new creature (2 Corinthians 5:17) whose spirit is susceptible of receiving the Holy Spirit (John 20:22, Acts 2:1–4).

Second, *God is Love* (1 John 4:16), and He vividly depicted His love by sending His only begotten Son to die on the cross as payment for the sins of mankind (John 3:16). Do you want to see and know what real and true love is like? Then, you should take a good look at God by reading, pray-reading, and meditating on His Word, the Bible, during the day and the wee hours of the night (Psalm 1:2). When you make God's Word your delight, He has promised to make your life fruitful (Psalm 1:3, Jeremiah 17:7–8). You should get to know God personally by committing your life to Him completely and by entering into a covenant relationship with the Maker and Keeper of your soul (Psalm 121:5; Job 35:10, 36:3). You should schedule daily to spend some meaningful time in prayer with God in the evening, during the morning, and at noon (Psalm 55:17). Your day should start with the evening prayer the day before. Try to be faithful, persistent, and consistent in your prayer life (Ephesians 6:18, Luke 18:1–8): God is constantly looking all over the world for people whose heart is perfect toward Him so that He can manifest Himself to them and intervene on their behalf (John 14:21, 2 Chronicles 16:9).

Third, *God is Light* (1 John 1:5), and He lives "in the light that no man can approach" (1 Timothy 6:16). Jesus, God in the flesh (John 1:14, 1 Timothy 3:16), is "the light of the world" (John 8:12, 9:5). In Him (Jesus) was life, and His life was the light of the world (John 1:4). Those that follow Jesus shall walk in the light and not in darkness and shall have the light of life (John 8:12). As the Spirit of the Lord moved upon the waters of the earth moments before creation (Genesis 1:2), His very first command was that there be light (Genesis 1:3). After the exodus of the Israelites from Egypt, the Lord led the people by day in a pillar of a cloud and by night in a pillar of fire to give them light (Exodus 13:21). Since the Lord is the salvation and the light of His people, they should fear no one (Psalm 27:1). The entrance of God's words gives light to His people (Psalm 119:130) because His word is a lamp unto their feet and a light unto their path (Psalm 119:105). The Lord shall be "an everlasting light" to His people (Isaiah 60:20), and He calls all of them children of light (1 Thessalonians 5:5, John 12:36).

Fourth, God is a *Consuming Fire* (Deuteronomy 4:24, Hebrews 12:29) who destroys sin as it is found in the lives of His enemies, the enemies of His people, and even the lives of His own people (Deuteronomy 9:3; Genesis 18:20–21, 19:12–25; 2 Kings 1:10–12; Isaiah 1:28; Leviticus 10:1–2; 2 Thessalonians 2:8). Sin must be atoned for by the blood of the sinner; otherwise, there is no remission for it (Hebrews 9:22). Prior to the exodus of the children of Israel, the Lord destroyed all the firstborns of the Egyptians while He "passed over" the firstborns of the children of Israel because He had ordered the Jewish families to kill a lamb, take of its blood, and "strike it on the two side posts and the upper post" of their homes so that He can "pass over" them and atone for their sins (Exodus 12). In similar fashion, Jesus Christ's hands were nailed to the cross, and His head was pierced by the crown of thorns that the Roman soldiers had thrust upon it.

In the Old Testament, God requested the killing of animals (lambs, goats, bulls, calves, pigeons, turtledoves) as sacrificial payments for the sins of the people. Actually, the sacrifices of those animals did not and could not really blot out the sins of one single human being (Hebrews 10:40). Those sacrifices anticipated and prefigured the killing of Jesus, the real PASSOVER Lamb of God who would die on the cross at Calvary to atone for all the sins of God's people (Matthew 1:21, Revelation 13:8, Genesis 3:15, Acts 20:28). Therefore, Satan, the fallen angels, and all the men and women in the history of the world whose sins are not covered by the blood of Jesus will all be consumed in the lake of "everlasting fire" prepared by God for them at the end of the world (Matthew 25:41, Revelation 20:15).

The knowledge of the existence of this Living God, the longing for fellowship with the Creator of the universe, and the fear of divine retribution are concepts that God has personally integrated deep within the confines of the human psyche (John 1:9; Acts 14:17, 17:27; Psalm 19:1–3). Man's natural inclination for the divine and the supernatural appears innate and instinctive; indeed man was formed "in the image and after the likeness" of His creator (Genesis 1:26), who has meticulously sprinkled the fertile seeds of eternity in his heart (Romans 1:19–20).

Every primitive society from every corner of the world from the Hutus in Central Africa to the Hurons of North America have left a spiritual legacy akin to the Sumerians in southeastern Iraq, the real harbingers of the Hebrews of the Middle East who would later provide the underpinnings for the propagation of the Jewish, Christian, and Muslim faiths: Man's spiritual aspirations are not bound by his physical constraints, they do indeed transcend his configuration of time and space.

The great biblical expositor, Saint Augustine, echoes the outcries of every individual that has ever walked upon the earth when he uttered the following poignant words:

> Yet man, this part of Thy creation, desires to praise Thee. Thou movest us to praise Thee; for Thou hast formed us for Thyself, and our hearts are restless till they find rest in Thee.

As such, in His Holy Scriptures, God asserts categorically that His fingerprints feature prominently in man and in every aspect of His marvelous creation:

> 18 For the wrath of God is revealed from heaven against all ungodliness and unrighteousness of men, who suppress the truth in unrighteousness, 19 Because what may be known of God is manifest in them, for God has shown it to them. 20 For since the creation of the world His invisible attributes are clearly seen, being understood by the things that are made, even His eternal power and Godhead, so that they are without excuse, 21 because, although they knew God, they did not glorify Him as God, nor were thankful, but became futile in their thoughts, and their foolish hearts were darkened. 22 Professing to be wise, they became fools, 23 and changed the glory of the incorruptible God into an image made like corruptible man—and birds and four-footed animals and creeping things.

The fingerprints of God are then not only expressed in His special revelation, the Bible, they are also exhibited in His general revelation, the natural world. If, in the Holy Scriptures, God has manifested Himself as triune: Father, Son, and Holy Spirit (Matthew 28:19, 2 Corinthians 13:14), is it simple serendipity that the universe should be composed of three components: time, space, and energy? Is it also a mere coincidence that time has three aspects: past, present, and future? Is it pure chance that space has three coordinates: length, width, and height? Is it normal fortuity that energy can be perceived under three prisms: matter in motion producing phenomena? Is it just happenstance that man, the crown jewel of God's creation, is tripartite (Genesis 2:7)? He is fearfully and wonderfully endowed with a spirit, a soul, and a body (1 Thessalonians 5:23). Is it also pure chance that man's spirit has three parts: conscience, intuition, and communion (Acts 17:16, 2 Corinthians 2:13, 1 Corinthians 5:3, Matthew 26:41, 1 Corinthians 16:18, Mark 2:8, Luke 1:47, John 4:23, Romans 1:9); or that man's soul embodies three elements: mind, emotion, and will (Proverbs 2:10, Lamentations 3:20, Deuteronomy 6:5, 1 Samuel 18:1, Psalm 84:2, Psalm 42:1); or that man's body is divided into three parts: the head, the trunk, and the limbs? Let's also recall that the Tabernacle that God ordered Moses to build to the exact specifications He had outlined to him earlier embodied three parts: the outer court, the holy place, and the holy of holies.

A REQUIEM FOR EVOLUTION

A triune God would be expected to leave traces of His handiworks all over His creation; and as a result, the entire universe provides an unmitigated declaration of the nature of its great Creator.

Are all the marvelous creatures living in the world today, are the earth, the sun, the moon, the planets, the stars, and all the galaxies, products of chance operating on random mutation over a long period of time, or were they all created by a superintelligent being? Let's consider some arguments making the case for the Living God as the Creator of the entire universe.

In his critically acclaimed opus magnum, *Signature in the Cell*, Stephen Meyer compares the following two sets of sequential letters and numbers:

AGTCTGGGACGCGCCGCCGCCATGATCATCCCTGTACGCTGCTTCACTTGTGGCAAGATC-
GTCGGCAACAAGTGGGAGCTTACCTGGGCTCTGCAGGCCGAGTACACCGAGGGGTGAG-
GCGCGGGCCGGGGCTAGGGGCTGAGTCCGCCGTGGGGCGGGCCGGGGCTGAGTCCGCC-
CTGGGGTGCGCGCCGGGGCGGGAGGCGCAGCGCTGCCTGAGGCCAGCGCCCATGAGC-
AGCTTCAGGCCCGGCTTCTCCAGCCCCGCTCTGTGATCTGCTTTCGGGAGAACC
01010111011010000110010101101110001000000110100101101110001000000111010001101-
00001100101001000000100001101101111011101010111001001110011011001010010010000000-
1101111011001100010000001101000011101010110110101100001010110111000100000011001-
0101110110011001010110111001110100011100110010000000110100101110100

(Reprint from *Signature in the Cell*)

Concerning the first set of data, the sequential set of letters, Dr. Stephen Meyer comments:

> This string of characters looks as if it could be a block encoded information, perhaps a section of text or machine code. That impression is entirely correct, for this string of characters is not just a random assortment of the four letters A, T, G, and C, but a representation of part of the sequence of genetic assembly instructions for building a protein machine—an RNA polymerase—critical to gene expression (or information processing) in a living cell.

The second set of data, the sequential set of numbers, entices Dr. Meyer to assert the following:

> This sequence also appears to be an information-rich sequence, albeit written in binary code. As it happens, this sequence is also not just a random array of characters, but the first words of the Declaration of Independence ("When in the course of human events…") written in the *binary conversion* of the American Standard Code for Information Interchange (ASCII). In the ASCII code, short specified sequences of zeros and ones correspond to specific alphabetic letters, numerals, or punctuation marks.

If the accumulation of the zeroes and ones in the second set of data elicits the careful intervention of an intelligent designer, isn't it equally plausible that the carefully arranged strings of *A*s, *C*s, *G*s, and *T*s (*A* stands for adenine, *C* for cytosine, *G* for guanine, and *T* for thymine—the four bases in the DNA that carry genetic information) in the first set of data should also warrant the handiwork of a superintelligent agent? In that regard, it is incomprehensible why so many scientists would demand the presence of intelligence in the second set of data while simultaneously denying its manifestation in the former.

In examining table 3, a few questions are in order. Since the presence of the three letters *A-U-G* (The cell uses sets of three of the aforementioned bases in the DNA as unit codes in its programmed instructions for the production of the various proteins it needs to build all the structures in all the organisms that are in the world.) yields the command to start and end the production of the various proteins for the cell to manufacture methionine, the protein needed to order the *start* of the production sequence (Programmers are quite familiar with the *Start* and *Stop* commands when writing a particular software.) of proteins in the production of the cells, tissues, organs, systems of organs, and organisms that populate our world today, who or what determines the presence of methionine at the *start* of the queue? Who or what determines the precise arrangement of codons (units of instructions in the DNA) in the DNA instruction code necessary for the precise production of a specific cell or tissue or organ or organ system or organism?

The gene software uses the commands UAA or UAG or UGA to *stop* or terminate a particular sequence of instruction; as such, how does the DNA software intuitively know where to *stop* the production of a particular protein in order to *start* another one? The software in the DNA entails specific instructions commanding the cell to *start* (AUG or GUG), thereby generating particular protein molecules necessary to manufacture the cells, the tissues, the organs, the organic systems of a particular organism.

Can there be specified information, the like warranted for the production of the sophisticated organic systems that permeate planet earth without the a priori presence of intelligence? Who wrote the software in the DNA to the exact specifications for the generation of so many wonderful creatures and living things manifest in our world today? Does not the precise coding of the DNA software necessitate the intervention of intelligence for both its design and implementation?

Moreover, the cell utilizes in a more elaborate and intensive fashion the same coding techniques and patterns that programmers use in the creation of sophisticated system and program software. The "Encode Project" that managed to identify precisely the entire genetic code of humans and various animals demonstrated without a shadow of doubt to the computer programmers peeking through the miniature confines of cellular biology that the cells employ coding strategies similar albeit more sophisticated than the most erudite programmers could fathom (see table 4).

For example, the so-called Junk DNA, parts of the DNA that seemingly do not include coding instructions, is used by the cell as an operating system, akin to the Windows 10, Mac-OS X, and Linux operating systems, that allows computers to command and control all the interactions that they undertake.

Moreover, the cellular information system embodies an automated error-correction system similar to those found in very sophisticated system programs. For instance, when writing with Microsoft

Word, the program will automatically correct a misspelled word. The cell information system contains a similar mechanism.

Furthermore, the cellular information system embodies a hierarchical system of files within folders to house various files of programming. Likewise, the cell has at its disposal numerous complete storage and retrieval information modules for short- or long-term storage and retrieval of files of information.

Additionally, the cellular information system can utilize a Nested Coding or Dual Coding mechanism for the encryption of data. The presence of information at the basic level of life and the operations of the cellular information system warrant the sine qua non intervention of an intelligent agent, the Living God of the universe.

Table 3

UUU Phenylalanine UUC Phenylalanine UUA Leucine UUG Leucine	UCU Serine UCC Serine UCA Serine UCG Serine	UAU Tyrosine UAC Tyrosine UAA STOP UAG STOP	UGU Cysteine UGC Cysteine UGA STOP UGG Tryptophan
CUU Leucine CUC Leucine CUA Leucine CUG Leucine	CCU Proline CCC Proline CCA Proline CCG Proline	CAU Histidine CAC Histidine CAA Glutamine CAG Glutamine	CGU Arginine CGC Arginine CGA Arginine CGG Arginine
AUU Isoleucine AUC Isoleucine AUA Isoleucine AUG Methionine START	ACU Theonine ACC Theonine ACA Theonine ACG Theonine	AAU Asparagine AAC Asparagine AAA Lysine AAG Lysine	AGU Serine AGC Serine AGA Arginine AGG Arginine
GUU Valine GUC Valine GUU Valine GUG Valine	GCU Alanine GCC Alanine GCA Alanine GCG Alanine	GAU Aspartic GAC Aspartic GAA Glutamic GAG Glutamic	GGU Glycine GGC Glycine GGA Glycine GGG Glycine

The DNA genetic code describing the exact amino acids that the various DNA base triplets elicit after transcription and translation in gene expression. Table 3 is a reprint from *Signature in the Cell* (page 102).

Table 4

"Design Patterns" Post "Encode Project"

1. "Junk DNA" as Operating System
2. Automated Error Correction
3. Files within Folders Hierarchical Filing System
4. Distributed Storage and Retrieval Information Modules
5. Nested Coding of Information (Dual Coding or Encryption) (https://www.youtube.com/watch?v=b7Vf6MvBiz8)

It is precisely this line of reasoning that enticed Dr. Stephen Meyer to articulate, in his masterpiece, *Signature of the Cell*, the presence of an intelligent source as the plausible agent responsible for the design and implementation of so sophisticated a program as the DNA software, after ruling out the theories of chance and necessity or a combination of the two as viable alternatives. Our venerable doctor provides three mains reasons for his conclusion:

First of all, there is in the entire universe no other known cause that can adequately explain the presence of the DNA software—what Dr. Stephen calls biological information, or specified information, or specified biological information—that tells the cell the types of proteins to produce and the right sequences of their production for the propagation of all the cells, tissues, organs, organic systems, and organisms in the world today.

Second of all, all the experimental evidence undertaken to recreate the undirected or unassisted accumulation of information in the cells have inadvertently confirmed the necessary intervention of an intelligent agent.

All the "prebiotic simulation experiments" undertaken under ideal and "realistic prebiotic conditions" always "generate biologically irrelevant substances" along with all "the desirable building blocks such as nucleotide bases, sugars, and amino acids." Regrettably, without the intervention of humans, all the "undesirable by-products" tend to react with the favorable and desirable building blocks to produce inert compounds such as melanoindin, a destructive chemical substance.

In order to prevent such negative "interfering cross-reactions," humans must override the intervening reactions by trapping, isolating, and removing all the undesirable reactants in order to produce the "nucleotides, sugars and amino acids" that make the building blocks necessary for the production of the desirable building blocks: once again, the presence of intelligent agents are necessary.

Moreover, all the sophisticated evolutionary algorithms, the complex computerized programs imitating the supposedly creative power of random mutation and natural selection, depend upon intelligent programmers to provide them with the right information warranted for the production of the building blocks—the nucleotides, sugars, and amino acids—forming all the living organisms active in our world today.

Third of all, Dr. Stephen Meyer relates that Intelligent Design is "the only known cause of specified information." "Undirected materialistic causes," our resident doctor of philosophy brilliantly articulates, "have not demonstrated the capacity to generate significant amounts of specified information."

On the other hand, "conscious intelligence," continues our savvy philosophe, "has repeatedly shown itself capable of producing such information." Dr. Meyer concludes:

> Conscious, rational intelligent agency-what philosophers call "agent causation," now stands as the only cause known to be capable of generating large amount of specified information starting from a nonliving state.

Moreover, Dr. Michael Behe unveils, in his magnificent book, *Darwin's Black Box*, what the field of biochemistry has revealed over the past few decades:

> The cumulative results show with piercing clarity that life is based on *machines*—machines made of molecules! Molecular machines haul cargo from one place in the cell to another along "highways" made of other molecules, while still others act as cables, ropes, and pulleys to hold cell in shape. Machines turn cellular switches on and off, sometimes killing the cell or causing it to grow. Solar-powered machines capture the energy of photons and store it in chemicals. Electrical machines allow current to flow through nerves. Manufacturing machines build other molecular machines, as well as themselves. Cells swim using machines, copy themselves with machinery, ingest food with machinery. In short, highly sophisticated molecular machines control every cellular process. Thus the details of life are finely calibrated, and the machinery of life enormously complex.

Life, in its most basic and detailed configurations, is made of machines! Molecular machines! Tiny microscopic machines that are more sophisticated, more effective, and more efficient than any piece of machinery the human mind has so far invented.

An example of such machines entails the bacterial flagellum with its complex motor drive system (figures 3A and 3B). A flagellum is a marvelous swimming device that some bacteria possess that is different than anything else observed in complex cells. It is a sophisticated "molecular machine" with a paddle (the green filament in figure 3B or the blue propeller in figure 3A) that interacts with the liquid during swimming, hooked to a complex motor drive system composed of a rotor (the purple S ring with its numerous light-brown M rings in figure 3A or the orange S ring with its numerous light orange M rings in figure 3B) around a stator (the studs and C rings in figure 3A).

Dr. Behe argues that the flagellum's motorized system has "the same mechanical elements as other rotary devices: a rotor (the rotating element) and a stator (the stationary element)," and as such, its system is deemed "irreducibly complex." Dr. Behe defines irreducible complexity as follows:

> A single system composed of several well-matched, interacting parts that contribute to the basic function, wherein the removal of any one of the parts causes the system to effectively cease functioning.

By making the case that the flagellum is irreducibly complex, Dr. Behe argues that the basic theory of evolution, natural selection acting on random mutation, could not have generated the flagellum with all its complex motorized systems.

Figure 3A. Schematic of a flagellum motor that bacteria use to swim

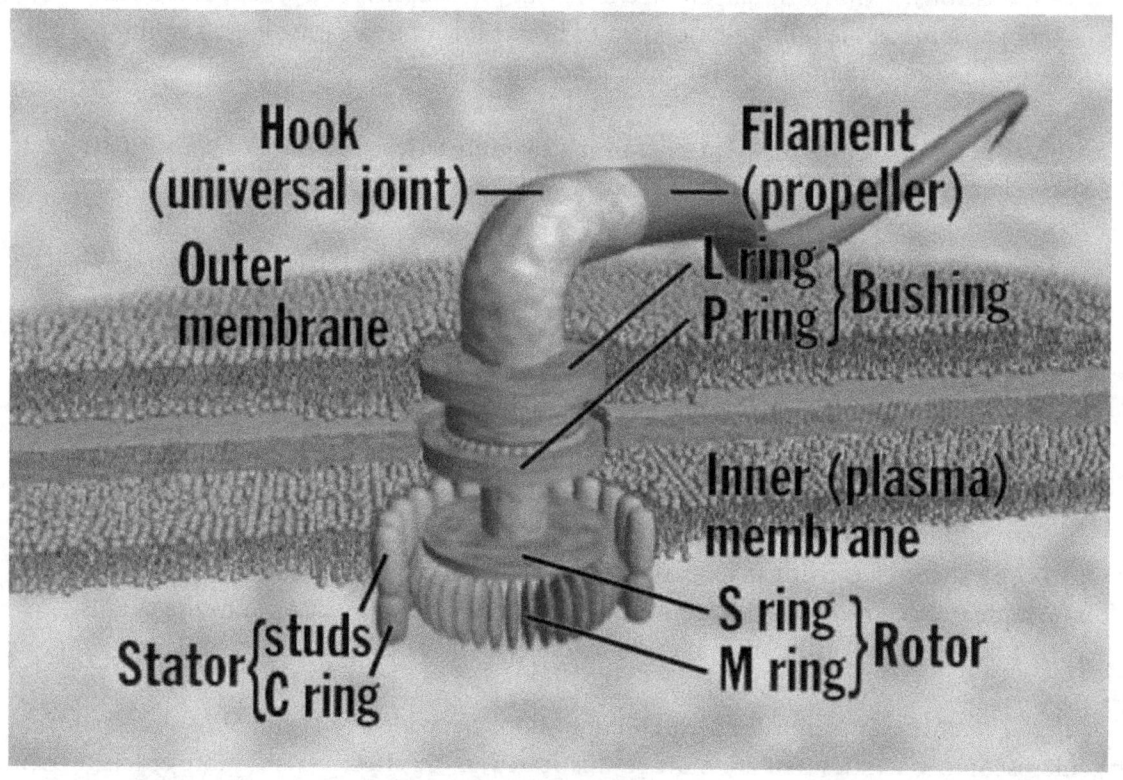

http://www.google.com/imgres?imgurl=http://www.phy.duke.edu/undergraduate/biophysics/bacterial-flagellum.jpg&imgrefurl=http://www.phy.duke.edu/undergraduate/biophysics/&h=480&w=720&sz=135&tbnid=6uKRmenpCxeYhM:&tbnh=90&tbnw=135&prev=/search%3Fq%3Dpicture%2Bbacterial%2Bflagellum%26tbm%3Disch%26tbo%3Du&zoom=1&q=picture+bacterial+flagellum&usg=__GNvzuBx31bS2nFobGHTUqElvgOk=&docid=iuWiHZwkrUgYlM&sa=X&ei=fqbCT5_0JpD0sQKwxNHyCQ&ved=0CGwQ9QEwAg&dur=2803

The Bacterial Flagellum

Figure 3B

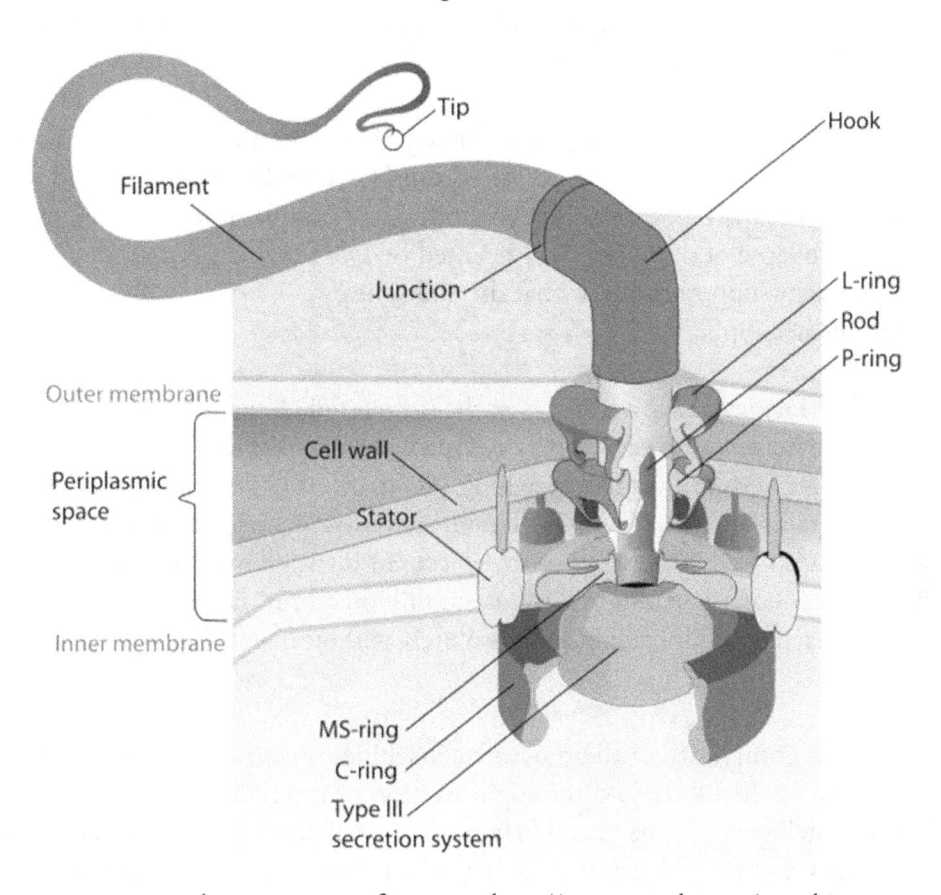

Figure labels: Tip, Filament, Junction, Hook, L-ring, Rod, P-ring, Outer membrane, Cell wall, Periplasmic space, Stator, Inner membrane, MS-ring, C-ring, Type III secretion system

<<note to layout: source of image>> http://www.google.com/search?sourceid=navclient&aq=1&oq=picture+flagel&ie=UTF-for

The two pictures of the flagellum depict an organism fashioned with tremendous sophistication, brilliant engineering, and magnificent beauty. Overwhelmed by the intricate design of the flagellum in particular, and of all living organisms in general, Dr. Beye remarks, "The elegant, coherent, functional systems upon which life depends are the result of deliberate intelligent design."

Even Richard Dawkins, a militant critic of Intelligent Design, when beholding the powerful evidence of living organisms for a Creator, was forced to compromise his views. "Biology," he denotes somewhat reluctantly, "is the study of complicated things that give the appearance of design."

Dr. Michael Denton, commenting on the microscopic machines directing and controlling all the dynamic activities taking place within the cell, opines:

> Protein molecules are the ultimate stuff of life. If we think of the cell as being analogous to a factory, then the proteins can be thought of as analogous to the machines on the factory floor which carry out individually or in groups all the

essential activities on which the life of the cell depends. Each protein is a sort of micro-miniaturized machine, so small that it must be magnified a million times before it is visible to the human eye.

The fields of biochemistry and molecular biology have, for the past six decades—from the time of the discovery of the chemical structure of the DNA by Dr. James Watson and Professor Francis Crick in 1953—slowly albeit surely been eroding the foundational structure of the theory of evolution: the total collapse of the system as presented by Darwin and his disciples of doom appear imminent and its ardent supporters know that the end is near.

Dr. Denton further stipulates:

> Molecular biology has shown that even the simplest of all living systems on earth today, bacterial cells, are exceedingly complex objects. Although the tiniest bacterial cells are incredibly small weighing less than 10 (–12) grams [ten to the minus 12 grams], each is in effect a veritable micro-miniaturized factory containing thousands of exquisitely designated pieces of intricate molecular machinery, made up altogether one hundred thousand million atoms, far more complicated than any machine built by man and absolutely without parallel in the non-living world.

The tremendous complexity of the molecular machines operating in the cell, the presence of specified information in the DNA, and the sophistication of the cellular information system make the case for a superintelligence as the most likely cause of all living organisms and cast doubt on the claim of evolutionists that natural selection acting on random mutation is responsible for the production of the living organisms, which, they assert, elicit only the appearance and not the actuality of design. The notion, forcefully advocated by evolutionists that natural selection by its ability to mimic the work of a designer refutes the design argument, entails a misguided conclusion that is easily falsified by the presence of cellular information, the sophisticated nature of molecular machines operating at the cellular level, and the efficacy of the cell's magnificent information system.

The fingerprints of the Living God are not only identified by the existence of microscopic living organisms, they are also easily manifest throughout the universe by the presence of our solar system, our galaxy, the Milky Way, and billions of galaxies, quasars, pulsars, supernovae, stars, and other bright luminaries sprinkled throughout the universe: "The heavens declare the glory of God," asserts the Holy Scriptures, "and the firmament shows His handiwork."

In their masterpiece, *The Privileged Planet*, astronomer Guillermo Gonzalez and philosopher and theologian Jay Richards make the argument that Earth's locus in the cosmos is ideally suited for discovery and measurability:

> We occupy the best overall place for observation in the Milky Way galaxy, which is itself the best type of galaxy to learn about stars, galactic structure, and the distant universe simultaneously; these are the three major branches of astronomy.

The two authors further relate that Earth and its immediate and distant environments were "designed" for "habitability," "measurability," and "discovery":

> The fact that our atmosphere is clear; that our moon is just the right size and distance from Earth, and that its gravity stabilizes Earth's rotation, that our position in our galaxy is just so; that our sun is its precise mass and composition—all of these facts and many more not only are necessary for Earth's habitability but also have been surprisingly crucial to the discovery and measurement of the universe by scientists.

The Moon represents the ideal planet to regulate the Earth's rotation around itself in a twenty-four-hour cycle; otherwise, the Earth could give birth to days lasting from a few hours (eight hours for instance) to very long days (thirty hours or more). The Moon also helps to maintain the Earth's rotational axis at a nearly constant tilt of around 23.4 degrees, thus allowing the Earth to experience its yearly cycle of four seasons (spring, summer, fall, and winter). The Moon's gravitational pull on the Earth also engenders the high and low tides; and using the light of the Sun, the Moon renders beautiful and bright even our darkest nights. Thus, the Moon represents a planet completely fine-tuned by its designer to help maintain life on planet Earth.

The Sun entails the right size and type of star to energize, illuminate, and regulate the Earth. The Sun provides the energy that plants utilize with carbon dioxide and water to produce sugar and oxygen. The wonderful fruits that we voraciously consume and a great deal of the oxygen in the air that we breathe are made possible by photosynthesis, a most crucial process without which life would be impossible on planet Earth. The light of the Sun warms and illuminates the Earth, and the sunlight's energy represents one of the most important drivers of the Earth's weather. Solar radiation plays a crucial role in the regulation of the Earth's climate, and the Sun's gravitational pull keeps the Earth in its proper orbit nearly 92.9 million miles away—located a few million miles too far, the Earth would cool to a frozen mass, threatening if not destroying life on planet Earth by reducing the availability of liquid water necessary for photosynthesis; orbiting a few million miles closer to the Sun, the Earth would watch its temperature rise considerably, thereby evaporating a great deal of the waters circulating on the surface of the Earth.

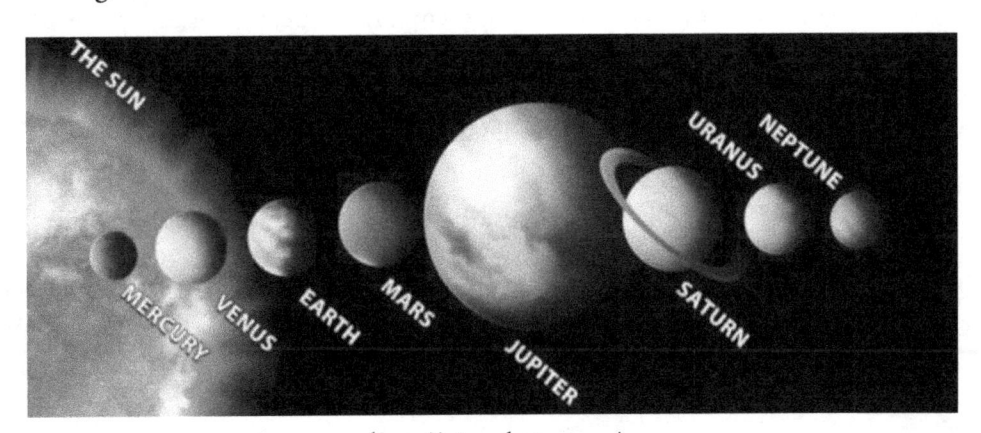

http://nineplanets.org/

http://solarsystem.nasa.gov/planets/

A bird's-eye view of our solar system

The beauty of our solar system is of the first order. The Sun stands brightly in the center of our solar system as the central illuminating force that provides direction, light, and energy to the orbiting planets. Saturn with its majestic and colorful rings and Jupiter with its less-pronounced albeit equally colorful rings serve as powerful shields that protect the Earth against the negative effects of the comets. It is remarkable how gravity has kept almost intact the routes of the orbiting planets around the Sun over the centuries.

The Earth, protected by Mars against the asteroid belt and regulated by its moon vis-à-vis sudden misdirection in its path, circles in arguably the ideal path that allows great visibility of the entire solar system. Not just a tiny blue dot in the company of spectacular and colorful neighbors, the Earth was chosen by its designer as the sole planet deemed necessary for the propagation of life in the solar system.

The Creator of the universe saw fit to locate our solar system in the outer edges of the Milky Way galaxy in order to make possible and visible the outer limits of the universe. The designer of the universe no doubt placed His earthly creatures in such a locus to allow them to be able to catch a good glimpse of His marvelous and glorious world.

In his critically acclaimed chef d'oeuvre, *Not a Chance*, Dr. R. C. Sproul deals a mortal blow to the theory (nowadays in vivid display in many scientific journals, research papers, academic manuals, and newspaper articles) that *chance* is the agent responsible for the creation of the universe. He brilliantly postulates:

Chance as a real force is a myth. It has no basis in reality and no place in scientific inquiry. For science and philosophy to continue the advance in knowledge, chance must be demythologized once and for all.

Moreover, Dr. Sproul brilliantly crystallizes the only four possible options (he studied the issue ad infinitum for many years, interviewed countless scientists, philosophers, and numerous thinkers for a probable fifth option to no avail!) vis-à-vis the origin of the universe:

Option 1: The cosmos is an illusion; it does not exist.
Option 2: The cosmos is self-existent (and eternal).
Option 3: The cosmos is self-created.
Option 4: The cosmos is created by something that is self-existent and eternal.

Option 1 can be quickly dismissed: It is a safe and evident assumption unless of course one suffers from delusion or schizophrenia.

Option 3 remains logically invalid: The cosmos must have been in existence prior to its self-creation! An entity cannot be and not be at the same time. That entails an obvious violation of one of the four fundamental laws of logic, the law of noncontradiction.

Option 2 constituted the darling of most scientists and philosophers until Einstein's theory of general relativity engendered the big bang theory, the principle that the universe exploded into existence nearly 14 billion years ago, thereby annulling the purported eternity and self-existence of the cosmos. After all, if the universe is still exploding, it must have an initial birth, a moment where time, space, and energy were confined into a point of singularity. Moreover, Edwin Hubble's discovery of the Cosmological Redshift (when a source of light is moving away from an observer, the light is red shifted) confirmed Einstein's mathematical prediction that the universe is expanding, and therefore, the universe must have had a beginning. Option 2 is thus falsified.

Option 4, as a result, remains the *only* viable alternative vis-à-vis the origin of the universe: It *must* have been *created* by something or someone that is self-existent and eternal. Most—if not all—scientists and philosophers now agree wholeheartedly with that premise; however, many of them part company when that "someone or something that is self-existent and eternal" is identified as the God of the bible.

In what may be considered the greatest debate of all time vis-à-vis the existence of God, Dr. Greg Bahnsen, one of the most accomplished Christian apologists in recent memory, dared Dr. Gordon Stein, one of the premiere articulators of the atheistic persuasion of our modern era, to defend the Transcendental Argument for the existence of God. Dr. Bahnsen argued the following:

> The transcendental proof for God's existence is that without Him, it is impossible to prove anything. The atheist world-view is irrational and cannot consistently provide the preconditions of intelligible existence, science, logic or morality. The atheist world-view cannot allow for laws of logic, the uniformity of nature, the ability of the mind to understand the world, and moral absolutes.

To better assimilate the tenets of the Transcendental Argument, one must pay heed to Dr. Bahnsen's focus on the "presuppositional conflict of world views" being waged between Christianity and atheism. As such, our philosopher du jour renders a general format of the concept of presupposition in his book *Van Til's Apologetic*:

> A "presupposition" is not just any assumption in an argument, but a personal commitment that is held at the most basic level of one's network of beliefs. Presuppositions form a wide-ranging, foundational perspective (or starting point) in terms of which everything else is interpreted and evaluated. As such, presuppositions have the greatest authority in one's thinking, being treated as one's least negotiable beliefs and being granted the highest immunity to revision.

Presuppositions can be properly utilized to demonstrate that both atheistic and non-Christian worldviews are irrational:

> The presuppositional apologist makes an internal critique of the non-Christian's espoused presuppositions, showing that they destroy the very possibility of knowledge or "proof." He maintains that only Christianity is a reasonable position to hold and that unless its truth is presupposed there is no foundation for an argument that can prove anything whatsoever. Thus it is irrational to hold anything but the truth of Scripture. The truth of Christianity is proved from the impossibility of the contrary.

How then can an atheist mount a serious case against the existence of God? How can he argue against the teaching of the Holy Scriptures, which unreservedly proclaim that the Almighty spoke the entire universe into existence? He has to use logic and rationality in his presentation. However, he cannot establish any foundational support for his use of logic and rationality based on his materialistic worldview, which cannot explain the rationale for such concepts.

The atheist cannot fall back on the notion that logic and rationality are consensuses of civilizations: their universality across all cultural barriers and nationalistic flavors precludes any sense of divergence.

The Word of God, however, provides ample justification for its foundational support and grounding of logic and rationality. As the Creator of the world, the earth and the human species (Genesis 1:1, 2:7; Psalm 90:2), God displayed His wisdom and power by speaking the present world order into existence (Genesis 1:3–26). The Bible firmly declares that it is God who keeps the present universe in operation (Hebrews 1:3). God is the personification of wisdom and knowledge (Colossians 2:3, Proverbs 21:30), and His rational mind is exhibited in His righteous judgments (Psalm 9:8, 96:13), in His love of righteousness (Psalm 33:5, 45:7) and in all of His creation (Psalm 97:6, Isaiah 61:11).

Therefore, man, created in the "image" and "likeness" (Genesis 1:26) of His maker, was endowed with a rational mind (Genesis 2:7, 1 Thessalonians 5:23) and the ability to use logic in order to conceive meaningful ideas, patterns of the righteous thoughts of His perfect creator (Isaiah 55:8 and 9).

The Word of God, therefore, grounds logic and rationality in the personhood of God Himself; as a result, the atheist must borrow from the Christian worldview logic and rationality, concepts that he cannot fully justify nor adequately explain, in order to argue against the existence of God and the truth of God's Word.

Furthermore, the atheist cannot explicate the raison d'être of scientific laws and formulas. Why is that two objects, no matter their size, exert a gravitational force toward each other (universal law of gravitation) valued as the multiplication by the gravitational constant G by the product of those two objects divided by the square of the distance between the two objects (Force = G ([M1 x M2]/d^2)? How can an atheist properly justify Hubble's law of cosmic expansion or Kepler's laws of planetary motion or Newton's laws of motion or the laws of thermodynamics or Archimedes's buoyancy principle or Einstein's theory of general relativity or Heisenberg's uncertainty principle?

Is it mere coincidence that nature operates according to precise mathematical formulas in the universe of the atom as well as the universe of the planets, suns, galaxies, pulsars, and nebulae? Is that just the way it is? Will the atheist hide behind the traditional rescuing device that science does not ask why but what and how? But why, pardon the pun, should the "who" variable be totally omitted from life's epic equation? What about the tiniest albeit plausible possibility that a certain "who" might actually be the eternal and all-powerful agent *necessary* for the existence of all things? As such, of the four question marks—who, what, how, and why—the who and why would seem to elicit at least as much inquiry as the other two.

The atheist would rather sacrifice the why question at the altar of the supposedly unacceptable who. The why inquiry must forever be abandoned, because it would then invariably lead to the who proposition; and as such, it needs never, never, never be asked! The tiniest and remotest *possibility* that a transcendent power could have created the entire universe must never be considered and must be avoided at all costs, less anyone be found accountable to a god whose jurisdiction must be opposed and whose very notion threatens the materialistic, epicurean, and existentialist joie de vivre of fools masquerading as wise.

Moreover, the atheist cannot establish any foundational support for the existence of objective moral standards and obligations. In "The God Debate II" between the atheist and neuroscientist Sam Harris (one of the Four Horsemen of the New Atheism; the other three? Richard Dawkins, Daniel Clement Dennett, and Christopher Eric Hitchens) and Dr. William Lane Craig, perhaps the most preeminent Evangelical Christian debater of our time, atheism was shown incapable of providing the ground for the manifestation of any objective morality.

Dr. Craig brilliantly argues that God's existence establishes the sine qua non condition for a "sound foundation for objective moral values and duties," and that God's nonexistence precludes any "sound foundation for objective moral values and duties."

"Moral values," Dr. Craig maintains, can only be truly and objectively "grounded in God," who is after all "the greatest conceivable Being," the "Highest Good," the only "Perfectly Good," and the "Locus and paradigm of moral value."

"God's own holy and loving nature," continues Dr. Craig, "provides the absolute standard against which all actions are measured," and that such a lofty standard is entirely independent of the subjective standards of humans.

Moral duties and obligations, the by-products of God's holiness, goodness, and love, consist of God's commandments that reflect His perfect love: "You shall love the Lord your God with all your heart, with all your soul, with all your strength, and with all your mind…and your neighbor as yourself." The standard atheistic retort is to ground objective moral standards and obligations in the natural world and to enunciate that they are the results of evolutionary human development or the effects of societal norms designed to provide for the well-being of humans with respect to their particular cultures. To that end, science philosopher Michael Ruse makes the following declaration:

> The position of the modern evolutionist is that humans have an awareness of morality because such awareness is of biological worth. Morality is a biological adaptation no less than hands and feet and teeth. Considered as a rationally justifiable set of claims about an objective something, ethics is illusory. I appreciate that when somebody says "Love thy neighbor as thyself," they think they are referring above and beyond themselves; nevertheless, such a reference is truly without foundation. Morality is just an end to survival and reproduction and any deeper meaning is illusory.

Richard Dawkins echoes the same sentiment:

> There is at bottom no purpose, no evil, no good, nothing but pointless indifference. We are machines for propagating DNA; it is every living object sole reason for being.

It remains clear why morality, rationality, logic, nature with all its magnificent creatures and its innumerable species of living things, its exquisite laws with their precise mathematical formulations, and the entire universe find their meaningful raison d'etre only in the confines of the God of the Bible: atheism, naturalism, humanism, and, to some extent, empiricism cannot explicate those concepts satisfactorily nor can they establish their proper foundation.

In that regard, irrationality and foolishness await anyone who "exalts [himself] against the knowledge of God," simply because "there is no wisdom, nor understanding, nor counsel against the Lord."

Chapter 4

His Living Words

Thy Words is a Lamp unto my Feet and a Light Unto my Path, Psalm 119:105

Behold, world, the Living Word of the Living God! Behold the Word of God in the words of sinful and mortal men! Behold the Word who was made flesh, who lived with us, walked with us, slept with us, ate with us, drank with us, whose words we heard, whose body we touched, and whose glory we beheld!

Behold God's Wisdom, the Brightness of His glory and the full Expression of His character! Behold the Lamb of God slain from the foundation of the world to take away the sin of the world! Behold the Seed of the Woman who destroys the works of the Devil!

Behold God's Passover Lamb sacrificed for the salvation of His people! Behold God's Great High Priest providing atonement for His people! Behold the Brass Serpent who gives healing to those bitten by the Old Serpent! Behold the Prophet of God who speaks His words to His people and the entire world!

Behold the Great Captain of our Salvation, the Judge of the world, the Redeemer who died on behalf of His own! Behold God's Chief Messenger, the King of kings with an everlasting kingdom, God's Faithful Scribe writing God's laws in the hearts of His people!

Behold the Repairer of the walls of the city of God! Behold the Real Mordecai who saves His people from their enemies! Behold the Day Spring from on high, the Great Shepherd feeding His people manna from heaven and leading them to green pastures! Behold the Bridegroom preparing an eternal city for His Bride!

Behold God's Suffering Servant who paid for the salvation of His people by the shedding of His own blood! Behold God's Weeping Prophet who endured tremendous persecution on their behalf! Behold the Son of Man and last Adam who came to destroy the works of the Devil!

Behold the Son of God maintaining the universe by the word of His power! Behold the Messiah anointed and sent by God to fill His people with His Holy Spirit! Behold the Burden Bearer giving rest to His people!

Behold the Mighty Savior redeeming His people from their sins! Behold Wonderful performing miracles for His loved ones, the Counselor leading His followers along the way, the Mighty God who purchased the church by the shedding of His blood! Behold the Everlasting Father bringing many sons to glory!

Behold the Prince of Peace who will bring real peace to the world, the Great Evangelist bringing good news to the people of the world, the Avenger of God's elects defending them against their accuser, the Devil! Behold the Root of Jesse and the Son of David who will inherit the kingdom forever, the Son of Abraham who inherits all His Father's possession!

Behold the Bread of Life feeding His people manna from heaven! Behold the Way to everlasting life, the Water of Life who quenches His people's thirst! Behold the Truth that sets His people free! Behold the Life bringing life to all His creatures and Eternal Life to His people!

Behold the Resurrection over whom death has no power, the Savior who has conquered death! Behold the Light of the World shining ever so brightly in a world full of darkness! Behold the Lord of the Living and the Dead!

Behold the Great Physician who has brought spiritual, psychological, and physical healing to His people! Behold the Rock of Offense over which many have stumbled and fallen! Behold the Firstfruits guaranteeing that God's harvest at the end of the world will produce many other fruits!

Behold the Cornerstone and the Chief Stone in the Eternal Edifice whose builder is the Lord Himself! Behold the Lord Jesus, the First Born from the dead, the Mediator between God and men, the Author and Finisher of our Faith, the Lord of Glory, the Alpha and Omega, the First and the Last, the Beginning and the End, the Bright Morning Star, the Lion of the Tribe of Judah, the One who is, who was, and is to come, the Lord, the Almighty, He that is holy, He that is true, the Amen, the Faithful, the True Witness, the Beginning of the Creation of God, the Possessor of heaven and earth, the Sustainer of the entire universe!

Behold the Bridegroom preparing an eternal habitation for His Bride! Behold the Builder of the Church, the Architect of the New Jerusalem, God's eternal city prepared for His people! Behold the Advocate of God's people defending them against Satan, their accuser!

Behold the Door letting God's people into paradise! Behold the True Vine bearing all kinds of great and lovely fruit into the Kingdom of God! Behold the Son of Man that came to seek and save the lost! Behold the Rock quenching the thirst of God's people with living water!

Behold Jesus, the Messiah, the Anointed One set apart for God's service! Behold God's Prophet speaking for God and speaking forth God into people! Behold God's Judge appointed to render a fair and righteous verdict to the living and the dead! Behold the Great I Am meeting all the needs of His people! Behold Emmanuel, God with us as our hope and our glory!

Behold, world, the Word! Behold the Word of the Living God in the words of sinful and mortal men!

The Bible depicts across its sacred pages a most unique individual, the Lord Jesus Christ. The Almighty God Himself, over the course of nearly fifteen hundred years, made His thoughts known to sinful and mortal men concerning His divine economy, His eternal plan worked out before the foundation of the world for the salvation of His redeemed people.

The unveiling of Jesus Christ throughout the pages of the Sacred Scriptures entails a powerful argument for God's existence. God spoke through Moses, Enoch, Abraham, Isaac, Jacob, Noah, Elijah, Elisha, Joshua, Samuel, Ezra, Nehemiah, Esther, Job, David, Solomon, Isaiah, Jeremiah, Ezekiel, Daniel, Hosea, Joel, Amos, Obadiah, Jonah, Micah, Nahum, Habakkuk, Zephaniah, Haggai, Zechariah, Malachi, Asaph and his family, Heman, the sons of Korah, Matthew, Mark, Luke, John, Paul, James, Peter, Jude, Mary the mother of Jesus, Adam, Eve, Sarah, Tamar, Judah, Rachel, Deborah, Jael, Bathsheba, Ruth, Mary Magdalene, Martha and her sister Mary, Elizabeth, the Samaritan Woman, the wife of Pilate, Rahab the prostitute, King Nebuchadnezzar, King Cyrus the Great, many other ordinary men and women, to present to the world one Person, the Lord Jesus Christ.

The consistency of the Bible in the unveiling of Jesus Christ throughout the biblical narrative constitutes yet another great indicator of the existence of God. All the biblical writers from Moses to John the Apostle could not have coordinated their stories to fit one theme.

The various pictures, parables, epic stories, tales of victory and defeat, the crimes of passion, the history of the nation of Israel, the conquests and annihilation of great empires, the rise and fall of great prophets, the selection and commission of priests and kings—all assume and presuppose the presence of Jesus and the existence of God.

The Bible contains statements so amazing that they could not have been penned by any mortal man. As a perfect example, let us consider Daniel 9:24 to 27:

> Seventy weeks are determined
> For your people and for your holy city,
> To finish the transgression,

> To make an end for sins,
> To make reconciliation for iniquity,
> To bring in everlasting righteousness,
> To seal up vision and prophecy,
> And to anoint the Most Holy.
> Know therefore and understand,
> That from the going forth of the command
> To restore and build Jerusalem
> Until Messiah the Prince,
> There shall be seven weeks and sixty-two weeks;
> The street shall be built again, and the wall,
> Even in troublesome times.
> And after the sixty-two weeks
> Messiah shall be cut off, but not for Himself;
> And the people of the prince who is to come
> Shall destroy the city and the sanctuary.
> The end of it shall be with a flood,
> And till the end of the war desolations are determined.
> Then He shall confirm a covenant with many for one week;
> But in the middle of the week
> He shall bring an end to sacrifice and offering.
> And on the wing of abominations shall be one who makes desolate,
> Even until the consummation, which is determined,
> Is poured on the desolate.

It is impossible for any human mind to conceive so elaborate a scheme of events culminating into the end of sins, the end of the transgression, the end of time, the coming of everlasting righteousness, the anointing of the Most Holy, the completion of the vision of end-time events, and the fulfillment of all biblical prophecy (for an in-depth analysis of Daniel 9:24–27, see chapter 8).

Who has determined those seventy weeks or seventy sevens (the Hebrew word transliterated *sa-bu-im* here can translate as "weeks" or "sevens") for the end of sins and to anoint the Most Holy? How long is each seven or week? How come seventy sevens or seventy weeks—actually 490 years!—from the command of King Artaxerxes to rebuild the city of Jerusalem, the year 458 BC, one lands directly at the precise date of the crucifixion of Jesus Christ in April 3, AD 33 as the Lamb of God was slain for the salvation of the world (Please remember to remove the year 0 in your mathematical operation!)?

Moreover, Daniel 9:24–27 infers that there exist seventy weeks or seventy sevens from the command of King Artaxerxes to the end of the world (See verse 27)! In that realm, Daniel 9 consists of a double prophecy, one leading to God's judgment of Christ for the payment of the sins of His people and the other to God's judgment of Satan, the fallen angels, and unsaved mankind for the payment of their own sins at the end of the world.

The four verses of Daniel 9 reveal the mind of God as He once more articulates in His own majestic and mysterious way the timings of the Judgment of Christ and the Judgment of the world.

Jesus uttered some amazing statements attesting to His divine nature and stature. Let us consider John chapter 3, verse 3 for instance: "Verily, verily, I say unto thee, except a man be born again, he cannot see the kingdom of God."

At first blush, one can quickly perceive that Jesus modifies twice His statement with the word *verily*. One affirmation would convey quite well Jesus's intent; nonetheless, the adverb *verily* repeated twice seems to indicate the presence of two additional personalities affirming the truth of the words of Jesus.

Continues Jesus, "Except a man be born again, he cannot see the kingdom of God." How can a man be born twice? Such a statement could not have been uttered by a natural human being.

Nature affords life one time! Death afterward comes knocking at the door. Jesus makes the second birth, the spiritual naissance of mortal man the sine qua non requirement for entrance into the kingdom of God. Such a kingdom entails a present state of affairs, the life of God, which regenerates or gives life to the dead spirit of man, and a future manifestation, the enjoyment of heaven and the New Jerusalem. The notion of the Kingdom of God necessitates the existence of God as its Creator, Executor, and King.

Jesus further articulated the most famous words in the history of the world: "For God so loved the world, that He gave His only begotten Son, that whoever believes in Him should not perish but have everlasting life."

When was the Son of God given as a testimony of God's love for the world? Again on April 3, AD 33, when Jesus was crucified for the sins of the world! The crucifixion of Jesus, a fact acknowledged by both biblical apologists and critics, provides to the world a powerful witness of God's love.

Another amazing statement from Jesus follows: "God is Spirit, and those who worship Him must worship in spirit and in truth." Hear, O world, the words of Jesus! The God of the Universe, the Creator of the heavens and the earth is Spirit! He is not flesh, and He is not matter.

There is a spiritual world after all, inaccessible to the most sophisticated telescopes and the most accurate microscopes, imperceptible to the human senses, and hidden to the minds of the most brilliant scientists, philosophers, and thinkers. Those who worship God, the Spirit, must do so using their spirit, their spiritual God-given organ capable of apprehending spiritual matters.

Sinful man, unfortunately, cannot use his spirit to communicate with God, the Spirit. The spirit of a natural man is inoperative (as a result of Adam's fall; see chapter 10) unless and until God, the Spirit, regenerates or quickens or enlivens his dead spirit, thereby allowing him to be "born again," a process Jesus delineates at length in John chapter 3.

The prediction by the Bible of the rebirth of the nation of Israel remains a solid proof regarding the supernatural nature of the Holy Scriptures as the true words of the Living God. Jesus made the prophetic utterance that biblical scholars of all stripes acknowledge as a referral to the events that enfolded in May 14, 1948 (Matthew 24: 32 to 35):

> Now learn this parable from the fig tree: When its branch has already become tender and puts forth leaves, you know that summer is near. So also, when you

see all these things, know that it is near—at the doors! Assuredly, I say to you, this generation will by no means pass away till all these things take place. Heaven and earth will pass away, but My words will by no means pass away.

Throughout the Holy Scriptures, God, the author of the Bible, symbolizes the nation of Israel as a fig tree (Jeremiah 8:13; Hosea 2:1–12, 9:10; Matthew 21:18–20; Mark 11:12–14, 20–21). Alluding to the events leading up to His return at the end of the world, Jesus picks up the symbolism of the fig tree bearing leaves in the aforementioned quote in order to indicate the nearness of His return.

The Holy Scriptures further pinpoint the exact years of the baptism and crucifixion of Jesus, two events acknowledged as facts by both biblical apologists and critics. Daniel 9:25 states:

> Know therefore and understand,
> That from the going forth of the command
> To restore and build Jerusalem
> Until Messiah the Prince,
> There shall be seven weeks and sixty-two weeks;
> The street shall be built again, and the wall,
> Even in troublesome times.

The command to "restore" and "build" Jerusalem took place in 458 BC when King Artaxerxes ordered Ezra to go rebuild the city of God; and since the Lord God differentiates the first seven weeks from the sixty-two weeks (Please, read again Daniel 9:25 very carefully), we are forced to believe that God wants us to consider the first seven weeks or seven sevens (seven weeks or seven sevens of years are equivalent to forty-nine years) as a Jubilee period of time of fifty years (Please see figure 4a, page 87, and chapter 8 where the seventy weeks or sevens are discussed in greater depth; and also read Leviticus 25, verses 8 to 18 for God's recommendation concerning the Jubilee Feast every fifty years); otherwise, the Lord God would not have separated the sixty-nine weeks or sixty-nine sevens of the seventy weeks or seventy sevens into three parts: the first seven weeks or the first seven sevens, the next 434 years or 434 sevens, and the remaining last seven weeks or last seven sevens.

We feel obliged to keep repeating the double meaning of the Hebrew word as *week* or *seven*: while it may be true that God wants us to consider the first path of the seventy weeks or sevens as actual years, the second path leads to a mysterious unit of time that is more than a year (Please again read the section on the seventy weeks or sevens in chapter 8 of this volume). In that regard, we will keep the focus on both the two words *week* or *seven* equally.

The Jubilee period to consider the first sevens or weeks is the fifty years from 457 BC to 407 BC (Again please check table 4a). Following that period, we can find the locus of the next sixty-two weeks or sevens as God Himself wisely divided those two time spans. Sixty-two weeks or sevens of years add up to 434 years (62 x 7), and running from 406 BC (The first Jubilee of fifty years is out of the picture now!), the year after the first seven weeks or sevens, for 434 years consecutively and adding one year to account for year 0 (We have to recoup the loss of one year when adding BC years to AD years) would lead us to the year AD 29 exactly as the year Jesus Christ was baptized by John the Baptist in the Jordan River.

As such, the Word of God predicted through the prophet Daniel nearly six hundred years before the fact the year of the introduction of Jesus to the people of Israel as He began His public ministry after His baptism. Now, read again Daniel 9 verses 24 to 27 very slowly while looking at table 4a. Daniel 9 verse 25 stipulates that from the command to rebuild Jerusalem until the arrival of the Messiah, there would be a total of seven sevens or weeks plus sixty-two sevens or weeks for a total of 483 years! As such, from the 483 years, remove the first seven sevens or weeks as warranted by verse 25 of Daniel 9 (Please, remark again that God took the time to separate the first seven sevens from the remaining sixty-two sevens: He could have stated here sixty-nine sevens as a whole; however, since God is perfect, precise, meticulous, and intentional in all that He says and does, He gave us our first clue to calculate precisely the events in Daniel 9). There then remain 434 years, the same years linking 406 BC to AD 29, the year Daniel 9:25 ("Until Messiah the Prince") predicted that the Messiah would appear to begin His ministry as God's Anointed One.

Table 4a

Jubilee Periods of Daniel 9

458BC	457BC	407BC	406BC	(YEAR0)	29AD	33AD
Sabbath year King Artaxerxes' Command To Ezra to Rebuild Jerusalem	Jubilee	Jubilee	Start of 434 years or Weeks		Jesus began His public Ministry End of 434 Years or Weeks	Jesus's Crucifixion

Surprisingly, we can arrive at the same year through another method that is used by both biblical and secular scholars. Luke 3 verse 1 relates that John the Baptist began his baptism ministry in the fifteenth year of the reign of Tiberius Caesar.

Accurate historical analysis focuses on the year AD 14 as the year Tiberius Caesar began his rule (Please, read Luke 3, and Google "Year Tiberius Caesar began to rule!"). As such, adding AD 14 to the fifteen years of Tiberius's rule (Luke 3:1) would yield again the year AD 29 as the year of Jesus's baptism before He began His public ministry. Most biblical and secular scholars agree on AD 29 as the year of Jesus's baptism, and that reinforces our belief that our Daniel 9 analysis is quite accurate.

Daniel 9 verse 24 also predicted quite accurately the year of Jesus's crucifixion:

> Seventy weeks are determined
> For your people and for your holy city,
> To finish the transgression,
> To make an end of sins,

> To make reconciliation for iniquity,
> To bring in everlasting righteousness,
> To seal up vision and prophecy,
> And to anoint the Most Holy.

When was reconciliation made for iniquity? When was sin annihilated? At the cross of course as the day and year (April 3, 33AD) that many biblical and secular scholars agree that Jesus Christ was crucified. Interestingly, the first path of the seventy weeks or sevens leads exactly to the year AD 33.

Let's trace that path: Seventy weeks or sevens of years add up to 490 years. Let's now begin again with the year 458 BC (Please, check table 4a again!) when King Artexerxes commanded Ezra to go rebuild Jerusalem, and let's add 490 years to 458 BC ($-458 + 490 = 32$); and we land at the year AD 32 to which we also add +1 to account for the loss of the year 0: we land exactly at the year AD 33! The reliability of the biblical record speaks volume on behalf of the True Writer of the Bible, the Living God Himself.

Even though the Living God, the Author of the Bible, has sprinkled the pages of the Holy Scriptures with images, pictures, and shadows of the Lord Jesus Christ, He has chosen in many passages of the Holy Scriptures to provide explicit numeric details of some specific events in the life of Jesus Christ that attest to the supernatural nature of the Word of God.

In Genesis 3:14 and 15, God Himself made the following proclamation to the Devil after he had successfully deceived Eve into eating of the forbidden fruit:

> Because you have done this,
> You are cursed more than all cattle,
> And more than every beast of the field.
> On your belly you shall go,
> And you shall eat dust
> All the days of your life.
> And I will put enmity
> Between your seed and her seed;
> He shall bruise your head,
> And you shall bruise His heel.

No other entity except the Living God, the Creator of the earth and the universe, could have uttered those words! The enmity at play here entails the warfare between God and His people, and Satan with his minions of fallen angels and all those whose names are not recorded in the Lamb's Book of Life (Ephesians 6:11–18). Those verses predicted the crucifixion of Jesus ("You shall bruise His heel") on Mount Calvary in AD 33. God, in His Holy Scriptures, was prophesying here that Jesus would destroy Satan and his kingdom at the end of the world in the lake of fire (Revelation 19:20, 20:10), while Jesus's heel, his temporary physical death, would be bruised in the process. Simply amazing!

A REQUIEM FOR EVOLUTION

In Exodus 12, the *Living God* included some remarkable details in His description of the sacrifice of the Passover Lamb:

> Then Moses called for all the elders of Israel and said to them, "Pick out and take lamb for yourselves according to your families, and kill the Passover Lamb. And you shall take a bunch hyssop, dip it in the blood that is in the basin, and strike the lintel and the two doorposts with the blood that is in the basin…For the Lord will pass through to strike the Egyptians; and when He sees the blood on the lintel and on the two doorposts, the Lord will pass over the door and not allow the destroyer to come into your houses to strike you."

It is interesting to note that God had instructed the Israelites to "pick out," "take," and "kill" the Passover Lamb, and to "dip" a "bunch hyssop" in the blood that was in the basin, and to "strike the lintel and the two doorposts with the blood."

The events surrounding the crucifixion of Jesus come into play here. The Synoptic Gospels (Matthew, Mark, and Luke) reveal that Jesus was examined (Matthew 21:23 to Matthew 22:46, Mark 11:27 to Mark 12:34, Luke 20:1 to Luke 20:40) and then "picked out" by the Jewish leaders and people, and he was "taken" to Mount Golgotha, where He was "killed."

Jesus died around 3:00 p.m. Jerusalem time on Friday April 3, AD 33, the same time when the Jewish people was celebrating the Passover Feast by killing thousands of Passover lambs as a memorial and in obedience to the commands God had given to Moses so that the Lord could "pass over" the door of their houses the night God was killing the Egyptian firstborns.

Striking the hyssop filled with blood against the lintel and the two doorposts depicted glaringly the blood of Jesus flowing from His hands as a result of the nails that pierced them and from His forehead as a function of the crown of thorns that pierced His forehead in numerous places. God's *Living Words* had thus predicted nearly fifteen centuries before AD 33 the crucifixion of Jesus!

More poignant details of Jesus Christ's crucifixion were predicted in Psalm 22. God caused the psalmist David to write verbatim many of the words that the Messiah would utter during His painful crucifixion nearly one thousand years before AD 33! "My God, my God," cried out David, "why have you forsaken me?" The same exact words constitute one of the seven final statements of Jesus at the cross!

We can readily understand why nearly one thousand years before the Cross, David would proclaim that "the Spirit of the Lord spoke by me, and His word was on my tongue." All the words of the Bible in the original manuscripts from which are derived countless versions of the Holy Scriptures are in fact the words of God echoed in the tongue of mortal men! Continues David in Psalm 22:

> For dogs have surrounded me;
> The congregation of the wicked has enclosed me.
> They pierced My hands and My feet;
> I can count all My bones.
> They look and stare at Me.

> They divide My garments among them,
> And for My clothing they cast lots.

The Holy Scriptures do not record any episode in David's life where his hands and feet were pierced and his garments, parted, were given by lottery. The Spirit of God enticed David to speak the words of someone enduring an awful and slow death during which he could observe that "all his bones are out of joint," his "heart…like wax…has melted within [him]," and that he can "count all [his] bones."

The Canonical Gospels (Matthew, Mark, Luke, and John) paint a vivid portrayal of the crucifixion of Jesus, and behold, it matches exactly the description in Psalm 22. All the prophetic utterances of David in Psalm 22 vis-à-vis the Lord Jesus Christ were fulfilled nearly one thousand years later during the life and death of the Messiah, the Lord Jesus Christ!

The prophet Isaiah, like David, was inspired by the Holy Spirit of God to depict in vivid details the crucifixion of Jesus Christ nearly eight hundred years before the Cross! Isaiah, in the fifty-third chapter of his book, tells the tale of a "despised and rejected…man of sorrows" who was "stricken for the transgressions of [His] people, and who "was wounded" and "bruised for [their] iniquities." That pitiful man was "oppressed" and "afflicted" without any verbal tirade, and being taken from "prison" and "judgment," he was led "as a lamb to the slaughter" and offered his soul as "an offering for sin."

In numerous picturesque words, God, through the auspices of various holy men, accurately predicted in the pages of the Holy Scriptures events that would materialize many centuries later, thereby attesting to the authenticity and truth of His words.

The prophet Zechariah was also instrumental in God's hands in relating very important details in the life of Jesus Christ. Zechariah 2:8–9 remarks:

> For thus says the Lord of Hosts: "He sent Me after glory, to the Nations which plunder you; for he who touches you touches the apple of His eye. For surely I will shake My hand against them, and they shall become spoil for their servants. Then you will know that the Lord of Hosts has sent Me."

Who is the "He" and who is the "Me" in those two verses? Who is sending whom? Who dares send the Lord of Hosts anywhere? A careful reading of the two verses would indicate that the Lord of Hosts is actually sending the Lord of Hosts! The Bible is filled with beautiful metaphors and mysterious double entendres that offer numerous insights in the life of our Living Lord and Savior Jesus Christ.

In that realm, Zechariah 3 presents one of the most epic debates in all of scripture involving Joshua and Satan and the "angel of the Lord" moderating the proceedings. Jude, one of the brothers of Jesus, comments in Jude 9 about that epic meeting:

> Yet Michael the Archangel, in contending with the Devil, when he disputed about the body of Moses, dared not bring against him a reviling accusation, but said: "The Lord rebuke you!"

Going back to Zechariah 3, we can read the account with greater insight:

> Then he showed me Joshua the High Priest standing before the Angel of the Lord, and Satan standing at his right hand to oppose him.
>
> And the Lord said to Satan, "The Lord rebuke you, Satan! The Lord who has chosen Jerusalem rebuke you!"

Blending the two accounts, we get the picture of Joshua, the High Priest, who is actually Michael the Archangel (Please, read Jude 9 again!), or Jesus, the Chief Messenger (Don't be thrown off by the word *Archangel* associated with Michael: the word *Arch* is really the word *chief* in this context, and the word *angel* can be translated as messenger or angel—the Greek word transliterated *archaggelos* consists of the word *arch*, which translates as the English *chief*, and the word *aggelos*, which warrants here the translation "messenger," and not the more common "angel."

Therefore, Michael the Archangel (bad translation!) is really Jesus, the Chief Messenger—not Joshua the Archangel, and not even Jesus the Archangel, for Jesus is not an angel—who is defending the body of Moses against the accusation of Satan in front of God.

Moreover, Michael can only be another name for the Lord Jesus Christ, for "there is one God and one mediator between God and man, the man Christ Jesus" (1 Timothy 2:5). He is after all the Chief Messenger. Let's then review the mysterious death of Moses on Mount Nebo as recorded in Deuteronomy 34, verses 5 to 7:

> So Moses the servant of the Lord died there in the land of Moab, according to the word of the Lord.
>
> And He buried him in a valley in the land of Moab, opposite Bel Peor; but no one knows his grave to this day.
>
> Moses was one hundred and twenty years old when he died.
>
> His eyes were not dim nor his natural vigor diminished.

Moses is dead, and God buried his body "in a valley in the land of Moab." However, "no one knows his grave to this day." Then why is Satan bringing to the Lord accusation against the body of Moses? Why would Satan need the physical body of Moses? What type of charges would or could Satan level against the corpse of the Lord's great servant? Is Satan worried that he does not know where God buried Moses? Why is Jesus contending with the Devil over the body of the Lord's great prophet? There is no record in the Scriptures of Satan's contesting the bodies of Enoch and Elijah, two other patriarchs who were raptured.

We suspect Satan's rants have nothing to do with the physical body of God's mighty servant. Could it be that God let it be known that He was in the process of creating a spiritual body for Moses, His dear servant, and that He decided to let Satan come to watch His newest handiwork?

Could it also be that Satan, knowing full well that Moses had murdered someone (Exodus 2:11–12), and had committed many other sins during his lifetime, protested that the Lord was not justified in giving Moses, a sinner, a spiritual body and bringing him into His holy heaven?

That seems to be the plausible reason Satan would be so upset. What right would God have in giving Moses—or anybody else for that matter—a spiritual body since Jesus had not yet gone to the Cross to pay for the sins of anybody?

Satan apparently was not aware that the Lamb of God, our Lord and Savior Jesus Christ, was slain for the sins of the world (John 1:29) from the foundation of the world (Revelation 13:8), and that Holy God was fully righteous (1 John 1:9) in giving His mighty servant his eternal spiritual body and taking him into His holy dwelling place. In that light, the Lord was justified in rebuking Satan, the accuser of the brethren (Revelation 12:10).

The Living God has hidden within the pages of the Holy Scriptures enough information that, when combined with secular data, can ascertain the date of the birth of Jesus Christ. We have already proven that the crucifixion of Jesus took place exactly on April 03, AD 33; and we now endeavor to search for the dates of the birth of Jesus Christ.

It had been nearly four hundred years since the last Old Testament prophetic utterings. The Living God had declared through the prophet Malachi that He would send His messenger John the Baptist right before the arrival of Jesus Christ. Just a few years remained before the end of the BC years when suddenly God started again to intervene overtly in the lives of mortal men in a most public fashion.

The year 6 BC was unlike any other for several magi, wise men, and kings from the East with a fair knowledge of astronomy, when they began to notice a special star shining brightly in the skies. Probably familiar with the Jewish Scriptures (The Jews had brought them to Babylon when they were deported to the land of Chaldea, and the Holy Scriptures fell in the hands of the Persians after they had conquered the Babylonian Empire), the magi must have come in contact with Numbers 24:17, which states the following:

> I shall see him, but not now: I shall behold him, but not nigh: there shall come a
> Star out of Jacob, and a Sceptre shall rise out of Israel, and shall smite the corners
> of Moab, and destroy all the children of Sheth.

The wise men and kings must have also stumbled upon Psalm 72 where King Solomon nearly a thousand years before the birth of Jesus had prophesied about kings worshipping the Messiah:

> The kings of Tarshish and of the isles shall bring presents:
> the kings of Scheba and Seba shall offer gifts.
> Yea, all kings shall fall down before him: all nations shall serve him.

Armed in all probability with their biblical knowledge for the birth of the child born king of the Jews, the magi, guided by the supernatural star that had appeared to them in their homeland, arrived in Jerusalem and announced to a troubled Herod, the present king of the Jews, and a startled Jerusalem, that they were in search of the child born king of the Jews.

Herod instantly gathered the scribes and Pharisees and queried from them the probable location of the birth of the new infant king. Their answer was categorical: "In Bethlehem of Judea!" They defended their answer by quoting the prophet Micah, who nearly seven hundred years earlier had uttered the following timeless prophetic declaration regarding the birthplace of the Messiah:

> But you, Bethlehem Ephrathah,
> Though you are little among the thousands of Judah,
> Yet out of you shall come forth to Me
> The One to be Ruler in Israel,
> Whose going forth are from old,
> From everlasting.

The magi, before leaving for Bethlehem, confided to the inquisitive tyrant Herod that their guiding star had first appeared to them two years earlier in their homeland and that it was the star that had led them to Jerusalem to pay homage to the new king.

Deeply insecure and cruel to the bone, Herod, seeing that the magi would not return to Jerusalem to tell him the exact location in Bethlehem of the new king, ordered the slaughter of all infants two years and under, according to the information he had acquired from the wise men.

History records that Herod died in April 4 BC (Josephus in *Antiquities 17.6.4* states that a lunar eclipse took place shortly before Herod's death on March 13, 4 BC). As a result, the wise men must have seen the star at least two years earlier, or more precisely the year 6 BC. The Messiah must have been alive in the year 6 BC, the year the star first appeared to the wise men and kings. We wish to introduce here Daniel 9, verse 25 (Please, go to chapter 8 for an in-depth analysis of Daniel 9, verses 24 to 27):

> Know therefore and understand,
> That from the going forth of the command
> To restore and build Jerusalem
> Until Messiah the Prince,
> There shall be seven weeks and sixty-two weeks:
> The street shall be built again, and the wall,
> Even in troublesome times.

Without elaborating here on the justification of the year 458 BC as the chosen starting year of Daniel's prophetic command, we notice at first the breakdown of the ending date as a mixture of seven weeks or seven sevens and sixty-two weeks or sixty-two sevens.

We revisit the rationale why God would choose to divide what obviously should have been sixty-nine weeks or sevens into two sets of data: the seven weeks or sevens and then the sixty-two weeks or sevens. We know full well from Leviticus 25 that seven weeks or seven sevens representing forty-nine years stand for a Jubilee period of time.

Could it be that God in breaking down the sixty-nine weeks as a period of seven weeks and then a period of sixty-two weeks is relating the birth of the Messiah to a Jubilee period of time?

We know that the Messiah was alive in 6 BC, and from the Jubilee table (See again table 4a), we also know that 7 BC was a Jubilee year. We suspect the reason that God has broken down the sixty-nine years is to indicate that the Messiah would be born in a Jubilee year, the year 7 BC actually! But what month was He born in 7 BC? Let's recalibrate a little.

The Living God decided to intervene as well in the lives of two important couples living hundreds of miles away from the country where the magi first witnessed the appearance of the miraculous star. Zacharias, a priest in the division of Abijah (the Living God had established twenty-four divisions in the Aaronic priesthood, table 4b), and his wife Elizabeth were well advanced in years, childless, and still praying and hoping for a baby.

In the middle of Zacharias's service in the temple, the Living God sent the angel Gabriel to announce to the priest that he and his wife Elizabeth would finally have a son they would name John (Luke 1:5–25).

Nearly sixty-five miles away from the activities in the temple of Jerusalem where the priest Zacharias ministered periodically according to the order of his priesthood, in the city of Nazareth dwelt a young virgin by the name of Mary engaged to a man named Joseph. The Living God sent an angel to declare to the Virgin Mary that she also would be soon pregnant with a child of the Holy Spirit, and that her cousin Elizabeth was sixth months pregnant of John, the forerunner of Mary's child (Luke 1:26–39).

The Living God also dispatched an angel to direct Joseph to accept Mary's pregnancy as an act of God and not a sign of unfaithfulness (Matthew 1:18–25).

When Mary visited Elizabeth to confirm the words of the angelic announcement, baby John leaped in Elizabeth's womb, and Elizabeth, filled with the Holy Spirit, paid homage to Mary and blessed the child in Mary's womb (Luke 1:39–45).

As a result, one can surmise that Jesus was conceived in Mary's womb about six months after the conception of John the Baptist, and that, assuming a full pregnancy by Mary, Jesus was born about fifteen months from the conception of John the Baptist (the six months of Elizabeth's pregnancy plus nine months of Mary's full pregnancy according to Luke 1, verses 36 and 56). Then if the time of John's conception can be determined with accuracy, the month of the birth of Jesus can also be ascertained.

The Bible, the Word of the Living God, relates in Luke 1 verse 5 that Zacharias, John's father, was of the course of Abia (a variation of the word *Abijah* found in 1 Chronicles 24:10). The Word of God surprisingly provides a complete listing of the twenty-four priestly courses in 1 Chronicles 24, verses 7 to 18 (see figure 4b).

Therefore, Zacharias of the priestly division of Abijah would have finished his course at the end of the second part of the fourth month of the Jewish Calendar. As a result, John the Baptist must have been conceived shortly after the fourth month (Tammuz 8 BC: keep a marker on table 4b and turn to table 4c) of the Jewish Sacred Calendar.

If the actual month of John's conception can be established, we can then infer the approximate month of the birth of the Messiah on a Jubilee year! The Sacred Year—not the Civil Year—is at play here (Please, focus on the last and first columns of table 4c). Beginning with the month Tammuz as the probable first month of John's conception (Month 1), we count fifteen months forward and land in the month Tishri as the probable month of Jesus's birth.

Therefore, we can somewhat boldly proclaim that sometime in the month of September or the month of October in the year 7 BC, the Messiah, Jesus Christ, was born in the city of Bethlehem in the land of Israel.

Figure 4b

The Twenty-Four Courses of the Priesthood of Aaron

Course	Name of Priest	Month
First	Jehoiarib	First (Part I)
Second	Jedaiah	First (Part II)
Third	Harim	Second (Part I)
Fourth	Seorim	Second (Part II)
Fifth	Malchijah	Third (Part I)
Sixth	Mijamin	Third (Part II)
Seventh	Hakkoz	Fourth (Part I)
Eighth	Abijah	Fourth (Part II)
Ninth	Jeshua	Fifth (Part I)
Tenth	Shecaniah	Fifth (Part II)
Eleventh	Eliashib	Sixth (Part I)
Twelfth	Jakim	Sixth (Part II)
Thirteenth	Huppah	Seventh (Part I)
Fourteenth	Jeshebeab	Seventh (Part II)
Fifteenth	Bilgah	Eighth (Part I)
Sixteenth	Immer	Eight (Part II)
Seventeenth	Hezir	Ninth (Part I)
Eighteenth	Aphsees	Ninth (Part II)
Nineteenth	Pethahiah	Tenth (Part I)
Twentieth	Jehezekel	Tenth (Part II)
Twenty-first	Jachin	Eleventh (Part I)
Twenty-second	Gamul	Eleventh (Part II)
Twenty-third	Delaiah	Twelfth (Part I)
Twenty-fourth	Maaziah	Twelfth (Part II)

(https://en.wikipedia.org/wiki/Priestly_divisions)

Figure 4c

The Jewish Calendar

Names of Months	Corresponds With	Number of Days	Month of Civil Year	Month of Sacred Year
TISHRI	September–October	30 days	1st	7th
HESHVAN	October–November	29 or 30	2nd	8th
CHISLEV	November–December	29 or 30	3rd	9th
TEBETH	December–January	29	4th	10th
SHEBAT	January–February	30	5th	11th
ADAR	February–March	29 or 30	6th	12th
NISAN	March–April	30	7th	1st
IYAR	April–May	29	8th	2nd
SIVAN	May–June	30	9th	3rd
TAMMUZ	June–July	29	10th	4th
AB	July–August	30	11th	5th

ELUL*	August–September	29	12th	6th

(Partial reproduction from the Liberty Annotated Study Bible, Kings James Version, Copyright 1988 by Liberty University).

---

* Hebrew months consisted of thirty and twenty-nine days alternatively. Their calendar year then only had 354 days. As a result, about every three years, an additional month of twenty-nine days, the month VEADAR, was introduced between the months ADAR and NISAN.

The Living God has not only hidden within the confines of His Living Words information concerning the timing of the birth of Jesus, He has also made numerous specific prophetic utterances vis-à-vis the life of the Messiah and their fulfillment in the life of Jesus Christ.

The Living Words of the Living God prophesied in Genesis 3:15—God must have uttered those words nearly eleven thousand years before the crucifixion, if Adam and Eve were created in the year 11013 BC, as the genealogies of Genesis seem to indicate—that Jesus, the Seed of Eve, the woman, would destroy Satan while the latter would "bruise his heel" (the death of Jesus at the Cross—Matthew 27:50, John 19:30, Mark 15:37, and Luke 23:46).

The Living Words of the Living predicted in Isaiah 7:14, nearly seven hundred years before his birth, that the Messiah would be born of a virgin: Jesus fulfilled that in Matthew 1, verses 18 and 25.

The Living Words of the Living God foretold, nearly seven hundred years before Joseph and Mary's trip to Bethlehem (Matthew 2:1 and Luke 2:4 to 7), that the Messiah would be born in the city of Bethlehem of Judea (Micah 5:2).

The Living Words of the Living God announced the ministry of John the Baptist as the forerunner of the Messiah nearly four hundred years (Malachi 3:1 and 4:1) before John the Baptist arrived on the scene in the year 8 BC (Luke 1:57 to 64).

The Living Words of the Living God proclaimed—nearly six hundred years before King Herod, in a futile attempt at killing the infant Jesus, ordered the massacre of all the children of Bethlehem two years old and under (Matthew 2:16 to 18)—that a great mourning and a tremendous weeping would take place as a result of a great slaughter of children (Jeremiah 31:15).

The Living Words of the Living God declared nearly seven hundred years before the birth of Emmanuel (Isaiah 7:14) that God would visit mankind in the person of Jesus Christ (Matthew 1:23 and 25) to save His people from their sins (Matthew 1:21).

The Living Words of the Living God related nearly five hundred years before Jesus's triumphal entry into Jerusalem (Luke 19:28 to 38) that the daughter of Jerusalem would rejoice greatly when she sees her king enter the city sitting on a donkey (Zechariah 9:9).

The Living Words of the Living God mentioned nearly one thousand years before the Resurrection (Acts 2:31) that Jesus Christ would be resurrected (Psalm 16:10).

The Living Words of the Living God articulated again nearly one thousand years before the Ascension (Acts 1:9) that Jesus Christ would ascend to heaven (Psalm 68:18).

The Same Living Words of the same Living God now prophesies boldly that Jesus is coming again to set up God's kingdom and to judge the world (Acts 1:11; Matthew 25:34; Revelation 22:12, 21:1 to 7, 20:11 to 15).

Behold, world, the Living Words of the Living God! Behold the Words of God in the words of sinful and mortal men!

Chapter 5

How to Study the Bible: A Poor Man's Biblical Hermeneutics

> But sanctify the Lord God in your hearts: and always be ready to give a defense to every man who asks you a reason for the hope that is in you, with meekness and fear (1 Peter 3:15).

The Living God has spoken! He has spoken indeed! He spoke the universe into existence out of nothing (Genesis 1). He uttered His mighty thunderous voice, and there was light. He shouted with the force of His might, and the firmament came to be. He ordered the waters of the earth to be gathered into one and caused the dry land to appear, thus forming the earth and the seas.

He commanded the earth to be filled with all kinds of trees, flowers, grass, and vegetation, and it was so. He brought out of nothing by the sheer force of His words the sun, the moon, the stars, and other luminaries to enlighten the skies, to keep time, and to account for signs and seasons.

He formed by the powerful words of His mouth the birds, the sea creatures, and the animals to populate the earth. He then spoke, albeit nonverbally, by creating man of the dust of the ground and by breathing into his nostrils the breath of life so that man could become a living soul.

Finally, God spoke His Word, the Holy Scriptures, into existence (2 Timothy 3:16). Actually, God's Word was already in existence before the creation of the universe. Eternal and self-existent, God's Word is divine and has no beginning and no end: "In the beginning," declare the Holy Scriptures (John 1 verse 1), "was the Word, and the Word was with God, and the Word was God!"

It remains a profound mystery why God, in the Holy Scriptures, would opt to call Jesus the Word. Is God insinuating that opening the Bible is tantamount to being ushered someway and somehow into His presence?

God has indeed spoken, but how do we know what He means? Why are there so many different interpretations of the Scriptures? Why so many sects and so many creeds? Are there any rules to accurate biblical interpretation? How do we attach meaning to the Word of God?

Theologians utilize the principles of hermeneutics in their attempt to understand the Holy Writ and dive in the process of exegesis in an effort to interpret a particular biblical text. Hermeneutics is exegesis plus. While the former tends to embrace the social, cultural, political, environmental, and historical context of all texts, the latter aims its tentacles at a specific and particular text—its lexicon, language, syntax, timing, author, and audience—to project meaning and understanding.

Biblical hermeneutics, in that lens, is thus biblical exegesis plus all the social, historical, political, environmental, and cultural factors deemed relevant in the interpretation of any biblical text. Let us be reminded that the principles and rules of hermeneutics and exegesis were developed by the academic world to study any document. Those principles, it is firmly believed here, when applied to the biblical text, are susceptible to provide meaningful value to any or all portions of the Word of God. Let's pass in review (Please see Table 5a) the salient points of Biblical Hermeneutics and ascertain afterward whether they constitute the main course in the proper comprehension of the Holy Scriptures.

The first step in analyzing a text through the lens of hermeneutics entails a review of the genre of that specific text—is it poetry, prophecy, a narrative, a prayer, a parable, a story, etc...?

The second step consists of a proper lexicon and syntax review. The words, the language and the grammar of the text, the language of the author and the people involved in the text must be adequately studied.

The third step entails the establishment of the relevant historical, political, and cultural environment susceptible of inspiring the author to write the text at play. The understanding of the terrain upon which the author stood should, it is argued here, be expected to help immeasurably in the comprehension of the text.

The fourth step may focus on the locus of a particular word-its setting in a verse, chapter and part of the book it finds itself. A good rule of thumb here is to accumulate all the locations of that word in the entire text and compare and contrast its meanings in those different settings.

The fifth step elicits the particular teaching of the text being analyzed: What was the information the author of the text intended to convey to his audience, and is that information relevant to the world of today?

Those are the main rules that theologians, historians, anthropologists, archeologists, and other researchers use to interpret the biblical text or any other ancient writing for that matter.

Those principles have been very successful in unraveling the meaning of ancient documents from all countries, societies, and cultures; however, the biblical text provides a big caveat against what is often called the historical-grammatical method of biblical interpretation.

We read from the Word of God the following:

> But the natural man does not receive the things of the Spirit of God, for they are foolishness to him; nor can he know them, because they are spiritually discerned.

The "natural man," the Word of God vividly proclaims, "does not receive the things of the Spirit of God." The Holy Scriptures differentiate between the "natural man" and the "spiritual man." "Unless one is born again," the Word of God further declares, "he cannot see the kingdom of God." What does it mean particularly to be "born again"? Can a man actually reenter his mother's womb to be born a second time? "Unless one is born of water and the Spirit," the Holy Scriptures retort, "he cannot enter the kingdom of God." "That which is born of the flesh is flesh," continues the Word of God, "and that which is born of the Spirit is spirit."

While hermeneutics is in the province of any man—the natural man, the social scientist, the modern philosopher, the Bible student—biblical hermeneutics, insist the Holy Scriptures, is the domain of the spiritual man "born again" by the Spirit of God. The modern biblical researcher who has not received regeneration, the second birth that only the Holy Spirit can grant, cannot understand "the things of the Spirit of God" depicted in the Bible, for they are altogether "foolishness to him," and he will not comprehend them.

"To you," that is the disciples upon whom He would breathe the Holy Spirit (John 20:22 and Acts 2:2–4), Jesus would proclaim, "It has been given to know the mystery of the kingdom of God." To those without the Holy Spirit, Jesus would offer the following dire warning:

> Seeing they may see and not perceive,
> And hearing they may hear and not understand;
> Lest they should turn, and their sins be forgiven them.

To the bitter cynics and petty critics lamenting unfairness, Jesus would not answer directly but would rather present the following prayer of thankfulness to God:

> I thank You Father, Lord of heaven and earth,
> That You have hidden these things from the wise
> And prudent and have revealed them to babes.

All the children of God born of His Holy Spirit then rejoice and cry in unison:

> Now we have received, not the spirit of the world,
> But the Spirit who is from God,
> That we might know the things
> That have been freely given to us by God.

It is true that the "natural man" can utilize the principles of hermeneutics to arrive at a similitude of biblical truth; however, he remains stubbornly alienated from the life of God, and without the Holy Spirit, who is able to transform him into a brand "new creature" (2 Corinthians 5:17), he remains incapable of understanding the spiritual truths emanating from the Holy Scriptures.

Since the principles of hermeneutics ignore the biblical prerequisite of regeneration, they have quietly disqualified themselves as the main course of action in the field of true biblical interpretation. While the exegetical and hermeneutical steps can provide a certain level of clarity and context to the biblical text, they do not lead necessarily to Jesus for life and salvation (John 5:39–40).

The Holy Scriptures are "God-breathed" with the specific purpose of teaching, convicting, correcting, and instructing the reader in the field of righteousness so that the child of God, born of His Spirit, may be properly equipped for every good work (2 Timothy 3:16). The acquisition of knowledge simply for its own sake should never be the primary focus of anyone researching the Holy Scriptures.

The Word of God furthermore calls the principles of hermeneutics into question in the following two verses:

> Now we have received, not the spirit of the world, but the Spirit who is from God, that we might know the things that have been freely given to us by God. These things we also speak, not in words which man's wisdom teaches but which the Holy Spirit teaches, comparing spiritual things with spiritual.

We have here a contrast of two teaching methodologies: the teaching that "man's wisdom teaches," and the teaching that the "Holy Spirit teaches." Let's remember that the principles of hermeneutics highlighted earlier were not, in general, overtly supported by any biblical verse. They were developed and implemented by social scientists in the fields of History, Sociology, Anthropology, Law, Geography, Psychology and Economics to elicit greater understanding of the research documents and materials in their purview for the accumulation and dissemination of knowledge. As such, those principles should be correctly labeled as the teaching that "man's wisdom teaches."

What then are the hermeneutical principles that the "Holy Spirit teaches?" Does the Word of God provide a methodology for studying its pages? Let's review a few biblical verses that shed light on the issue of true biblical hermeneutics.

First of all (See table 5b), the Bible student must have the Holy Spirit of God, that is, he/she must be born again.

To the natural man, to the unsaved, to the man or woman upon whom the Lord has not breathed His Holy Spirit, to the wicked and to the Godless, to the atheist and to the agnostic, to the disputer and to the wise of this world, the Word of God makes the following solemn pronouncement:

> What right have you to declare my statutes,
> Or take My covenant in your mouth,
> Seeing you hate instruction
> And cast My words behind you?
> When you saw a thief, you consented with him,
> And have been a partaker with adulterers.
> You give your mouth to evil,
> And your tongue frames deceit.
> You sit and speak against your brother;
> You slander your own mother's son.
> These things you have done, and I kept silent;
> You thought that I was altogether like you;
> But I will rebuke you,
> And set them in order before your eyes.
> Now consider this, you who forget God,
> Lest I tear you in pieces,
> And there be none to deliver:
> Whoever offers praise glorifies Me;
> And to him who orders his conduct aright
> I will show the salvation of God.

Those are incredible words of warning to the nonchalant biblical researcher who approaches the Word of God with a laissez-faire attitude: he/she faces the deadly rebuke of Almighty God, the Creator and the Ruler of the entire universe.

Jesus prophecies in Matthew 15 the sorry state of affairs for those who come to His Word without a sincere heart:

> These people draw near to Me with their mouth,
> And honor Me with their lips,
> But their heart is far from Me.
> And in vain they worship Me,
> Teaching as doctrines the commandments of men.

The ultimate goal of the Word of God is that the kingdom of God might be established on earth at it is in heaven (Matthew 6:10), and those who come to the Holy Scriptures without receiving the Holy Spirit of God, and those who search the Holy Scriptures without coming to Jesus for life (John 5:39–40) cannot and will not enter into the kingdom of God (John 3:3 and 5). They are spiritually dead! They are out of fellowship with the Living God of the Bible, and they cannot receive any meaningful and salvific revelation from the Word of God.

Second of all, the Bible student must be humble. In the book of Matthew chapter 11 verse 25, Jesus makes the following insightful remark:

> I thank You, Father, Lord of heaven and earth,
> That You have hidden these things from the wise
> And prudent and have revealed them to babes.

Jesus thereby lets it be known that God, the Father, the Lord of heaven and earth, withholds and hides biblical truth from the intellectually bright, the doctors, and sages of the world and has opted to reveal them to "babes," those that are poor in spirit and humble. Too many prominent biblical researchers rely on their intellectual prowess, their natural knowledge and wisdom and their impeccable judgment to opine on the Word of God. To them Jesus declares that they will never attain a proper understanding of God's Word: God will simply not allow them to arrive at biblical truth because of their arrogant attitude toward Him and His word: "The humble," the Word of God relates, "[God] guides in justice," and "the humble," continue the Holy Scriptures, "[God] teaches His way."

"Whom," asks the Living God in the book of Isaiah, chapter 28, verse 9, "shall [I] teach knowledge?" "And whom," wonders the Almighty, "shall [I] make to understand doctrine?" Without baited breath, the Lord of the heaven and earth answers His own questions: "Them that are weaned from the milk, and drawn from the breasts."

The Creator of the universe cannot tolerate anyone with "a haughty look and a proud heart" (Psalm 101:5), and He has already "rebuked" and "cursed" the "proud," because he/she continually "err[s] from His commandments" (Psalms 119:21). The Holy Scriptures (Proverbs 16:5) assert unabashedly that "every one that is proud in heart is an abomination to the Lord" and that "though they join forces, none will go unpunished." Finally, concludes the Holy Scriptures, the proud "know[s] nothing" and is "destitute of the truth," and his/her teaching is in opposition to the "wholesome words…of our Lord Jesus Christ" because he/she assumes that "godliness is a means of gain" (1 Timothy 6:3–5).

The Lord God Almighty has announced to the world that he has decided to "destroy the wisdom of the wise" and to "bring to nothing the understanding of the prudent" (1 Corinthians 1:19). Why then would God be so distrustful of the "wisdom of the world" and so perturbed at the "understanding of the prudent?" Listen, world, to His justification as articulated in the Holy Scriptures:

> I'll turn wisdom on its head,
> I'll expose so called experts as crackpots.
> So where can you find someone truly wise,
> truly educated, truly intelligent in this day and age?
> Hasn't God exposed it all as pretentious nonsense?
> Since the world in all its fancy wisdom never had a clue
> when it came to knowing God,

> God in His wisdom took delight in using
> what the world considered dumb…
> to bring those who trust Him into the way of salvation.

Third of all, the Bible student must be in spirit and in communion with God when studying the Word of God. What does it entail to be in spirit (See chapter 10 for a greater analysis of the spirit of man)? The Word of God declares that man is composed of a body, a soul, and a spirit (1 Thessalonians 5:23), in the pattern of God, who is Father, Son, and Spirit. Genesis 2:7 makes the following assertion:

> And the Lord God formed man of the dust of the ground,
> And breathed in his nostrils the breath of life;
> And man became a living soul.

Man, "formed of the dust of the ground," was transformed into a "living soul" when God "breathed into his nostrils the breath of life." Man's personhood thus originates from the interaction between God's "breath of life," the spiritual element, with man's body, the physical element, the product of the "dust of the ground."

The spirit of man, the breath that God blew into his nostrils, is composed of three parts: conscience, intuition, and communion (Please, see chapter 10 as a foundation for that statement). All three parts of the spirit of the regenerated man or woman is fully active and functional. As a result, he/she is able to commune with God and worship Him "in spirit and in truth" (John 4:24, Philippians 3:3); he/she is capable of being prompted by God into action or inaction (2 Corinthians 2:13, Acts 19:21); he/she is also apt to be troubled (John 13:21), crushed (Psalm 34:18), and provoked (Acts 17:16) in his spirit.

The spirit of the natural, unregenerate, and unsaved man or woman—dead and inoperative since the fall of Adam—is not able to commune with God and is unresponsive to the promptings of the Holy Spirit. Nonetheless, in His wisdom, God has allowed the conscience of the spirit of the natural man or woman to remain active as a small, quiet, peaceable, internal witness within man of the perfect attributes of God (Please see chapter 9 for a detailed analysis of the attributes of God!). That is why the natural man or woman can be troubled, crushed, and provoked in the presence of sin in his life and the lives of others.

Thus, the Bible student, with a dead and unregenerate spirit, searching and researching the Holy Scriptures for truth, may be likened to an expensive glove without the benefit of a human hand: it may be attractive and useful for cosmetic reasons but unreliable and useless for its primary function.

Fourth of all, the Bible student must pray that the Holy Spirit open his/her mind to spiritual truth. This is quite possibly the most important step in the field of true biblical hermeneutics and the most overlooked by biblical researchers. The disciples of Jesus were told on numerous occasions by Jesus Himself that He would eventually return to Jerusalem and "suffer many things of the elders and chief priests and scribes, and be killed, and be raised again the third day." This detailed and specific Word from the Lord never registered in the minds and hearts of the disciples until after Jesus was risen and manifested Himself to them. We read from the Gospel of Luke chapter 24, verses 44 and 45 the following:

> Then He [Jesus] said to them, "These are the words which I spoke to you while I was still with you, that all things must be fulfilled which were written in the Law of Moses and the Prophets and the Psalms concerning Me." And He opened their understanding, that they might comprehend the Scriptures.

In the practice of biblical hermeneutics, Bible researchers must allow these words to resonate in their hearts and minds every time they turn to the Holy Scriptures: "And He opened their understanding, that they might comprehend the Scriptures." The principles of hermeneutics, although valid and apropos in the interpretation of any other text, fall short when the Holy Scriptures are involved: divine intervention is indispensable!

Lydia, a merchandise dealer from the city of Thyatira (Acts 16:14), illustrates the pathway that renders possible the understanding of biblical truth. The Word of God relates that "she worshipped God," which means that she was already a child of God whose spirit was regenerated; and she was in communion with the Holy Spirit. When she heard the voices of the apostle Paul and his companions, the Lord "opened" her heart so that she could understand their teaching and receive their message.

Fifth of all, the Bible student must persevere in his/her quest for spiritual truth. In the seventeenth chapter of the book of Acts, the apostle Paul and Silas, His companion, had preached the message of the Gospel in the city of Thessalonica to mixed results: a great number of devout Greeks and many important women of the city believed; however, many of the Jews who did not receive the message of the Gospel assembled a group of the common people and created a great tumult in the entire city against the apostle Paul and his companions.

To remedy the situation, the Christian brothers of Thessalonica quickly sent Paul and Silas by night to the city of Berea. The Jews and the other citizens of Berea, the Word of God asserts, were more "noble" than those of Thessalonica, and they received the Word of God readily and "searched the scriptures daily, whether those things were so."

The Bereans, in their quest for spiritual truth, "searched the scriptures daily" to ascertain the truth of the message. Perseverance is critical in the search of biblical truth. God takes pleasure in hiding spiritual truth in His Word (Proverbs 25:2), and He expects the student of His Word to take great delight in searching it out.

The parable of the persistent widow of Luke 18 applies here as well: If the unrighteous and unjust judge was finally forced to agree to render justice to the widow because of her persistence, the Lord, out of the goodness of His heart, will most likely agree to open the heart and mind of His child inquiring from Him concerning the truth of a particular biblical passage. Persistence finally pays.

Sixth of all, the Bible student must learn to harvest all the spiritual truths scattered throughout the books of the Holy Scriptures. The Word of God incites every child of God born of His Holy Spirit to echo the words of the psalmist in Psalm 119, verse 11:

> Your word I have hid in my heart,
> That I might not sin against you.

How can a child of God hide the Word of God in his/her heart? God provides the answer in the book of Joshua 1, verse 8:

> This Book of the Law shall not depart from your mouth,
> But you shall meditate in it day and night,
> That you may observe to do according to all that is written in it.
> For then you will make your way prosperous, and then you will have great success.

The Bible student must endeavor to become familiar with the great truths of the Holy Scriptures by spending considerable time in reading, pray-reading, and meditating on God's Word. "Be diligent," commands the Lord to the sincere Bible student, "to present yourself approved to God, a worker who does not need to be ashamed, rigthy dividing the word of truth."

To "rightly" differentiate the Word of God, the Bible student must learn to meditate on all the various parts of the biblical text, the fairly easy or simple parts as well as the seemingly complicated or tedious. In that realm, the Bible student must be continually reminded of 2 Timothy 3, verses 16 and 17:

> ALL SCRIPTURE is GOD-BREATHED and is useful for teaching, rebuking, correcting and training in righteousness, so that the child of God may be thoroughly equipped for every good work.

The entire biblical text in its original form is inspired by God and is profitable for teaching the legitimate Bible student the truth of the Word of God. Those who question the divine inspiration of the Bible are not children of God and cannot expect to understand the Holy Scriptures, which appropriately describe the terrible predicament of the unregenerate researcher of the Word of God in 1 Corinthians 2:14:

> But the natural man does not receive the things of the Spirit of God, for they are foolishness to him; nor can he know them, because they are spiritually discerned.

Seventh of all, the Bible student must learn to compare *spiritual things* with *spiritual*. This is the heart of true biblical hermeneutics. In 1 Corinthians 2:12 and 13, we read (Please, consider here the King James Version for a more accurate translation of the original Greek!):

> 12 Now we have received, not the spirit of the world, but the spirit which is of God; that we might know the things that are freely given to us of God.

> 13 Which things also we speak, not in the words which man's wisdom teacheth, but which the Holy Ghost teacheth; comparing spiritual things with spiritual.

The Holy Spirit, the Word of God instructs us, has a unique and particular teaching methodology that consists in comparing *spiritual things* with *spiritual*. In His infinite wisdom, God has chosen a style of pedagogy distinct from any other. The Word of God elaborates in Isaiah 28:9 and 10:

> Whom shall [the Holy Spirit] teach knowledge? And whom shall He make to understand doctrine?
> Them that weaned from the milk, and drawn from the breasts.
> For precept must be upon precept, precept upon precept, line upon line, line upon line, here a little, and there a little.

The Holy Spirit reveals that in order to comprehend the Holy Scriptures, the true Bible student must learn to transpose "precept upon precept, precept upon precept" and "line upon line, line upon line," as He (the Holy Spirit) unveils truth "here a little, and there a little."

A perfect example of the Holy Spirit's genre of pedagogy finds its locus in Galatians 4, verses 21 through 31:

> Tell me you who desire to be under the law, do you not hear the law? For it is written that Abraham had two sons: the one by a bondwoman, the other by a freewoman. But he who was of the bondwoman was born according to the flesh, and he of the freewoman through promise, which things are symbolic, which is Hagar—for this Hagar is Mount Sinai in Arabia, and corresponds to Jerusalem which now is, and is in bondage with her children—but the Jerusalem above is free, which is the mother of us all. For it is written:
>
> Rejoice, O barren, who do not bear! Break forth and shout, you who are not in labor! For the desolate has many more children than she who has a husband.
>
> Now we, brethren, as Isaac was, are children of promise. But, as he who was born according to the flesh then persecuted him who was born according to the Spirit, even so it is now. Nevertheless what does the Scripture say? "Cast out the bondwoman and her son, for the son of the bondwoman shall not be heir with the son of the freewoman." So then, brethren, we are not children of the bondwoman but of the free.

What is the Holy Spirit teaching here? How does one make sense of so many spiritual truths? Let's return to the Holy Spirit's principle of "precept upon precept, precept upon precept, line upon line, line upon line, here a little, and there a little," also known as the principle of "comparing spiritual things with spiritual" (Please, check out appendix 6 for the biblical definition of the word *salt*).

This passage (Please, see table 5c), a fair representation of the entire book of Galatians in which it finds its locus, was originally addressed to the believers of the churches of Galatia, a region of modern Turkey, as a powerful antidote to the teaching of a group of Jewish individuals that had infiltrated the churches in order to advocate the obedience of the Jewish Law as a prerequisite for salvation (Galatians 1:6–9, 6:12 and 13).

Actually, the audience of the passage is more inclusive than simply the believers of Galatia and their Jewish proselytes. In order to properly identify the audience of the passage in view, we need to go back to the book of Genesis where God introduces us to Abraham.

God spoke to Abraham the following words in Genesis 12, verses 2 and 3:

> I will make you a great nation;
> I will bless you
> And make your name great;
> And you shall be a blessing.
> And I will bless those who bless you,
> And curse him who curses you;
> And in you all the families of the earth shall be blessed.

Let's keep in mind here that God promised that "in [Abraham] *all the families of the earth* shall be blessed." How then has God blessed "all the families of the earth" through Abraham?

First of all, God has made Abraham "the father of all those who believe" (Romans 4:11). In other words, all those who have received "the faith of Jesus Christ" (Galatians 2:16, 20, 3:22; Romans 3:22), which is also called the "the faith of Abraham" (Romans 4:16), have Abraham as their spiritual father (James 2:21, Romans 4:16).

Second of all, Abraham, it is argued in these pages, could be considered also the physical father of all those born according to the flesh and do not believe. Please, do not cry sacrilege! Do not shout heresy! We could plainly see here a spiritual proportion inferred by many verses in the Word of God: Isaac, the son of Abraham according to the promise (Genesis 12:2–3, 17:21, 21:1–3) is to all the spiritual children of Abraham who believe (Galatians 4:28, Romans 4:16, 11, 3:22) as Ishmael, the son of Abraham according to the flesh (Galatians 4:23, Genesis 16:15) is to all the physical children of Abraham who do not believe (John 8:37, 56, 3:6)!

Thus, every one, born into this world, who does not believe is a partaker of the blessing of Abraham in that he or she is born into this world and has a physical existence. How can Abraham be a blessing to "all the families of the earth" when most families of the peoples of the world are not saved and are headed for eternal perdition in the lake of fire? It is argued here that in the contrast of the two Abraham's sons, if Isaac is a representation of all of Abraham's children according to the promise of God, the elects of God, therefore Ishmael, the son of Abraham born according to the flesh, must also be a representation of all the individuals in the history of the world born according to the flesh.

The two sons of Isaac, Esau and Jacob, represent respectively the same spiritual truths as Ishmael and Isaac: the children of the Devil and the children of God. "I loved Jacob," says the Almighty, the God of the universe, "and I hated Esau, and laid his mountains and his heritage waste for the dragons of the wilderness."

Why was Esau hated and Jacob loved? In His own divine prerogative, God rejected Esau, who sold His birthright for a bowl of soup (Genesis 25:27–34) and was characterized as a fornicator and "a profane person" (Hebrew 12:16) by the Word of God. Esau, also known as Edom, begot the Edomites, among the greatest enemies of the nation of Israel. Esau typifies unregenerate and unsaved mankind eager to trade a life of intimate and constant fellowship with the God of the universe for the temporary pleasures of the moment.

On the other hand, Jacob, twin brother of Esau and also known as Israel, was loved by God, who had chosen him to inherit the birthright even before the birth of the twin brothers (Romans 9:11). It is not by accident that God is identified in the Holy Scriptures as the God of Abraham, the God of Isaac, and the God of Jacob (or Israel) (1 Chronicles 29:18, Matthew 22:32), typifying the triunity of the Godhead—God the Father, God the Son, and God the Holy Spirit (Galatians 4:6, Matthew 28:19).

In that regard, if Abraham typifies God the Father and Isaac God the Son, then Jacob is a type of God the Spirit. Jacob, originally a cunning deceiver, represents sinful mankind who has been washed, justified, sanctified, and transformed by the Holy Spirit into a new creature destined to inherit the blessing of eternal life in the New Jerusalem (1 Corinthians 6:11, 2 Corinthians 5:17, Daniel 12:2, John 5:28–29).

In the book of Romans chapter 1, verses 28 through 32, the Word of God lists a number of characteristics depicting the ungodly, the children of the Devil. They are described in the following manner (Please see table 5c):

> And even as they like to retain God in their knowledge, God gave them over to a reprobate mind, to do those things which are not convenient;
>
> Being filled with unrighteousness, fornication, wickedness, covetousness, maliciousness;
>
> Full of envy, murder, debate, malignity, whisperers, backbiters, haters of God, despiteful, proud, boasters, inventors of evil things, disobedient to parents, without understanding, covenant breakers.

What is then the covenant that the ungodly, the unrighteous, the children of the Devil are accused of breaking? It is quite naturally the Covenant of the Law of God! As such, every one born into this world is automatically under the Covenant of the Law of God and is accountable to it. The unmet and unkempt requirements of the Law prominent in the lives of the children of the Devil constitute the legal charge and the incriminating evidence that warrant eternal damnation in hell.

The children of God, justified by the *Faith of Jesus Christ* (Galatians 2:16, 3:22), are not under the Covenant of the Law but under the Covenant of Grace (Romans 6:14, Hebrews 8:6–13).

Hagar, the slave woman and concubine of Abraham, gives birth to a child of the flesh, while Sarah, the freewoman and wife of Abraham, engenders a child of the Spirit (Galatians 4:25, 29). "Except a man be born of water and of the Spirit," says Jesus, "he cannot enter into the kingdom of God," because "that which is born of the flesh is flesh, and that which is born of the Spirit is spirit" (John 3:4 and 5).

There is indeed a great line of demarcation between the children of the flesh and the children of the Spirit. The children of the flesh have experienced only a physical birth along with a dead or inactive spirit whereas the children of the Spirit have undergone a radical transformation: the Spirit of God has quickened their spirits, thereby making them active and operational and susceptible of interacting with the Holy Spirit.

Hagar represents the Jerusalem "which is now," a type of Babylon, the Harlot, the mother of the children of the Devil, while Sarah typifies the New Jerusalem, the city of God, the Bride of Christ, and the mother of all of God's children (Galatians 4:25 and 26; Revelation 17:1–6, 21:10–27).

The Covenant of the Law was given on Mount Sinai in Arabia whereas the Covenant of Grace relates to Mount Zion in heaven (Galatians 4:25, 26, Exodus 19 and 20, Revelation 21:1–7).

The fruitful concubine, Hagar, has more children (symbolized by 2/3) than the children of the temporarily barren wife, Sarah (symbolized by 1/3). The Word of God in Zechariah 13, verses 8 and 9:

> "And it shall come to pass in all the land,"
> Says the Lord,
> "That two-thirds in it shall be cut of and die,
> But one-third shall be left in it:
> I will bring the one-third through the fire,
> Will refine them as silver is refined,
> And test them as gold is tested.
> They will call My name,
> And I will answer them.
> I will say, 'This is my people';
> And each one will say, 'The Lord is my God.'"

God has mysteriously decided to represent the children of the Devil, the lost, unsaved mankind by the symbolic fraction 2/3, and His children, regenerated mankind, those whose spirit the Holy Spirit has quickened by the symbolic fraction 1/3 (Please, see chapter 8, about the fear of the number 666!).

The Word of God declares that there are only two types of people in the world: the regenerated children of God and the unregenerate children of the Devil. The Holy Scriptures also identify them as the sheep and the goats (Matthew 25:21–46). The sheep are destined for eternal life in the New Jerusalem and the New World that God will create, while the goats are headed for eternal punishment in hell with Satan and all the fallen angels.

All the men and women born into this world are creatures of God (Genesis 1:27, 2:7) and not necessarily His children. One must be born of God (John 1:13), receive His Spirit (Galatians 3:14), and become "a new creature" (2 Corinthians 5:17 and Galatians 6:15) in order to become one of His children.

The slave concubine, along with her children, the children of the Devil, all those born into this world who have not received the Spirit of God and whose name is not found in God's Book of Life, the Devil, and all the fallen angels, will all be cast into hell (Galatians 4:30, Revelation 20:15, Matthew 25:41).

On the other hand, the free married wife with all her children, the children of God, will inherit paradise, heaven, the New Jerusalem, where they will spend eternity with Christ and all God's holy angels and creatures (Galatians 4:30 and 31; Revelation 21:1–7, 10–27).

The student of the Word of God must learn to wait on the Lord for guidance in the search of spiritual truth. Jesus made known to His disciple that in their quest for direction they should wait for the coming of the Holy Spirit into their lives, for He alone could and would "guide [them] into all truth" and would "tell [them] things to come" (John 16:13).

Moreover, the resurrected Christ gave two of His disciples a practical application on their need to wait on Him in their search for spiritual truth. Jesus approached two of His disciples on the road to Emmaus as they tried to make sense of the events that had befallen Him a few days before (Luke 24:13–35). And, "beginning at Moses and all the prophets," the Word of God states, Jesus "expounded unto them in all the scriptures the things concerning Himself;" however, relate the Holy Scriptures, "their eyes were restrained, so that they did not know Him" until moments later, long after Jesus's exhaustive exposition of the Scriptures, "their eyes were opened, and they knew Him."

In the presence of the most knowledgeable, the most eloquent and the greatest teacher in the history of the world, the eyes of the most sensitive, the most attentive, and the most careful unsaved Bible student will be "restrained" so that he/she can see neither the Lord of the Scriptures nor the Lord in the Scriptures!

Such a condition will remain until the Lord, on His own timing and volition, decides to open the eyes of the blind and the understanding of the blockhead. The duty of the true Bible student is to remain patient, persistent in prayer, and await the manifestation of the Lord.

Thus God, in Galatians 4:21 to 31, differentiates between two kinds of people: His children for whom He has prepared an eternity of bliss in the New Heaven, the New Earth, and the New Jerusalem in the company of all His holy angels and the entire cast of heavenly creatures, and the children of the Devil for whom He has prepared eternal destruction in the lake of fire, also known as hell, a place reserved for all the fallen angels, the Devil, and all his children.

Dear reader, are you a child of God or a child of the Devil? There is no other group, no other class! If you were to die today, where would you go? Are you predestined for an eternity of bliss with God the Father, God the Son, God the Holy Spirit, the holy angels, the heavenly creatures, and all the saints? Or are you destined for everlasting destruction with the Devil, the fallen angels, and all the children of the Devil?

If you are not convinced of your status as a child of God, the Word of God commands you *right now* to repent, turn to the Living God, who most assuredly will have mercy on your soul. Then, with a contrite heart and a lowly spirit, say the following prayer:

> Eternal God, thank you for creating me in Your image and likeness. Thank You for making it possible for me to hear Your voice telling me to turn from my sins to You, the Living and True God. Thank You for sending Jesus Christ, Your Son, to die as a ransom for my sins. Thank You for the Holy Spirit that has given life to my spirit, thus making me Your child and You my Father. Grant me the strength to live in Your presence day by day through prayer, the reading of Your Word, and the fellowship of my brothers and sisters in Your church. I thank You for saving my soul and for giving me eternal life, and I pray this prayer in the Name of my Lord and Savior Jesus Christ, amen!

Hallelujah! Praise the Lord! Welcome, my dear brother or sister, to the family of God! Now, you are qualified to start studying the Word of God. If you are already a believer and a child of God, the Word of God commands you to "be diligent to present yourself approved to God, a worker who does not need to be ashamed, rightly dividing the word of truth" (2 Timothy 2:15) (For a more detailed hermeneutical analysis of the Word of God, please, see appendix 6).

Table 5a

Hermeneutics = Exegesis Plus
("Wisdom of Man's Teaching")
1 Corinthians 2:13

1. Literature Review	Analysis of the genre of the text: is it poetry, prophecy, a narrative, etc.?
2. Lexicon and Syntax Review	Analysis of the vocabulary and grammar of the text.
3. History and Culture Review	Analysis of the history and culture that gave birth to the author of the text, and the history and culture of the people to whom the text is addressed.
4. Context Review	Analysis of a word in the environment of its verse, chapter, and book, or of a verse in the environment of its chapter and book, or of a chapter in the environment of its book and the entire Bible.
5. Text Review	Analysis of the teaching of the text.

Table 5b

Biblical Hermeneutics
("Holy Spirit's Teaching")
1 Corinthians 2:13

1.	The Bible student must have the Holy Spirit, that is, he/she must be born again.	Psalm 50:16–23, Matthew 15:8–9, John 3:3–6.
2.	The Bible student must be humble.	Matthew 11:25; Psalm 25:9; Isaiah 28:9; Psalm 101:5, 119:21; Proverbs 16:5; 1 Timothy 6:3–5; 1 Corinthians 1:19–21.
3.	The Bible student must be in spirit and communion with God when studying the Word of God.	1 Thessalonians 5:23; Genesis 2:7; John 4:24; Philippians 3:3; 2 Corinthians 2:13; Acts 19:21, 17:16; John 13:21; Psalm 34:18.
4.	The Bible student must pray that the Holy Spirit open his/her mind to spiritual truth.	Luke 24:44–45, Acts 16:14.
5.	The Bible student must persevere in his/her quest for spiritual truth.	Acts 17:1–11, Proverbs 25:2, Luke 18.
6.	The Bible student must learn to collect and recollect spiritual truths scattered throughout all the books of the Holy Scriptures.	Psalm 119:11; Joshua 1:8; 2 Timothy 2:15; 2 Timothy 3:16; 1 Corinthians 2:14.
7.	The Bible student must learn to compare spiritual things with spiritual.	1 Corinthians 2:12 and 13, Isaiah 28:9 and 10, Galatians 4:21 to 31.
8.	The Bible student must learn to wait on the Lord for guidance in the search of spiritual truth.	John 16:13, Luke 24:32, 44, and 45.

Table 5c

The Children of the Devil and the Children of God:
A Contrast of Two Different Types of People

	Children of the Devil	Children of God
1.	Ishmael: Son of Abraham according to the flesh (Genesis 16:15; Galatians 4:29; John 3:6, 8:37, 56; Romans 9:8).	Isaac: Son of Abraham according to the promise: Genesis 12:2–3, 17:21, 21:1–3; Galatians 4:28; Romans 4:11; Galatians 2:16, 20, 3:22; Romans 3:22, 4:16; James 2:21.
2.	Esau, also known as Edom, symbolizes the children of the Devil, those destined for eternal damnation (Malachi 1:3, Genesis 25:27–34, 36:9 and 43).	Jacob, also known as Israel, typifies the children of God destined for eternal life in the New Jerusalem (Malachi 1:2b, Romans 9:11, Galatians 4:6, Matthew 28:19, 1 Corinthians 6:11, 2 Corinthians 5:17, Daniel 12:2, John 5:28–29).
3.	Children of the Devil under the Covenant of the Law of God (Romans 1:28–32).	Children of God under the Covenant of Grace (Galatians 2:16, 3:22; Romans 6:14; Hebrews 8:6–13).
4.	Hagar, slave woman and concubine of Abraham, gives birth to a child of the flesh (Galatians 4:25, 29).	Sarah, free woman and wife of Abraham, gives birth to a child of the Spirit (4:29 John 3:4 and 5).
5.	Hagar represents Jerusalem, "which is now," Babylon, the Harlot, the mother of the children of the Devil (Galatians 4:25, Revelation 17:1–6)	Sarah represents the New Jerusalem, the city of God, the Bride of Christ, and the mother of all of God's children (Galatians 4:26, Revelation 21:10–27).
6.	The Covenant of the Law was given in Mount Sinai in Arabia (Galatians 4:25, Exodus 19 and 20).	The Covenant of Grace relates to Mount Zion in heaven (Galatians 4:26, Revelation 21:1–7).
7.	Fruitful concubine has more children (symbolized by 2/3) than married wife (Zechariah 13:8).	Wife, temporarily barren, has children of her own (symbolized by 1/3) (Zechariah 13:9).

8.	The goats, unregenerate mankind, are headed for eternal punishment (Matthew 25:41–46).	The sheep, the regenerated children of God, are destined for eternal life (Matthew 25:31–40).
9.	Creatures of God (Genesis 1:27, 2:7)	Children of God (John 1:13; Galatians 3:14, 6:15; 2 Corinthians 5:17).
10.	Concubine and her children are to be cast out and are forever lost in hell (Galatians 4:30, Revelation 20:15, Matthew 25:41).	Wife with all her children, the sons of God, are heirs with Christ in the New Jerusalem forever in the presence of God (Galatians 4:30, Revelation 21:1–7, 10–27).

Chapter 6

A View of Time through the Prism of Biblical Chronology and Modern Dating Methods

He has made **EVERYTHING** *beautiful* **IN ITS TIME**
ECCLESIASTES 3:11

> Thou, even thou, art Lord alone: thou hast made heaven, the heaven of heavens, with all their host, the earth, and all things that are therein, the seas, and all that is therein, and thou preservest them all; and the host of heaven worshippeth thee. (Nehemiah 9:6)

"All scripture," we are told in 2 Timothy 3:16, "is given by inspiration of God, and is profitable for doctrine, for reproof, for correction, for instruction in righteousness." Actually, that translation does not fully display all the contours of that passage. Young's Literal Translation of the Hebrew more appropriately states: "Every writing is God-breathed, and profitable for teaching, for conviction, for setting aright, for instruction that is in righteousness."

All the words and all the numbers of the Bible were then actually and mysteriously breathed by God into the spirits, the hearts, and the minds of God's chosen holy prophets; as such, the words and numbers of the Bible became the actual words of eternal God in the words of mortal men. "For the prophecy," the word of God further relates in 2 Peter 1:21, "came not in old time by the will of man: but holy men of God spoke as they were moved by the Holy Spirit."

Although it is semantically correct, as most Bible preachers and scholars do, to speak of Peter as the articulator of the previous verse, it is actually more accurate to pontificate that God or the Holy Spirit declares such and such through the apostle Peter.

It is very troubling to behold renowned theologians labeling the genealogical records of Genesis 5 and 11 as "boring" and "uninformative," and to hear various Bible expositors declaring that the Bible is "corrupt" on account of "numerical deficiencies." Other biblical lecturers make the case that scribal errors make the biblical numbers unreliable.

Are the numbers of the Bible unreliable? We will make the case in this chapter that they are "God-breathed" by presenting the Biblical Timeline as proof of the accuracy and dependability of all God's words.

One of the most important verses in the formulation of the Biblical Timeline entails 1 Kings 6:1:

> And it came to pass in the four hundred and eightieth year after the children of Israel come out of the land of Egypt, in the fourth year of Solomon's reign over Israel, in the month of Ziv, which is the second month, that he began to build the house of the Lord.

That remarkable verse establishes a powerful link between our present Julian Chronology and the biblical chronology. History teaches us that the division of Solomon's kingdom occurred in 931 BC.

Let's recall that the kingdom was divided the same year that Solomon died in 931 BC. King Solomon had reigned forty years before his death. Adding forty years to 931 BC would yield 971 BC as the year that Solomon began to reign. First Kings 6:1 states that Solomon began building the temple the fourth year of his reign; as such, we need to subtract four years from 971 BC to arrive at 967 BC in order to establish a perfect linkage between 1 Kings 6:1 and the timing of the beginning of the Exodus of the children of Israel out of Egypt.

First Kings 6:1 relates that same fourth year of Solomon's reign is the 480th anniversary of the Exodus. Adding 480 years to 967 BC yields 1447 BC, the undisputable date of Israel's Exodus out of Egyptian soil.

The second great biblical verse that helps us connect our present calendar to the biblical calendar is Exodus 12:40. We read verses 40 and 41 from that significant passage of the Holy Scriptures the following:

> Now the sojourn of the children of Israel who lived in Egypt was four hundred and thirty years. And it came to pass after the four hundred and thirty years—on that very same day—it came to pass that the armies of the Lord went out from the land of Egypt.

Adding 430 years to 1447 BC brings us to 1887 BC, the year that Jacob and his entire family migrated to Egypt. Let us remember that Jacob was 130 years when he and his entire family migrated to the land of the Pharaohs (Genesis 47:9).

Adding 130 years to 1887 BC yields 2007 BC as the year of Jacob's birth. The Bible records that Isaac was then sixty years old when Jacob was born (Genesis 25:26). The year of Isaac's birth would therefore be 2067 BC.

Abraham, for his part, was one hundred years old when Isaac was born: adding one hundred years to 2067 BC gives 2167 BC as the year that Abraham was born! Amazing, isn't it?

Now, almost every Bible scholar agrees that Abraham was indeed born, as we have just computed, in 2167 BC. The major controversy in the configuration of the Biblical Timeline starts in linking Abraham to Noah, as Genesis 11 purports to show, and Noah to Adam, as Genesis 5 apparently claims. We need to pay particular attention to a few caveats before attempting to make sense of the aforementioned two chapters.

First, the verb *beget* sprinkled throughout those two chapters does not elicit an immediate father-and-son relationship as many Bible scholars have indicated. Let us examine respectively Matthew 1:7–11 with 1 Chronicles 3:10–14 as an example.

> And Solomon begat Roboam; and Roboam begat Abia; and Abia begat Asa; and Asa begat Josaphat; and Josaphat begat Joram; and Joram begat Ozias; and Ozias begat Joatham; and Joatham begat Achaz; and Achaz begat Ezekias; and Ezekias begat Manasses; and Manasses begat Amon; and Amon begat Josias; and Josias begat Jechonias and his brethren, about the time they were carried away to Babylon.
>
> And Solomon's son was Rehoboam, Abia his son, Asa his son, Jehoshaphat his son, Joram his son, Amaziah his son, Azariah his son, Joash, his son, Jotham his son, Ahaz his son, Hezekiah his son, Manasseh, his son, amon, his son, Josiah his son.

While Matthew relates that Joram "begat" Ozias who in turn "begat" Jotham, 1 Chronicles 3 clearly states that Joram's son was not Ozias, but instead Amaziah; and Amaziah's son was Azariah, who apparently "begat" Jotham.

Therefore, Matthew apparently considers the following father-son relationships: Joram, Ozias, Joatham; whereas 1 Chronicles 3 posits Joram, Amaziah, Azariah, Joash, and Jotham in the same light.

If Abraham was born in 2167 BC (Please, see table 7d), Terah, who was born 130 years earlier, was born in 2297 BC (Genesis 11:32 and Genesis 12:4, and consider Genesis 11:10 to 26 for the other references); Nahor, born 148 years earlier, was born in 2445 BC (Genesis 11:24–25); Serug, born 230 years earlier, was born in 2675 BC; Reu, born 239 earlier, was born in 2914 BC; Eber, born 464 years earlier, was born in 3617 BC; Salah, born 433 years earlier, was born in 4050 BC; Arphaxad, born 438 years earlier, was born 4488 BC. That was also the same year that Shem died, five hundred years after the Flood.

Therefore, we are certain that Noah's Flood took place in 4990 BC! And Noah was six hundred years old when the Flood arrived: Noah was then born in 5590 BC. And Lamech was 182 years old when Noah was born; as such, Lamech was born in 5772 BC. And Methuselah was born 187 earlier: he was born in 6741 BC. Enoch was born 365 years earlier: he was born in 7106 BC. Jared was born 962 years earlier: he was born in 8068 BC. Mahaleel was born 895 years earlier: he was born in 8963 BC. Cainan was born 910 years earlier: he was born in 9873 BC. Enoch was born 905 years earlier. Enosh was born in 10778 BC. Seth was born 105 years earlier: he was born in 10883 BC. And finally, Adam was 130 years when Seth was born: *Adam was then born* in 11013 BC (Again table 7d lists the proper references)!

Bishop Usher's misguided computation of the genealogies of Genesis 5 and 11 has led many to believe that the Bible has postulated that Adam was born nearly seven thousand years ago, a date, as we have just shown, elicits no biblical justification.

Biblical mathematics has given us the year 11013 BC as the year of Adam's creation, the year that the Lord God Almighty created light (day 1); the firmament (day 2); plant life (day 3); the sun, moon, and stars (day 4); the sea creatures and the fowls of the air (day 5); animal life and mankind (day 6).

The Word of God seems to make the case that all the aforementioned creatures hail from 11013 BC. Is that an accurate configuration? Are the numbers of the Bible relevant and accurate? Is the earth four and a half billions years old as modern science seems to indicate? Let's analyze various dating methodologies to see if they are in agreement with the biblical chronology.

Scientists of a bygone era maintained that the oceans could be used as a legitimate tool to figure out the age of the earth (We will summarize in the next few paragraphs the analysis of a very important short book on that matter, *Let the Oceans Speak*). In that regard, those trained researchers posit that rivers continue to transport chemicals and sediment in solution from erosion of the continental mass; and as such, they theorize that "most of the solid materials dissolved in the sea originated from the weathering of the crust of the earth."

In that light, Herald Ulrik Sverdrup, Martin W. Johnson, Richard Fleming, in their masterpiece, *The Oceans*, hypothesize that a great deal of the earth's history can be apprehended from the biological, physical, and chemical contents of the oceans. Thus, they argue that the knowledge of the amounts of the chemical elements in the sea can be compared with the amounts entering the seas each year by the weathering of the continental mass to render an approximate age of the earth.

In fact, using that methodology, scientists initially conjectured that the earth was nearly one hundred million years old! The development of radioactive decay measurements would soon replace the data coming from the oceans, and scientists would reconfigure the age of the earth at 4.5 billion years!

It was prematurely believed that radioactive decay would yield more accurate measurements than the information stemming from the oceans; and scientists, eager to find justification for the theory of evolution, ignored the possibility that both methodologies, undertaken through the lens of the principles of modern science, should yield the same conclusion vis-à-vis the age of the earth. As such, the oceans were abandoned in favor of the atoms.

We believe that scientists were too quick to put aside the data coming from the oceans; after all, if they can know both the chemical contents of the elements in the sea and the amount of the chemicals entering the sea each year, they should be able to approximate the age of the earth.

Moreover, since the earth, along with its continents and oceans, is believed to be four and a half billion years old, the continents and the oceans must remain in a state of equilibrium; otherwise, all the continents would have by now drifted into the open seas.

Even now, geologists continue to believe that the chemical composition of both ocean water and the ocean floor rocks stems from the erosion or weathering of continental rocks; and if the erosion of the continental rocks was of long duration, the amounts of the chemicals in both the ocean waters and the ocean floor should be equal to the amounts of those chemicals in the continental rocks.

As a result, if both the amounts of the elements in the sea and in the sea floor and the rate of the erosion of the elements from the continental mass can be accurately known, then the amount of time needed to bring about the equilibrium of the elements in the ocean and in the continent can be fairly ascertained, thereby establishing as closely as possible the age of the earth.

Geologists have been able to determine the amounts of chemicals in both the oceans and the continental mass. As such, they should be able to estimate the amount of time it took for the present amounts of chemicals in the oceans to accumulate to their present levels.

Interestingly, Harald Ulrik Sverdrup, Richard H. Fleming, and Martin W. Johnson relate (table 6b) the estimated amount of chemicals that should be deposited in one kilogram of ocean water from six hundred grams of weathered continental rocks over a period of 260 million years.

A thorough analysis of the elements in table 6b does not reveal any type of relationship between the elements as they are found in ocean water and in the continental mass. For example, iron and aluminum should be respectively 1,000,000 (100/0.0001) and 100,000 times (100/0.001) more abundant in ocean water if they were in exact proportion with the continental rocks; and bromine and chlorine would be respectively 20 and 67 times less abundant if they were in exact proportion with the continental rocks.

The precipitation of chemicals to the bottom of the ocean floor could be one of the reasons accounting for a lack of direct relationship of the proportion of the elements in the ocean as compared to their proportion in the continental rocks.

Nonetheless, it remains apparent that most of the chemicals present in ocean water appear far below their expected values: only ten of the elements noted in table 6b (calcium 1.9 times more abundant, sodium 65 times more abundant, potassium 2.6 times more abundant, magnesium 10 times more abundant, sulfur 300 times more abundant, chlorine 6,700 times more abundant, strontium 5 times more abundant, bromine 2,000 times more abundant, baron 240 times more abundant, and iodine 25 times more abundant) have exceeded their expected value, thereby suggesting that the oceans must be very young. In other words, most if not all of the elements would have equaled or exceeded their saturated values in many or at least a few parts of the world if the oceans were very old.

Moreover, since an estimate of the average annual quantity of elements flowing into the oceans from the rivers of the world can be established, scientists can determine the age of the oceans by dividing the quantity of an element present in unsaturated condition in ocean solution by the annual quantity of that element flowing from the rivers. Table 6b sheds light on the number of years it would take for various elements to exist in ocean solution.

Therefore, 560,000 years (table 6c) would have been required to generate the amount of gold present in ocean solution, 2,100,000 years for silver, 18,000 years for nickel, 45,000,000 years for magnesium, and 260,000,000 years for sodium.

A more careful consideration of table 6b reveals a very interesting tale. Many of the elements present in solution in ocean water are in short supply, thereby implying a short amount of time was warranted for their continental erosion into the ocean. For example, it would take aluminum 100 years of erosion time, titanium 160 years, chromium 350 years, iron 140 years, niobium 300 years. In fact, nineteen of the elements in the oceans required less than one thousand years of continental erosion.

What do those short amounts of time represent? How should anyone interpret the little amount of time warranted for so many elements to drift from the continental rocks into the oceans?

Those short amounts of time no doubt indicate that the oceans could be indeed very young. The paucity of so many elements in ocean water as compared with the amounts that should be present if the oceans were very old constitutes the big elephant in a room filled with foolhardy evolutionists eager to find any evidence justifying their theory of macroevolution.

What are the ramifications for sodium with 260,000,000 years, magnesium with 45,000,000 years, lithium with 20,000,000 years, strontium with 19,000,000 years, and potassium with 11,000,000 years? Those vast amounts of time might simply indicate that continental erosion is not the only factor at play here: God could have created the oceans already saturated with vast amounts of those chemicals.

Moreover, after examining the evidence presented by ocean sediments, Maurice Ewing wrote the following:

> In more than 300 places over vast areas of the Atlantic, we have now measured with sound echoes the depth of the sediment on top of the bed-rock of the ocean floor. These measurements clearly indicate thousands of feet of sediments on the foothills of the Ridge. Surprisingly, however, we have found that in the great flat basins on each side of the Ridge this sediment appears to be less than 100 feet thick, a fact so startling that it needs further checking.

For its part, a great deal of the Pacific floor contains sediments less than one hundred meters in depth; in fact, some areas carry sediments amounting to twenty meters in depth!

Therefore, the presence in ocean solution of so many chemicals that could have been accumulated within the past one thousand years seems to support the young earth theory; and that notion is also complemented by the presence of a thin layer of sediments on the ocean floor.

As a result, one can ascertain that the accumulation of various chemicals in the oceans and in the ocean floor does not contradict the creation story of Genesis, which seems to indicate the creation of the first man in the year 11,013 BC.

A REQUIEM FOR EVOLUTION

Could the study of the oldest trees in the earth also shed some light on the age of the earth? If the earth is indeed nearly 4.5 billion years old, shouldn't we find somewhere in the earth trees that are one million years old, or one hundred thousand years old, or even ten thousand years old?

In that regard, let's review the top ten oldest known trees in the world to find out whether they also support the young earth theory.

The General Sherman, a giant sequoia that stands 275 feet tall, is located in the Sequoia National Park and is believed to be nearly 2,700 years old.

So far, we have endeavored to present arguments in defense of a young ocean and a young earth. The genealogies of Genesis 5 and 11 have led us to believe that Adam was in all likelihood created in the year 11013 BC. The absence or paucity in ocean solution and in the floor of the oceans of chemicals that should have accumulated over the purported millions or even billions of years since the formation of the oceans and the continental masses tends to support the apparent notion of a young earth.

Moreover, the nonexistence of a single living tree more than eight thousand years old seems to add fodder to the young earth hypothesis.

However, the data in radiometric dating lends support to an old earth hypothesis. Let's consider some of the tenets of radiometric dating (also called radioactive dating) and lay the foundation for an old earth theory in juxtaposition to the young earth hypothesis.

Radiometric dating is analogous to an hourglass (See figures 1 and 2). Turning the glass upside down would allow sand to precipitate from the top to the bottom of the glass. Radioactive atoms emulate the behavior of sands as they fall from the top to the bottom of a glass. As one can determine precisely the time it takes for all the sands to precipitate to the bottom of a glass, so one can pinpoint the time it would take for all the atoms of a radioactive element to disappear.

There is, nonetheless, a slight difference between the hourglass where the amount of falling sands remain steady until the end and the number of decays from a specific number of radioactive atoms where the number of atoms is reduced with each successive atomic decay. In other words, it will take a specific amount of time for half of the atoms to decay and the same amount of time for the remaining half (that is, 1/4 and then 1/8; again see figures 1 and 2) and so on.

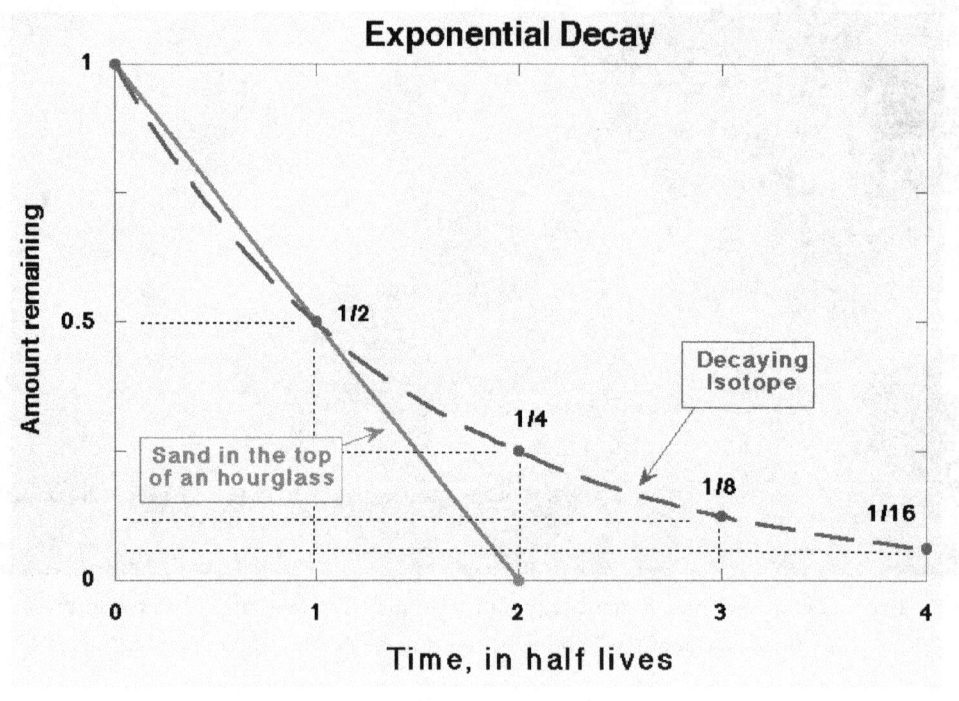

http://asa3.org/ASA/resources/Wiens.html

Figure 1. The exponential decay of radioactive elements stands compared to the rate of change of sand from the top to the bottom of an hourglass (taken from *Radiometric Dating: A Christian Perspective* by Dr. Roger C. Wiens).

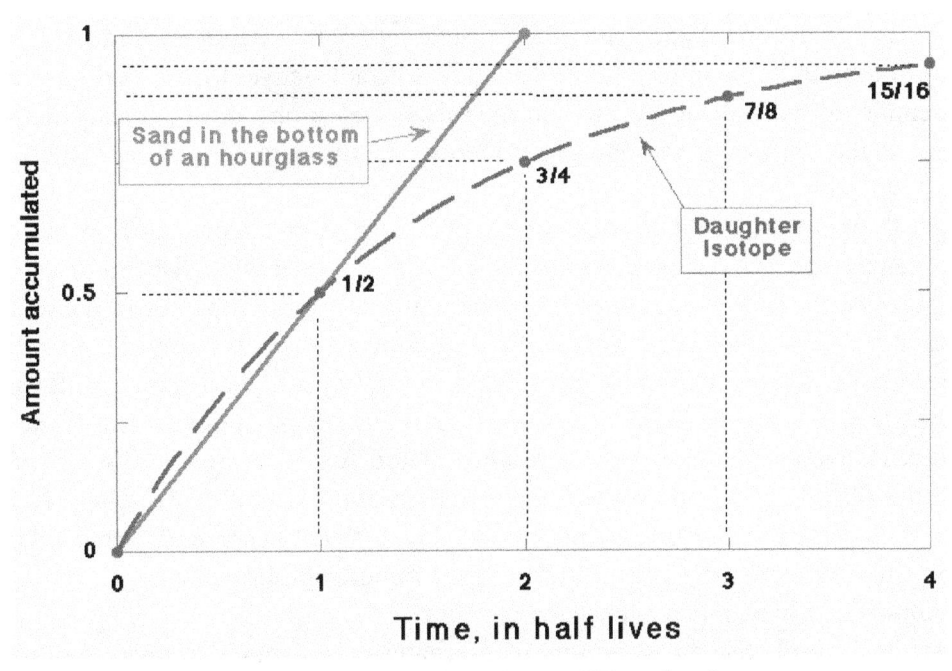

Figure 2. The daughter isotope or element increases precipitously at first and then slows down after each half-life (from *Radiometric Dating: A Christian Perspective*).

Moreover, the rate of change of radioactive decays remains constant and cannot be influenced by changes of temperature or pressure or any other means, whereas the hourglass can be influenced simply by shaking the glass different ways or by placing the glass in a vehicle with great speed.

Radiometric dating of rocks and other items indicate how much time has elapsed since the passing of some event. For example, for igneous rocks, the passing event may entail the hardening or cooling of the rock from lava or magma. In other cases, the event might entail the amount of time an animal or a plant has been dead.

There are now about forty distinct radiometric dating procedures available, each one originating from a different radioactive isotope. Table 6a presents a partial listing of some radioactive isotopes with their daughter isotopes and half-lives. Samarium-147, for instance, is used to date items that are very old—one hundred billion years or more; and Carbon-14 can be effective in dating items that are less than sixty thousand years old: the rather large range of half-lives is designed to fit in a variety of items based on their age.

In other words, isotopes with considerably long half-lives take a long time to decay; as a result, they are used to date items that are very old, while isotopes with short half-lives cannot be used for the same old items because all the atoms of the parent isotope would have already disappeared. As a result, they are used to date items that are young.

How does radiometric dating actually work? We will focus on igneous rocks as a practical illustration. Let's remember that the event being dated here entails the moment when the rock was formed from lava or magma. When the molten material cools, it hardens, and its atoms are not allowed to move around. Daughter atoms, the results of radioactive decays, that develop are then frozen and remain in the same location within the rock. Those atoms can be considered as the sands accumulating at the bottom of the hourglass. Identifying the date of the rock entails a two-step mechanism.

First of all, one must calculate both the number of daughter atoms and the number of the remaining parent atoms, and one must determine the ratio between them. Second of all, the half-life is used to figure out the time it took to produce that particular ratio of parent-to-daughter atoms.

Let's examine now how precisely radiometric dating works. Let's consider first the potassium-argon technique (We are thankful in that regard to Dr. Roger C. Weins for his marvelous work, *Radiometric Dating: A Christian Perspective*). Potassium is quite popular in the crust of the earth. One of its isotopes, Potassium-40, decays into Calcium-40 and Argon-40 by two distinct mechanisms. That's not however a big issue since the ratio of the amounts of those two daughter products is well-known: 88.8 percent turns to Calcium-40, and 11.2 percent becomes Argon-40. Dating rocks with the potassium-calcium mechanism can become a rather complicated affair since it's not always possible to know the initial amount of calcium present.

On the other hand, the potassium-argon mechanism is a much simpler commodity. Since argon is a gas, it tends to leave a rock any time a rock melts into magna or lava. Whenever the molten product cools off and hardens, any remaining argon left is trapped inside the rock. As such, any savvy scientist is able to measure the ratio of Potassium-40 to Argon-40 to determine the age of the rock.

Critics of radiometric dating point out that rocks dated several million years old by the potassium-argon method were actually a few years old. However, that particular methodology with its half-life of 1.26 billion years was not intended to measure items that are a few years old. The false reading is due to dating a daughter argon without a parent. In that regard, it is always recommended to corroborate the results obtained through radiometric dating with other nonradiometric techniques.

The argon-argon technique, although as nearly as old as the other radiometric techniques, is seldom attacked by critics. In that technique, the rock under investigation is placed close to the center of a nuclear reactor for a specific amount of time. The rock is then heated as much as possible in a furnace so that both the Argon-40 and the Argon-39 (which represents the potassium) inside the rock can be analyzed.

The heating is increased periodically so that the ratio of Argon-40 to Argon-39 can be measured under increasing sets of temperatures. If the Argon-40 stems from a decay of potassium, it would materialize at the same temperatures as the potassium derived from the Argon-39, and in the same proportion. In case of excess of Argon-40, a different set of ratios of Argon-40 to Argon-39 would materialize, thereby hindering the heating steps to agree with each other.

We will take a detour from the various techniques that have been developed in order to establish their import vis-à-vis the age of the earth. In that regard, our upper limit consists of the age of the oldest rocks, which all have been dated to nearly four billion years.

The study of meteorites has brought to the forefront a most interesting phenomenon: they are all about 4.56 billion years old! Those meteorites, fragments of the asteroids circulating around the earth, were created in space and then cooled off rather quickly afterward.

Therefore, almost all their rocks were formed within a few million years. Since all the rocks of the asteroids have not melted again after their creation, their ages have been set in stone (pardon the pun here): again 4.56 billion years! It is believed in the scientific community that all the planets and all the asteroids in our solar system were created at nearly the same time; therefore, the age of the earth is believed to be 4.56 billion years.

The age of the earth can also be ascertained by analyzing another set of factors. There are many more parent isotopes than those listed in table 6a; nonetheless, most of them do not exist anymore: they have exhausted their half-lives. In fact, it is believed that "every single element has radioisotopes that no longer exist on Earth!"

As a result, when all the radioactive isotopes that exist naturally and those that do not are carefully studied, a very interesting phenomenon ensues: almost all the radioactive isotopes with half-lives much less than half a billion years can no longer be found anymore. That is clearly conclusive justification that the solar system was created quite a while longer than those young half-lives! The earth in that light appears indeed very old.

Moreover, radiometric dating has been positively and carefully cross-referenced with various nonradiometric age indicators. Tree rings, for example, have been positively cross-checked with Carbon-14 dates. Dendrochronology or Tree Dating can be calibrated with Carbon-14 for up to 11,800 years, while other nonradiometric dating procedures can take the calibration with the longer radiometric dating techniques for up to 100,000 years.

The calibration of Carbon-14 with several nonradiometric methods goes as far back as 50,000 years! One technique entails the finding of natural layers produced over much longer periods of time than tree rings. For example, sediment layers, "varves," form yearly patterns in lakes and bays. Those layers, much like tree rings, can be counted; and many go back longer than tree rings.

Yet another method of calibration with radiometric dating involves "recently-formed carbonate deposits" found in various caves. All those methods of calibration synchronize quite harmoniously with the radiometric dating techniques that have been developed over the years.

Arguably, the ideal nonradiometric way to measure time longer than dendrochronology would involve Ice Cores, the seasonal variations in polar ice from Antarctica and Greenland. The snow layers deposited in the winter are much more different than those made in the spring, summer, and fall. As a result, those layers can be counted just like tree rings.

Ice Cores can be acquired by drilling in the ice caps of Greenland and Antarctica with specialized drilling rigs that are able to penetrate 9,000 feet of snow and bring to the surface a long core of ice in the process. Those cores, carefully analyzed, reveal layers that exist as far back as 160,000 years!

Coral reefs' annual layering can be used to date various sections of coral. It is well-known that coral grows at a fairly stable rate of about one centimeter per year, and that those layers are quite visible to the naked eye.

Many other nonradiometric dating methods—thermoluminescence, electron spin resonance (ESR), cosmic-ray exposure dating—have corroborated the results of the radiometric dating techniques to make the conclusive claim that the earth is very old.

Our analysis so far has simultaneously made the case for both a very young and a very old earth! How do we then synchronize both sets of findings?

Someone may argue here that God made everything very recently but with the appearance of age. This idea was immortalized by Philippe Henry Gosse in his book *Omphalos: An Attempt to Untie the Geological Knot*.

Nonetheless, by integrating our biblical finding of the chronologies of Genesis 5 and 11 with the scientific discoveries provided by various radiometric and nonradiometric dating techniques, it appears that God did create Adam and Eve nearly thirteen thousand years ago, and the earth as well as the rest of the universe quite possibly billions of years before.

Table 6a

Half-Lives of Various Radioactive Isotopes

Radioactive Isotope (Parent)	Product (Daughter)	Half-Life (Years)
Samarium-147	Neodymium-143	106 billion
Rubidium-87	Strontium-87	48.8 billion
Rhenium-187	Osmium-187	42 billion
Lutetium-176	Halfnium-176	38 billion
Thorium-232	Lead-208	14 billion
Uranium-238	Lead-206	4.5 billion
Potassium-40	Argon-40	1.26 billion
Uranium-235	Lead-207	0.7 billion
Beryllium-10	Boron-10	1.52 million
Chlorine-36	Argon-36	300,000
Carbon-14	Nitrogen-14	5,715
Uranium-234	Thorium-230	248,000
Thorium-230	Radium-226	75,400

(Reprinted from *Let the Oceans* Speak: http://may-212011.com/downloads/LetTheOceansSpeak.pdf)

A REQUIEM FOR EVOLUTION

Table 6b

Chemical Elements in Sea Water and in Continental Rocks

Element	Sea Water	Potential Supply of Sea Water	Solution (% in 600g of rock, mg/kg)
Silicon	4	165,000	0.002
Aluminum	0.5	53,000	0.001
Iron	0.002	31,000	0.0001
Calcium	408	22,000	1.9
Sodium	10769	17,000	65
Potassium	387	15,000	2.6
Magnesium	1297	13,000	10
Titanium	……..	3,800	?
Manganese	0.01	560	0.002
Phosphorous	0.01	470	0.02
Carbon	28	300	9
Sulfur	901	300	300
Chlorine	19,353	290	2,700
Strontium	13	250	5
Barium	0.05	230	0.02
Rubidium	0.02	190	0.1
Fluorine	1.4	160	0.9
Chromium	p	120	?
Zirconium	p	120	?
Copper	0.01	60	0.02
Nickel	0.0001	60	0.0002
Vanadium	0.0003	60	0.0005
Tungsten	…………	41	?
Lithium	0.1	39	0.2
Cerium	0.0004	26	0.002
Cobalt	p	24	?
Tin	p	24	?
Zinc	0.005	24	0.02
Yttrium	0.0003	19	0.002
Lanthanum	0.0003	11	0.003
Lead	0.004	10	0.04
Molybdenum	0.0005	9	0.005
Thorium	0.0005	6	0.01
Cesium	0.002	4	0.05
Arsenic	0.02	3	0.7
Scandium	0.00004	3	0.001
Bromine	66	3	2000
Boron	4.7	2	240
Uranium	0.015	2	0.8
Selenium	0.004	0.4	1
Cadmium	p	0.3	?
Mercury	0.00003	0.3	0.001
Iodine	0.05	0.2	25
Silver	0.003	0.06	0.5
Gold	0.056	0.003	0.3
Radium	0.093	0.066	0.05

(Reprinted from *Let the Oceans Speak*: http://may-212011.com/downloads/LetTheOceansSpeak.pdf)

Table 6c

Possible Number of Years of Chemicals in Ocean Solution (Years)

Element	Year	Element	Year
Lithium	2.0×10^7	Gadolinium	5.0×10^5
Beryllium	150	Tin	1.0×10^5
Sodium	2.6×10^8	Antimony	3.5×10^5
Magnesium	4.5×10^7	Cesium	4.0×10^4
Aluminum	100	Barium	8.4×10^4
Silicon	8.0×10^3	Lanthanum	440
Potassium	1.1×10^7	Cerium	80
Calcium	8.0×10^6	Praseodymium	320
Scandium	5.6×10^3	Neodymium	270
Titanium	160	Samarium	180
Vanadium	1.0×10^4	Europium	300
Chromium	350	Gadolinium	260
Manganese	1,400	Dysprosium	460
Iron	140	Holmium	530
Cobalt	1.8×10^4	Erbium	690
Nickel	1.8×10^4	Thulium	1,800
Copper	5.0×10^4	Ytterbium	530
Zinc	1.8×10^5	Lutetium	450
Gallium	1.4×10^3	Tungsten	10^3
Germanium	7.0×10^3	Gold	5.6×10^5
Rubidium	2.7×10^5	Mercury	4.2×10^4
Strontium	1.9×10^7	Lead	2.0×10^3
Yttrium	7.5×10^3	Bismuth	4.5×10^4
Niobium	300	Uranium	5.0×10^5
Molybdenum	5.0×10^5	Thorium	350
Silver	2.1×10^6		

(Reprinted from *Let the Oceans Speak*: http://may-212011.com/downloads/LetTheOceansSpeak.pdf)

Chapter 7

The Patterns of the Biblical Timetable

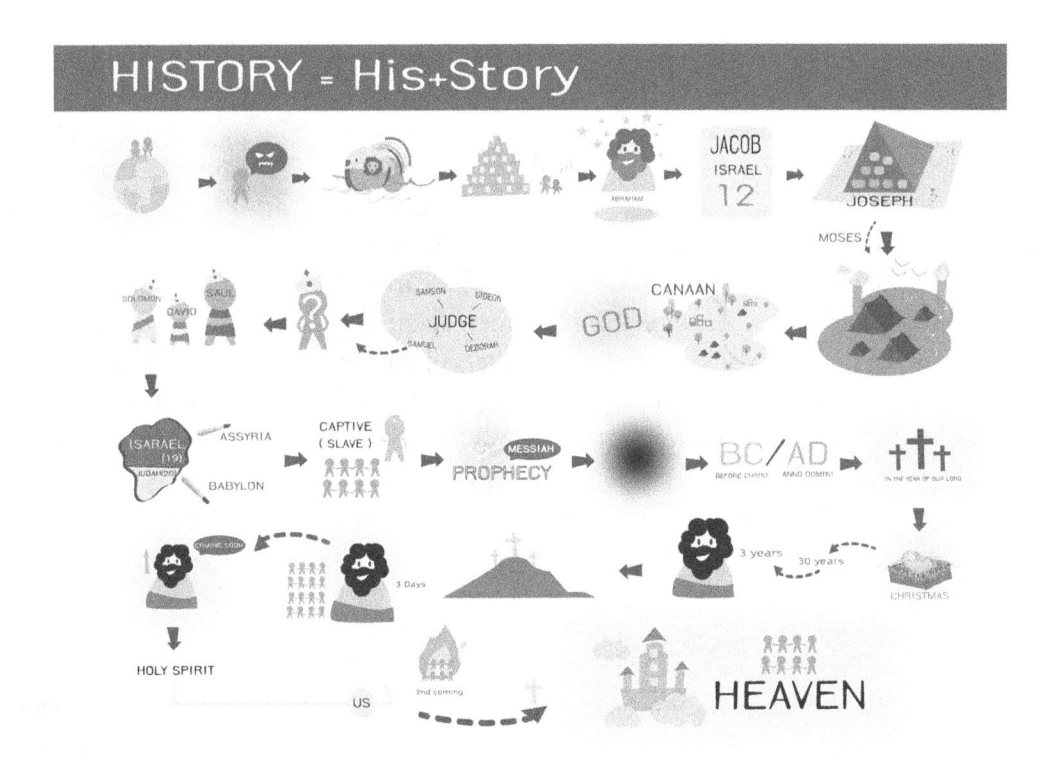

> Who hath wrought and done it, calling the generations from the beginning? I the Lord, the first, and with the last. (Isaiah 41:4)

We now stand on the threshold of the creation of time, space, and energy. The Lord God Almighty, the great Creator of the heavens and the heaven of heavens, in the presence of His morning stars singing in perfect harmony and His mighty angels shouting joyously, and in anticipation of the upcoming six days of creation of the present world, was about to create out of nothing the point of singularity, the entire universe confined in a single point, the size of a primordial atom. Sounding like a mighty flowing river, the Lord God, with a few simple words stemming from His voice of thunder, mixed together the four great forces—gravity, electromagnetism, nuclear, and radioactivity—into a single super force, an infinitely small and extremely hot pressurized gas.

Suddenly, His majestic voice slowly rising to match the solemn occasion, the Great Creator commanded the baryons—essentially the protons and neutrons squeezed in tight formations inside the point of singularity—to multiply exponentially: they did instantly, thus disturbing the status quo of equilibrium among the point's primordial elements. And the Lord God observed the baryogenesis process, and behold, it was good.

The Lord God issued a second set of commands, and behold, a gigantic explosion—the all too familiar big bang—took place. God's wonderful creatures witnessed a "cosmic inflation," a process whereby the superhot, dense, and pressurized ball of gas doubled multiple times its size in fractions of a second, and space increased at a speed several times the speed of light.

As this incredibly hot, dense, and pressurized ball of fire cooled down, various elementary particles combined to form the elements, planets, stars, and galaxies of today: The universe indeed had a very big inning.

The trinity of materials needed for the formation of the universe—time, space, and energy—was created, each with its triune elementary components: time—past, present, and future; space—length, width, and height; and energy—electrons in motion inducing phenomena. Indeed! The Triune God has left His fingerprints all over His created universe.

11013 BC (See table 7d) was an explosive year! Adam arrived on the scene to be shortly joined by Eve, his beautiful bride. God finally had His human agents in place in order to trap His cosmic foe, Lucifer, in the flesh. Bitten by the deceptive snake, Adam and Eve were no longer energized by the light of God's glorious holiness; the deadly venom of the serpent added a draconic element in the innocent bloodstream of the new couple, rendering effectively both the husband and his wife mortal- actually dead spiritually, then physically and psychologically.

Cain and Abel, their firstborn sons, had their DNA corrupted by their parents' satanic element. Man is sadly born a sinner by inheritance! Seth, born in 10883 BC, was not the exception to the deadly rule.

It is remarkably interesting that Enoch, the seventh generational patriarch from Adam, lived 365 years (should we recall here that a year is about 365 days?)! It is of great import that Enoch "walked with God after he begat Methuselah three hundred years." As a result of such a close walk with God for so long a time, he was raptured, becoming the perfect type of the church that will be raptured by God after walking with Him the full and perfect allotment of time that God, in His divine wisdom, had appointed.

4990BC (again see table 7d) stands out as the most important year since the creation of Adam in 11013 BC. It was the year of the worldwide flood that destroyed every human in existence, except Noah and his seven immediate family members. We should note here that the Flood took place exactly 6,023 years from the creation of Adam: twenty-three years added to a full six thousand! God brought His first great judgment on the world after an even set of years plus twenty-three!

The Seventy Weeks of Daniel 9 pinpoints AD 33 as the year of Christ's crucifixion. Is it by accident that the judgment of Jesus Christ on the cross is inclusively 5,023 from the judgment of the Flood, twenty-three years added to a full even number, this time 5,000!

The Bible reports that God has "made of one blood all nations of men for to dwell on the face of the earth, and hath determined the times before appointed, and the bounds of their habitation."

In 2167 BC, God brought to life a child in the pagan city of Ur named Abram. Abram, later renamed Abraham, was mightily used by the Lord to be the father of the physical and spiritual Israel as well as the Arab nations.

Abraham's son Isaac, born in 2067 BC, gave birth to the first man to be called Israel, Jacob, in 2007 BC. Jacob and his family, fleeing a famine that had spread all across the land of Palestine, fled to Egypt in 1877 BC. Exactly 430 years later, nearly two million Israelites, led by Moses, took part in the great Exodus and returned to the land of the promise, Palestine.

It is remarkable that God had prophetically announced to Abraham the complete predilections of the generations of his children nearly six hundred years before their enslavement to Egypt (Please, see table 7a):

> Know of a surety that thy seed shall be a stranger in a land that is not theirs, and shall serve them; and they shall afflict them four hundred years. And also that nation, whom they shall serve, will I judge; and afterward they shall come out with great substance.

As a fulfillment of the divine prophecy, Jacob, at the request of Joseph, his son and now the second in command in the Egyptian kingdom, migrated along with his entire family to Egypt to avoid the years of famine that God had proclaimed to Pharaoh in two similar dreams.

The time of Jacob's trouble, mentioned in Jeremiah 30:7, corresponds to the seven years of famine of Genesis 41 that compelled Jacob and his family to purchase food in Egypt. Joseph, on account of that "great tribulation," invited his father, Jacob, and the rest of his family to relocate in Egypt.

It is amazing to discover that the number 7 would again be featured in another "great tribulation" endured by the nation of Israel from the death of Israel's godly king Josiah in 609 BC to the capture of Babylon by the Medes and Persians in 539 BC. The prophet Jeremiah had prophesied earlier that God would punish the nation of Israel a period of seventy years (Jeremiah 25:11–12, 2 Chronicles 36:21).

The number 7 was again in full display during the seven months when the Arc was captured by the Philistines. That "great tribulation" is identified in 1 Samuel 4:21 as Ichabod, the departure from Israel of the presence of the glory of God.

In that light, the Seventy Weeks or Sevens of Daniel 9 must be considered the antitype of all the aforementioned "great tribulations," as they point simultaneously to the Judgment of God on our Lord and Savior Jesus Christ in AD 33 and Judgment Day at the end of the world.

Are those patterns simple coincidences of time or parts of a grandiose plan of a wise planner? Is the timing of the events of the Bible the undirected product of chance or the calibrated unveiling in time of God's great salvation program? We read in Galatians 4:4, "But when the fullness of the time was come, God sent forth His Son made of a woman, made under the sun."

The Lord God always acts "when the fullness of time has come." In other words, God is never too early, and He is never too late: He is always on time! In that light, let's reminisce in a fuller way the Four Generations prophecy that the Lord God made to Abraham with regard to the sojourning of the children of Israel in Egypt:

Know certainly that your descendants will be strangers in a land that is not theirs, and will serve them, and they will afflict them four hundred years. And also the nation whom they serve I will judge; afterward they shall come out with great possessions. Now as for you, you shall go to your fathers in peace; you shall be buried at a good old age. But in the *Fourth Generation* they shall return here, for the iniquity of the Amorites is not yet complete.

Exodus 12:40 to 41 renders the historical verdict concerning the stay of Israel in Egypt:

Now the sojourn of the children of Israel who lived in Egypt was four hundred and thirty years. And it came to pass at the end of the four hundred and thirty years—on that very same day—it came to pass that the armies of the Lord went out from the land of Egypt.

What then were the four generations that made up the 430 years of Israel's sojourning in Egypt? We read in Exodus 6:16 to 20 the following:

And these are the names of the sons of Levi according to their generations; Gershon, and Kohath, and Merari: and the years of the life of Levi were an hundred thirty and seven years. The sons of Gershon; Libni, and Shimi, according to their families. And the sons of Kohath; Amram, and Izhar, and Hebron, and Uzziel: and the years of the life of Kohath an hundred thirty and three years. And the sons of Merari; Mahali and Mushi: these are the families of Levi according to their generations. And Amram took him Jochebed his father's sister to wife; and she bare him Aaron and Moses: and the years of the life of Amram were an hundred and thirty and seven years.

Exodus 7:7 gives us the age of Aaron when he and Moses spoke to Pharaoh: he was eighty-three years old. Exodus 6:20 relates the length of the generation of the patriarch that preceded *Aaron*: Amram's generation lasted 137 years; and Exodus 6:18 brings to light the length of the generation of the patriarch that lived before Amram: Kohath's generation endured 133 years.

We have so far found the timings of the last three of the four generations of the children of Israel God had prophesied would sojourn in Egypt (Genesis 15, particularly verse 16): the generation of Kohath (133 years), the generation of Amram (137 years), and the generation of Aaron (83 years), which is equivalent to the age of Aaron at the time of the Exodus. The only missing generation entails the generation of Levi, which is equal to the time Levi spent in Egypt. How can we ascertain the amount of time Levi spent in Egypt?

We know that Levi died when he was 137 years old (Exodus 6:16); what then is the amount of years Levi lived in Egypt? If we can find Levi's age the year Jacob and his entire family moved to Egypt, we can find a satisfying answer to our question.

The Bible indicates in Genesis 29:31–35 that Leah bore four children to Jacob, Levi being the third child. Since Jacob married Leah after his first seven years of service to Laban (Genesis 29:20–26), we can posit here that Levi in all likelihood was born the third year of Jacob's marriage to Leah (or some time very close to the third year) or Jacob's tenth year of service to Laban.

Joseph, on the other hand, was born close to the last six years of Jacob's service to Laban (Genesis 30:23–25). Since Joseph was thirty-nine (he was made ruler in Egypt at thirty [Genesis 41:46]), and he made himself known to his brothers during the second year of famine that succeeded the seven years of great harvest (Genesis 45:6, 41:28–30), his older brother Levi, the third son of Leah and Jacob (Genesis 29:31–35), must have been twenty-one years older than he was, or sixty years old when he (Levi), Jacob, and his entire family moved to Egypt.

Levi must have been sixty years old because the three generations that followed him in Egypt (please, review the Prophecy of the Four Generations of Genesis 15:16), the generation of Kohath (133 years), the generation of Amram (137 years), and the generation of Aaron (83 years) add up to 353 years; and as such, 77 years are needed to make the 430 years that the children of Israel spent in Egypt (Exodus 12:40 and 41). As the leader of the four generations in Egypt (Exodus 6:16–20), Levi *must* have spent 77 years in Egypt after arriving in that country at the age of sixty (Remember he lived to be 137 according to Exodus 6:16).

Therefore, a chart of the Four Generations of Genesis 15:16 would look like the following:

Table 7a

Generation	Leader of Generation	Number of Years
Generation#1	Levi	77
Generation#2	Kohath	133
Generation#3	Amram	137
Generation#4	Aaron	83
TOTAL		430

Please, note again that the total 430 years that the four patriarchs (Levi, Kohath, Amram, and Aaron) spent in Egypt is exactly equal to the years the children of Israel spent in the land of the Pharaohs according to Exodus 12:40 and 41, thus fulfilling God's prophecy of the Four Generations of Genesis 15:16.

The year 1447 BC (See table 7d) was the year the children of Israel finally left Egypt; and since they spent forty years wandering in the wilderness, they must have arrived in the Promised Land in the year 1407 BC (Exodus 16:35; Numbers 14:34, 32:13).

First Kings, chapter 6, verse 1 establishes a very important time bridge in the history of the nation of Israel. We read in that most significant verse the following:

> And it came to pass in the four hundred and eightieth year after the children of Israel had come out of the land of Egypt, in the fourth year of Solomon's reign over Israel, in the month of Ziv, which is the second month, that [Solomon] began to build the house of the Lord.

We learn from that passage that 480 years elapsed between the Exodus and the construction of Solomon's temple. In other words, the wilderness sojourn, the conquest of the Promised Land by Joshua, the periods of the judges, the reigns of King Saul and King David, and the fourth year of Solomon's reign in which he began the construction of the temple make up the 480 sequence spoken here.

As a result, subtracting 480 years from 1447 BC, the year the children of Israel left Egypt, yields 967 BC as the fourth year of King Solomon's reign (1 Kings 6:1); 967 BC stands out as well as the year that King David died, thus ending the four-year coregency with Solomon, his son (King Solomon was not allowed to begin construction of the temple until the death of David, his father, according to 1 Chronicles 28:3).

David then must have started his reign in 1007 BC, since he ruled over the nation of Israel for a period of forty years (1 Kings 2:11 and 2 Samuel 5:4); and Saul, David's predecessor, in all likelihood began to reign in the year 1047 BC (like David, he also ruled Israel for forty years according to Acts 13:21). Therefore, the period of the judges in Israel must have ended in 1047BC in order to coincide with the first year of Israel's first king, Saul.

How long did the period of the judges last? What are some of the noticeable patterns in that era in the history of the nation of Israel? Since the children of Israel arrived in the Promised Land in 1407 BC and Saul began his reign in Israel in 1047 BC, subtracting those two numbers yields 360 years as the length of time of the period of the judges.

Do the Holy Scriptures provide additional support for those 360 years? A more detailed analysis of the period of the judges reveals a very interesting proposition. Adding the years that the land had rest to the years the nation of Israel was judged (See table 7b), we obtain exactly 360 years! Please, notice the extra 111 years at the bottom right of the chart. At first glance, one might surmise that they should be added to the 360 years for a total of 471 years; however, one must realize that the 111 years occurred simultaneously as the 360 years: we have already calculated that the period of the judges lasted 360 years (Please, remember that 1407 – 1047 = 360).

We are, therefore, able to establish an accurate chronology of the times of the judges (Please, see table 7c). We know that the children of Israel entered the Promised Land in the year 1407 BC. The Word of God gives us the next chronological clue in Judges 3:11: "And the land had rest forty years." That should be equivalent to the years 1407 BC to 1367 BC during which the conquest of the Promised Land took place. In fact, Joshua 14:7–10 and Deuteronomy 2:14 would indicate that the entire conquest occurred during the first seven years of the initial forty years. Moreover, the children of Israel fell into slavery to the king Cushanrishthaim for eight years during the same forty years before they were rescued by Othniel (Judges 3:9).

The next time clue occurred in Judges 3:30: "And the land had rest for eighty years." This would be the years 1367 to 1287 BC. In that period of time, the nation of Israel went served King Eglon of Moab for eighteen years, according to Judges 3:31. God chose Ehud (Judges 3:15) and Shamgar (Judges 3:31) to deliver Israel from King Eglon.

The next time clue took place in Judges 5:31: "And the land had rest forty years." That would entail the years 1287 to 1247 BC. In those years, King Jabin of Canaan afflicted the nation of Israel for twenty years (Judges 4:3). Then, God used Barak and the prophetess Deborah to rescue his people from the tyranny of the king (Judges 4 and 5).

The next time clue can be found in Judges 8:28: "And the country was quiet for forty years in the days of Gideon." That period involved the years 1247 to 1207 BC. In that time, the nation of Israel served Median for seven years (Judges 6:1). God used Gideon to save His people (Judges 7:14). Then Abimelech, one of the sons of Gideon, ruled the nation of Israel for three years (Judges 9:22), from the year 1207 to the year 1204 BC.

Then Tola judged Israel for twenty-three years (Judges 10:7 and 8), from the year 1204 BC to the year 1181 BC. After Tola, Jair judged the nation of Israel for twenty-two years, from the year 1181 BC to the year 1159 BC. During that period of time, God used the Philistines and the children of Ammon to oppress the nation of Israel for eighteen years (Judges 10:7 and 8).

Then, Jephthah judged six years (Judges 12:7, from 1159 BC to 1153 BC); afterward, Ibzan judged seven years (Judges 12:9, from 1153 BC to 1146 BC); then, Elon judged ten years (Judges 12:11, from 1146 BC to 1136 BC); and Abdon judged eight years (Judges 12:14, from 1136 BC to 1128 BC).

The next time clue is given in Judges 15:20: "And [Samson] judged Israel in the days of the philistines twenty years." That takes us from the year 1128 BC to the year 1108 BC. Concerning this particular Philistine oppression, we read in Judges 13:1, "Again the children of Israel did evil in the sight of the Lord, and the Lord delivered then into the hand of the Philistines for forty years."

The next time clue occurs in 1 Samuel 4:18, where we are told that Eli judged Israel for forty years: that would be from 1108 BC to 1068 BC. We then learn that the Ark was captured by the Philistines for seven months (1 Samuel 6:1) or almost one year. That probably happened during the years 1068 and 1067 BC.

We finally arrive at Samuel's judgeship. Although a clear-cut reference to Samuel is not indicated in 1 Samuel 7:2, it must be inferred. The twenty years indicated in that verse must refer to the time during which Samuel judged Israel. That would take us from the year 1067 BC to the year 1047 BC when Saul became the first king of the nation of Israel.

The Bible provides a detailed chronology of all the kings that would rule over the nations of Israel and Judah after the division of Solomon's kingdom in 931 BC. The detailed description of the events that unfolded during the ruling of those kings as well as the accurate delineation of the timings of their reign are powerful indicators of the truthfulness, dependability, and reliability of the Holy Scriptures. Let's examine the biblical record concerning the status of each of those kings.

As we saw earlier, Saul, the first Jewish king, reigned in Israel from 1047 BC to 1007 BC (Acts 13:21). He was followed by King David, arguably the greatest Jewish king who ascended to power in the year 1007 BC. King David would rule over the nation of Israel during the span of forty years, from 1007 BC to 967 BC (1 Kings 2:11, 2 Samuel 4:4 and 5).

First Kings, chapter 6, verse 11 reveals that there were 480 years between the Exodus out of Egypt and the fourth year of King Solomon at which time he began to build the temple. As a result, 1447 BC, when the Exodus happened minus 480 years would take us to the year 967 BC, the fourth year of Solomon's reign: he must have begun ruling in 971 BC. Therefore, we can ascertain a coregency between King David and King Solomon of four years, from the year 971 BC to the year 967 BC. King Solomon would have reigned in Israel from 971 BC to 931 BC since he reigned over the nation of Israel for forty years (1 Kings 11:42 and 2 Chronicles 9:30).

After the death of Solomon in 931 BC, the Jewish kingdom was divided (Please, see table 7e). Rehoboam, a bad king (2 Chronicles 12:14), the son of King Solomon, reigned over Judah seventeen years, from the year 931 BC to the year 914 BC (2 Chronicles 12:13). Over the ten tribes of Israel reigned Jeroboam, a very wicked king (1 Kings 14:9). He ruled over the Ten Tribes of Israel for a period of twenty-two years (1 Kings 14:20), from the year 931 BC to the year 910 BC.

While Jeroboam was still ruling over the Ten Tribes of Israel, Abijah, the son of Rehoboam, took over the Tribe of Judah after the death of his father. A bad king, Abijah only reigned for three years (1 Kings 15:2), from the year 914 BC to the year 911 BC.

Asa, the son of Abijah, took control of the Tribe of Judah after the death of his father during the twentieth year of the reign of Jeroboam (1 Kings 15:9). A good king, Asa reigned in Jerusalem for forty-one years, from the year 911 BC to the year 870 BC.

During the second year of Asa's ruling over Judah, Nadab, the son of Jeroboam, assumed the throne over the Ten Tribes of Israel. Like his father, Jeroboam, he was a bad king (1 Kings 15:26), and he would reign for only two years, from the year 910 BC to the year 909 BC.

In the third year of Asa's kingship, Baasha conspired against King Nadab of Israel and assassinated him (1 Kings 15:27). He then killed all the sons of Jeroboam in order to fulfill the Lord's prophecy to bring destruction to the entire house of Jeroboam (1 Kings 15:29). A bad king, Baasha walked in the way of Jeroboam and enticed the people of Israel to sin (1 Kings 16:2). He would reign in Israel for twenty-four years (1 Kings 15:33), from the year 909 BC to the year 886 BC.

Elah, the son of Baasha, took over the Ten Tribes of Judah in the twenty-sixth year of the reign of Asa, king of Judah. Like his father, he was a bad king given to binge drinking (1 Kings 16:9): he would reign for only two years (1 Kings 16:8), from the year 886 BC to the year 885 BC. He was assassinated by his servant Zimri, a captain of half his chariot guards (1 Kings 16:9).

Zimri, the new king of Israel, "slew all the house of Baasha" (1 Kings 16:11). His murderous spree was a fulfillment of the Word of God pronounced against the house of Baasha by the prophet Jehu (1 Kings 16:12). Another bad king of Israel, Zimri managed to rule for only seven days during the year 885 BC. He committed suicide by burning "the king's house over him" (1 Kings 16:18).

Half of the people then made Tibni king, and the rest made Omni king following the death of Zimri in the year 885 BC. (1 Kings 16:21). The followers of Omni overwhelmed those of Tibni, who subsequently died. As a result, Omni, another bad king, reigned in Israel for twelve years (1 Kings 16:23), from the year 885 BC to the year 874 BC.

Ahab, the son of Omni, began ruling in Israel after the death of his father. One of the worst kings of Israel, Ahab, in the thirty-eighth year of the reign of Asa in Judah, acquired the throne in 874 BC, and he reigned in Israel for twenty-two years (1 Kings 16:29): He died in battle in the year 853 BC.

In the fourth year of the reign of Ahab over Israel, Jehoshaphat, the son of Asa, began ruling over the Tribe of Judah in the year 871 BC. One of the better kings of Judah, Jehoshaphat reigned in Jerusalem for twenty-five years (1 Kings 22:42); and he died in 846 BC.

In the seventeenth year of the reign of Jehoshaphat (1 Kings 22:51), king of Judah, in the year 854 BC, Ahaziah, the son of Ahab, began to rule over the Ten Tribes of Israel. Another bad king who caused Israel to sin (1 Kings 22:52), Ahaziah ruled for only two years; and he died after falling "through a lattice in his upper chamber" (2 Kings 1:2) in the year 853 BC.

Over the Tribe of Judah, Jehoram, the son of Jehoshaphat, had an eight-year coregency (2 Kings 8:16) with his father that began in the year 854 BC, two years before another Jehoram (2 Kings 1:17), also known as Joram (2 Kings 8:16), another son of Ahab, took over the kingship over the Ten Tribes of Israel. King Jehoram did not walk with the Lord as his father, King Jehoshaphat, and he "did evil in the sight of the Lord" (2 Kings 8:18) and died in the year 842 BC after ruling over Judah for eight years (2 Kings 8:17).

The aforementioned Jehoram, also known as Joram, the son of Ahab, began to rule over the Ten Tribes of Israel in the year 853 BC, two years after Jehoram, the son of Jehoshaphat, took over the Tribe of Judah (2 Kings 1:17). Like his father, Ahab, Joram was a bad king, and he reigned over the Ten Tribes twelve years, from the year 853 BC to the year 841 BC.

In the twelfth year of the reign of King Joram, the son of Ahab, in the year 842 BC, Ahaziah, the son of Jehoram, king of Judah, began to reign over the Tribe of Judah. He was a bad king who ruled for only two years. Ahaziah and Jehoram, the son of Ahab, were killed the same day by Jehu in the year 841 BC (2 Kings 9:14 to 29).

When Athaliah, the mother of King Ahaziah, knew that her son was murdered, she proclaimed herself queen over Judah in the year 841 BC and proceeded to kill "all the royal heirs" (2 Kings 11:1). She was a bad ruler who reigned over the Tribe of Judah for six years, as she was overthrown and killed on the orders of the great Jewish priest Jehoida in the year 835 BC.

Jehu, the son of King Jehoshaphat, who had murdered in the same day Ahaziah, king of Judah, and Joram, king of Israel, became the king of Israel in the year 841 BC, the same year that Athaliah took control of the Tribe of Judah. King Jehu also slew forty-two brothers of Ahaziah, king of Judah (2 Kings 10:13 and 14) and the worshippers of Baal (2 Kings 10:18 to 25).

King Jehu excelled in executing the Lord's judgment on the house of King Ahab and in destroying Baal from Israel (2 Kings 10:28 and 30); however, he "took no heed to walk in the law of the Lord God of Israel with all his heart" and repeated the sins of Jeroboam, king of Israel, in inciting the nation of Israel to sin (2 Kings 10:31). Jehu died in 813 BC after ruling over the Ten Tribes of Israel for twenty-eight years (2 Kings 10:36).

During Athaliah's reign of terror over Judah, when she murdered "all the royal heirs," Jehosheba, sister of King Ahaziah and daughter of King Joram, hid the infant Joash, the son of King Ahaziah, in the temple for six years (2 Kings 11:1 and 2). The following year when he turned seven and after the assassination of Athaliah, Joash was declared king of Judah by the priest Jehoida in the year 835 BC.

A reasonably good king (2 Kings 12:2), Joash (also known as Jehoash) ruled over the Tribe of Judah for forty years (2 Kings 12:1), and he was assassinated by his servants in the year 795 BC (2 Kings 12:20).

The Lord had promised Jehu that his sons would rule over Israel up to the fourth generation (2 Kings 10:30). As such, after the death of Jehu, his son, Jehoahaz, became the ruler of Israel in the year 813 BC. King Jehoahaz "did that which was evil in the sight of the Lord" during his reign of seventeen years (2 Kings 13:1 and 2). And he died in the year 796 BC.

Two years before the death of his father, King Jehoahaz, Jehoash, his son, King Jehu's grandson, began to rule over Israel in the year 798 BC. (He began his rule in the thirty-seventh year of the reign of Joash, king of Judah according to 2 Kings 13:10.) He "did that which was evil in the sight of the Lord" (2 Kings 13:11) during his reign of sixteen years (2 Kings 13:10); and he died in the year 782 BC.

In the second year of the reign of Jehoash, king of Israel, in the year 796 BC, Amaziah, the son of King Joash, began to rule in Judah. Like his father, he was a good king who "did that which was right in the sight of the Lord" (2 Kings 14:3). However, he challenged King Jehoash of Israel to his downfall. King Jehoash came to Jerusalem, broke down the walls of Jerusalem, and "took all the gold and silver, and all the vessels that were found in the house of the Lord, and in the treasures of the king's house, and hostages, and returned to Samaria" (2 Kings 14:13 and 14). And like his father, Amaziah died in a conspiracy by his servants in the year 767 BC after ruling Judah for twenty-nine years (2 Kings 14:2 and 19).

Commenting on the calendar of the kings of Judah and Israel, R. P. Bendedek relates that Jeroboam II began to reign in Israel in the year 792 BC (http://www.kingscalendar.com/cgi-bin/index.cgi?action=viewnews&id=551). Another bad king of Israel, Jeroboam II, King Jehu's great-grandson, died in the year 751 BC, after ruling Israel for forty-one years (2 Kings 14:23).

Azariah or Uzziah, the next king over Judah after the death Amaziah, must have begun ruling in 789 BC since the biblical record indicates that in his thirty-eighth year of power, Zechariah took control of Israel after the assassination of his father, Jeroboam II, in the year 751 BC (2 Kings 15:8). He was a good king who reigned over Judah for fifty-two years (2 Kings 15:2 and 3), and he died in the year 737 BC.

Zechariah, King Jehu's great-great-grandson, began to reign in Israel in the year 751 BC as a fulfillment of God's promise to Jehu that his children up to the fourth generation would reign in Israel (2 Kings 10:30 and 2 Kings 15:12). He was publicly assassinated by Shallum, the son of Jabesh (2 Kings 15:10) after ruling for only six months (2 Kings 15:8). Another bad Israeli king, he must have relinquished power in the year 750 BC since his successor, Shallum, began ruling in Israel during the thirty-ninth year of King Uzziah's reign (2 Kings 15:13).

Thus, Shallum terminated King Jehu's lineage from the throne of Israel as the Lord had prophesied to Jehu. His began ruling in the year 750 BC and lasted only one month (2 Kings 15:13) after he was assassinated by Menachem.

As a result, Menachem began ruling over Israel in 750 BC. He was yet another bad Israeli king (2 Kings 15:18) who ruled the nation for ten years (2 Kings 15:17) and died in the year 740 BC.

Menachem's son, Pekahiah, began ruling over Israel in the year 740 BC. A bad king (2 Kings 15:24), he only ruled for two years as he was assassinated by Pekah, one of his captains, in the year 738 BC.

Back in Judah, Uzziah (also called Azariah) would die the following year (737 BC) after ruling over Judah for fifty-two years (2 Kings 15:2). Since King Uzziah was struck by the Lord with leprosy (2 Kings 15:5), his son Jotham began ruling on his behalf in the year 738 BC, about one year before his death (2 Kings 15:5). Like his father, King Jotham was a good king (2 Kings 15:34) who led Judah until his death in 718 BC.

Pekah, brother of King Pekahiah (they were both sons of Remaliah according to 2 Kings 15:25 and 27), began to reign over the Ten Tribes of Israel in 738 BC. Like all the kings who ruled over the Ten Tribes of Israel, he was a bad king (2 Kings 15:28). He was assassinated by Hoshea in 718 BC after ruling Israel for twenty years (2 Kings 15:27 and 30).

Hoshea became the last king to rule over the Ten Tribes of Israel. He took control of the nation in 718 BC after murdering King Pekah. Like all the previous nineteen kings of Israel before him, Hoshea was a bad king who "did that which was evil in the sight of the Lord, but not as the kings of Israel that were before him" (2 Kings 17:2). In the sixth year of his reign, Shalmaneser, king of Assyria, came and besieged the land of Judah; and after three years, the king of Assyria carried the Ten Tribes of Israel into captivity (2 Kings 17:3 to 6) in the year 709 BC.

Therefore, we can declare that the kingdom of Israel lasted exactly 222 years, since the division of the kingdom took place in 931 BC (931 BC minus 709 BC yields 222 BC).

The Word of God indicates that King Hoshea became the ruler of Israel in the twelfth year of the reign of Ahaz, king of Judah (2 Kings 17:1). As a result, Ahaz must have ascended to power in Judah in the year 730 BC. His sixteen years of rule in Judah were marked by disobedience to the commands of the Lord (2 Kings 16:2 to 4). Against him came Rezin, king of Syria, and Pekah, king of Israel (2 Kings 16:5). Then King Ahaz appealed to Tiglathpileser, king of Assyria, to come to his rescue: he did by capturing Samaria, the capital of Israel, and by slaying King Rezin of Syria (2 Kings 16:9). King Ahaz died in the year 714 BC, and his son Hezekiah became the next king of Judah.

King Hezekiah of Judah must have been installed as king in the year 715 BC, for he became king in the third year of the reign of Hoshea, who had taken control of the Ten Tribes of Israel in the year 718 BC (2 Kings 18:1). One of the best kings of Judah (2 Kings 18:6 and 7), Hezekiah withstood the siege of Sennacherib, king of Assyria, against Judah by praying and seeking the help of Isaiah, one of the Lord's great prophets. The Lord answered Hezekiah's prayer by destroying in one night the entire Assyrian army—185,000 men! Defeated and disillusioned, Sennacherib returned to his country where he was murdered by his two sons (2 Kings 19:35 to 37). King Hezekiah reigned in Judah for twenty-nine years (2 Kings 18:2), and he died in the year 686 BC.

In order to account for the 110 years for the last six kings of Judah and for the captivity of Judah by Babylon in 587 BC (Please, see table 7e), Manasseh, the son of Hezekiah, must have come to power in the year 697 BC. His evil rule—Manasseh is arguably the worst of all the kings of Judah (2 Kings 21)—over the Tribe of Judah (2 Kings 21:2) lasted fifty-five years (2 Kings 21:1), from the year 697 BC to the year 642 BC.

Upon the death of his father, Manasseh, Amon became the next king of Judah in the year 642 BC. He followed in his father's footsteps in committing evil in the sight of the Lord (2 Kings 21:20), and his reign lasted only two years as he was assassinated by some of his servants in the year 640 BC.

Amon's son, Josiah, began to rule after the death of his father in the year 640 BC at the tender age of eight years. Judah's last great and good king (2 Kings 22:2 and 2 Kings 23), Josiah's reign lasted thirty-one years (2 Kings 22:1): he died in battle in the year 609 BC.

King Josiah's son, Jehoahaz, took over the throne on behalf of his father in the year 609 BC. He was an evil king (2 Kings 23:32) who reigned for only three months as he was deposed by Pharaoh Necho, the king of Egypt, who installed his brother, Eliakim, whom he called Jehoiakim, in his place in the year 609 BC. Jehoiakim's reign of evil (2 Kings 23:37) lasted eleven years.

Jehoichin, Jehoiakim's son, began to rule in the year 608 BC. His eleven years of power were characterized as evil (2 Kings 24:9); and during his reign, Nebuchadnezzar, king of Babylon, besieged Judah's capital, Jerusalem, and carried Jehoichin, his mother, his wives, his officers, and the leaders of Judah to Babylon (2 Kings 24:12 to 16).

Therefore, in the year 597 BC, Nebuchadnezzar proclaimed Mattaniah, Jehoichin's uncle, king of Judah and changed his name to Zedekiah. As the last of Judah's kings, Zedekiah "did that which was evil in the sight of the Lord" (2 Kings 24:19), and in the ninth year of his reign, King Nebuchadnezzar besieged Jerusalem for two years (2 Kings 25:1 and 2). Afterward, Jerusalem and the temple were destroyed, and King Zedekiah, captured alive, was "bound…with fetters of brass" and carried to Babylon (2 Kings 25:5 to 7). As a result, the Tribe of Judah was officially destroyed in the year 587 BC, and the nation of Israel disappeared from the face of the earth.

Table 7b

The 360 Years of the Judges	Israel in Servitude	
Israel in slavery to Cushanrishathaim	8 yrs	Judges 3:8
The land rested 40 years		Judges 3:11
Israel in slavery to Eglon	18 yrs	Judges 3:14
The land rested 80 years		Judges 3:30
Israel in slavery to Jabin	20 yrs	Judges 4:3
The land rested 40 years		Judges 5:31
Israel in slavery to Median	7 yrs	Judges 6:1
Gideon judges 40 years		Judges 8:28
Abimelech rules 3 years		Judges 9:22
Tola judges 23 years		Judges 10:2
Jair judges 22 years		Judges 10:3
Israel in slavery to Philistines	18 yrs	Judges 10:8
Jephthah judges 6 years		Judges 12:7
Ibzan judges 7 years		Judges 12:9
Elon judges 10 years		Judges 12:11
Abdon judges 8 years		Judges 12:14
Israel in slavery to Philistines	40 yrs	Judges 13:1
Samson judges 20 years		Judges 15:20
Eli judges 40 years		1 Samuel 4:18
Ark captured 1 year	Philistines kept Ark for 7 months, rounded to 1 yr	1 Samuel 6:1
Samuel judges 20 years		1 Samuel 7:2
Total	360 years	111 yrs

Table 7c

Event	Years
Entrance into Promised Land	1407BC
First 40 years: Joshua's conquest of Canaan and Othniel's deliverance	1407 BC–1367BC
Next 80 years: Ehud's deliverance and Shamgar's deliverance	1367 BC–1287BC
Next 40 years: Deberah and Barak's deliverance	1287 BC–1247BC
Gideon's judgeship	1247 BC–1207BC
Abimelech's reign	1207 BC–1204BC
Tola's judgeship	1204 BC–1181 BC
Jair's judgeship	1181 BC–1159 BC
Jephthah's judgeship	1159 BC–1153 BC
Ibzan judgeship	1153 BC–1146 BC
Elon's judgeship	1146 BC–1136 BC
Abdon's judgeship	1136 BC–1128 BC
Samson's judgeship	1128 BC–1108 BC
Eli's judgeship	1108 BC–1068BC
Ark captured by Philistines	1068 BC–1067BC
Samuel's judgeship	1067 BC–1047BC
Saul's reign	1047 BC–1007 BC
David's reign	1007 BC–967 BC
Solomon's reign	971 BC–931 BC
Construction of temple begins	967 BC

A REQUIEM FOR EVOLUTION

Table 7d

Timetable of some of the major events in the Bible

Event	Year
1. Creation of Adam	11013 BC
2. Birth of Seth	10883 BC (Genesis 5:3)
3. Birth of Enosh	10778 BC (Genesis 5:6)
4. Birth of Cainan	9873 BC (Genesis 5:11)
5. Birth of Mahaleel	8963 BC (Genesis 5:14)
6. Birth of Jared	8068 BC (Genesis 5:17)
7. Birth of Enoch	7106 BC (Genesis 5:20)
8. Birth of Methuselah	6741 BC (Genesis 5:23)
9. Birth of Lamech	5772 BC (Genesis 5:27)
10. Birth of Noah	5590 BC (Genesis 5:28–29)
11. The Flood	4990 BC (Genesis 7:6)
12. Birth of Arphaxad	4488 BC (Genesis 11:10–11)
13. Birth of Salah	4050 BC (Genesis 11:12–13)
14. Birth of Eber	3617 BC (Genesis 11:14–15)
15. Birth of Peleg	3153 BC (Genesis 11:16–17)
16. The Tower of Babel	3153–2914BC (Genesis 10:25)
17. Birth of Reu	2914 BC (Genesis 11:18–29)
18. Birth of Serug	2675 BC (Genesis 11:20–21)
19. Birth of Nahor	2445 BC (Genesis 11:22–23)
20. Birth of Terah	2297 BC (Genesis 11:24–25)
21. Birth of Abraham (Terah was 130)	2167 BC
22. Birth of Isaac	2067 BC (Genesis 21:5)
23. Birth of Jacob	2007 BC (Genesis 25:26)
24. Jacob and Family moved to Egypt (Jacob 1:30)	1877 BC (Genesis 47:9)
25. Exodus from Egypt	1447 BC (Exodus 12:40)
26. Entrance into Promised Land	1407 BC (Exodus 16:35)
27. Construction of Solomon's temple	967 BC (1 Kings 6:1)

Table 7e

History of the Kings of Judah and Israel

Judah		Israel	
Rehoboam	931 BC–914 BC	Jeroboam	931 BC–910 BC
Abijam	914 BC–911 BC	Nadab	910 BC–909 BC
Asa	911 BC–870 BC		
Jehoshapat	871 BC–846 BC*	Baasha	909 BC–886 BC
Jehoram (Joram)	854 BC–842 BC*	Elah	886 BC–885 BC
Ahaziah (Jehoahaz)	842 BC–841 BC	Zimri	885 BC (7 days)
Athaliah (Azariah)	841 BC–835 BC	Tibni	885 BC
Joash (Jehoash)	835 BC–795 BC	Omni	885 BC–874 BC*
Amaziah	796 BC–767 BC*	Ahab	874 BC–853 BC
Uzziah (Azariah)	789 BC–737 BC*	Ahaziah	854 BC–853 BC
Jotham	738 BC–718 BC*	Joram (Jehoram)	853 BC–841 BC
Ahaz	730 BC–714 BC*	Jehu	841 BC–813 BC
Hezekiah	715 BC–686 BC	Jehoahaz	813 BC–796 BC
Manasseh	697 BC–642 BC	Jehoahaz (Joash)	798 BC–782 BC
Amon	642 BC–640 BC	Jeroboam II	792 BC–751 BC
Josiah	640 BC–609 BC	Zechariah	751 BC–750 BC
Jehoahaz	609 BC	Shallum	750 BC
Jehoiakim (Eliakim)	609 BC–598 BC	Menahem	750 BC–740 BC
Jehoiachin (Coniah)	608 BC–597 BC*	Pekahiah	740 BC–738 BC
		Pekah	738 BC–718 BC
Zedekiah (Mattaniah)	597 BC–587 BC	Hoshea	718 BC–709 BC

---

* coregency

Chapter 8

An Attempt at Correcting Various Misunderstood Biblical Concepts

The secret things belong to the Lord our God, but those things which are revealed belong to us and to our children forever, that we may do all the words of this law. (Deuteronomy 29:29)

Hexakosioihexekontahexaphobia: The Fear of the Number 666

Why are so many people afraid of the number 666? Why did President Ronald Wilson Reagan (Anyone can quite obviously perceive that the words *Ronald*, *Wilson*, *Reagan* contain each 6 letters, thus forming a perfect 666!) and his wife, Nancy, upon leaving the presidency and the White House, opted to change the number of their Bel-Air, Los Angeles, California house from 666 to 668?

In an article vis-à-vis the phobia that the number 666 generates, Lisa Fritscher depicts the following interesting story:

> One of the most famous examples of how pervasive the fear of the number 666 can be, is [sic] the renaming of a famous highway in the American Southwest. U.S. Highway 666 was so named by the American Association of State Highway officials in 1926. Its name was selected according to officials naming guidelines, as it were the sixth spur off U.S. Highway 66 (the infamous 66).
>
> Over time, the New Mexico section of Highway 666 proved to be statistically dangerous. Skeptics believe that this was due to the road being improperly designated or maintained for increasing traffic loads. However, many believed that it was actually the road's name that caused accidents and fatalities. This was magnified in public awareness. Soon Highway 666 became known as the Devil's Highway.
>
> In 1985, Route 66 was decertified due to the emerging interstate system, although many areas chose to pick up the historic route as a reclassified state road. Nonetheless, this opened the door for a possible name change to the now orphaned Highway 666.
>
> Over time, sections of the Devil's Highway were absorbed by other state systems or removed altogether for interstate expansion. The original road was largely ignored, leading the New Mexico section of the highway to be known as one of the nation's 20 most dangerous highways.
>
> In 2003, the Devil's Highway was officially renamed U.S. Highway 491. The renaming coincided with a series of road construction projects designed to improve the highway's safety. Although many believe that the highway's now vastly improved safety record is due to the construction and not the name change, it is worth noting that the official dedication featured a Navajo medicine man who supposedly removed the highway's curse.

The genesis of the fear of the number 666 stems from Revelation 13:18, which states the following:

> Here is wisdom. Let him who has understanding calculate the number of the beast, for it is the number of a man. His number is 666.

Young's Literal Translation of this verse from the original Greek is along the following line:

> Here is the wisdom! He who is having the understanding, let him count the number of the beast, for the number of a man it is, and its number [is] 666.

Actually, it is interesting that the Word of God does not include any article in front of the word *man* in the original Greek: "for the number of man it is" would entail a more faithful and truthful translation. Let us restate the point: God does not indicate in the original Greek that the number 666 is the number of "a" man, but the number of "man!" This is a perfect case where the Devil is in the details.

Many scholars and Bible students make the erroneous assumption that God in this verse is referring to a specific man—the Antichrist. He is *not*! He would have, in His perfect divine wisdom, preceded the word *man* by the all-significant article *a* if He were so inclined. We will demonstrate shortly the important value of the omission of the article.

The revelation that God posits that 666 is "the number of man" and not "the number of a man" repudiates vividly the most common understanding of the subject matter.

Since comparing spiritual things with spiritual entails one of the great tenets of biblical hermeneutics, let us examine a few places in the Word of God where the number 666 is prominently displayed.

First of all, let us consider 2 Kings 1:2–15 where the prophet Elijah calls fire from heaven upon King Ahaziah's messengers:

> Now Ahaziah fell through the lattice of his upper room in Samaria, and was injured; so he sent messengers and said to them, "Go, inquire of Ball-Zebub, the god of Ekron, whether I shall recover from this injury." But the angel of the Lord said to Elijah the Tishbite, "Arise, go up to meet messengers of the king of Samaria, and say to them, 'Is it because there is no God in Israel that you are going to inquire of Baal-Zebub, the god of Ekron?' Now therefore, thus says the Lord: 'You shall not come down from the bed to which you have gone up, but shall surely die.'" So Elijah departed.
>
> And when the messengers returned to him, he said to them, "Why have you come back?" So they said to him, "A man came up to meet us, and said to us, 'Go, return to the king who sent you, and said to him, "Thus says the Lord: 'Is it because there is no God in Israel that you are sending to inquire of Baal-Zebub, the god of Ekron? Therefore you shall not come down from the bed to which you have gone up, but you shall surely die.'"
>
> Then he said to them, "What kind of man was it who came up to meet with you and told you these words?" So they answered him, "A hairy man wearing a leather belt around his waist." And he said, "It is Elijah the Tishbite."
>
> Then the king sent to him a captain of fifty with his fifty men. So he went up to him; and there he was, sitting on the top of a hill. And he spoke to him: "Man of God, the king has said, 'Come down!'" So Elijah answered and said to the captain of fifty, "If I am a man of God, then let fire come down from heaven and consume you and your fifty men." And fire came down from heaven and consumed him and his fifty. Then he sent to him another captain of fifty with his fifty men. And he answered and said to him: "Man of God, thus has the king

said, 'Come down quickly!'" So Elijah answered and said to them, "If I am a man of God, let fire come down from heaven and consume you and your fifty men." And the fire of God came down from heaven and consumed him and his fifty.

Again, he sent a third captain of fifty with his fifty men. And the third captain of fifty went up, and fell on his knees before Elijah, and pleaded with him, and said to him: "Man of God, please let my life and the life of these fifty servants of yours be precious in your sight. Look, fire has come down from heaven and burned up the first two captains of fifties with their fifties. But let my life be precious in your sights."

And the Angel of the Lord said to Elijah, "Go down with him; do not be afraid of him." So he arose and went down with him to the king.

Where in the world, you might ask, is the mysterious number 666 in this passage? Well, let us recall that the first two captains of fifty with their fifty were consumed and destroyed whereas the third captain of fifty with his fifty was spared. In three separate (3/3 to be arithmetically correct!) scenarios, 2/3 of the participants (the first two groups) were destroyed, while the last 1/3 (the last captain of fifty with his own fifty) was spared.

Simple and basic arithmetic reveals that 2/3 is equal to 0.666, while 1/3 is equivalent to 0.333. Let us remember from Revelation 13:18 that 666 was the number of man. As such, is God using the passages of 2 Kings and Revelation 13 to indicate that 2/3 of mankind belongs to Satan (The beast of Revelation 13: see a commentary on the Antichrist in this chapter) as they are destined to be burned up, totally consumed, and destroyed by the fire of God, while the remaining 1/3 identifies with God's people as they will be spared and ushered into heaven, God's paradise promised to them before the foundation of the world?

The Bible offers, with the great king David, yet another interesting episode illustrating the number 666. Let's recapitulate one of King David's great battle against the Moabites as outlined in 2 Samuel 8:1–2:

> After this it came to pass that David attacked the philistines and subdued them. And David took Metheg Ammah from the hands of the Philistines. Then he defeated Moab. Forcing them to the ground, he measured them off with a line. With two lines he measured off those to be put to death, and with one full line those to be kept alive. So the Moabites became David's servants, and brought tribute.

We have yet another story from the Word of God with a familiar pattern: again 2/3 of the participants (well, 0.666 if you are fearful of fractions!) were put to death, and the remaining 1/3 (or 0.333) was kept alive and became David's servants.

Is it just a coincidence that the Holy Scriptures link two seemingly isolated stories with two-thirds of the participants of both stories receiving damnation (isn't 666 the number of man?) while the remaining one-third of both accounts obtains underserved mercy (let's recall here the basic definition of salvation)?

It is quite interesting that God, through the auspices of the prophet Zechariah (chapter 13, verse 8), makes the following shocking declaration:

> "And it shall come to pass in all the land," says the Lord, "that two-thirds in it shall be cut off and die, but one-third shall be left in it."

Moreover, God boldly proclaims in verse 9 the following:

> I will bring the one-third through the fire, will refine them as silver is refined, and test them as gold is tested. They will call on My name, and I will answer them. I will say, "This is My people"; and each one will say, "The Lord is my God."

Indeed, to compute the number of the beast warrants a lot of wisdom (Revelation 13); it is, after all, the number of man—unsaved mankind, to be more specific—associated with the great dragon, the Devil depicted in Revelation 13 as a menacing beast coming out of the sea with venom and fury in order to steal, kill, and destroy.

The corollary of our identification of the number 666 with the people of Satan surprisingly leaves us with the number 333 as a clear reference to the people of the Living God. If 666 is the number of man, 333 must then be the number of regenerate man, a "refined" mankind recreated after the pattern of the Second Adam (1 Corinthians 15:45), Jesus Christ Himself, the Son of the Living God.

The Seventy Weeks or Seventy Sevens of Daniel 9

Welcome, ladies and gentlemen, to the greatest literary passage of all time! The most erudite paragraphs of William Faulkner, the greatest lines of tragedy of William Shakespeare, the most articulate lectures of Gertrude Stein, the most famous novels of Frantz Kafka, the most emotionally poignant rhymes of John Milton, the most recognizable prose of Samuel Beckett, the most modern short stories of Anton Chekhov, the most memorable fictions of Marcel Proust, the most suspense-filled novels of Fyodor Dostoyevsky, the funniest tales of Geoffrey Chaucer, the most influential books of Charles Dickens, the most sentimental comments of Miguel Cervantes, the most important essays of George Orwell, the most moving poems of Charles Baudelaire, the most instructive fables of Jean de Lafontaine, the most epic plays of Jean Racine, the most satirical jokes of Jean-Baptiste Poquelin (Moliere), the most influential writings of Leo Tolstoy, and the most memorized verses of Tu Fu put together cannot match the literary, historical, and prophetic import of the last four verses of Daniel 9.

If anyone harbors a shard of skepticism vis-à-vis the veracity of the Bible, he/she should spend some time researching the last four verses of Daniel 9. No human intellect can produce so elaborate a scheme that dares to accurately describe the pinpoint timing of the epic events signaling the end of the world. Only someone with a priori access to the classified chronological information detailing the exact and precise unfolding of all the events in the history of the world could prophetically articulate the major historical circumstances ushering in the judgment of Christ for the sins of His people and the judgment of Antichrist for his sins and the sins of his people.

Let's set the stage for the events leading to Daniel's vision. The Lord God, in His divine sovereignty and wisdom, selected Abraham of Ur of the Chaldees (ancient Babylon and now "modern" Iraq) and ordered him to leave his country, his kindred, and his father's house to inhabit a land that He would show him (Genesis 12).

The Lord God promised to bless Abraham, to make his name great, to transform his descendants into a great and mighty nation, and *to bless all the people of the world through him!* Abraham, obedient to the divine revelation, left with his family and settled in the land of Canaan where the Lord God made a twofold covenant with him: a material, earthly, and temporary covenant, the type and harbinger of a spiritual, heavenly covenant that will last forever and will endure throughout eternity. Let's remark what the Lord relates to Abraham in Genesis 15:18:

> On the same day the Lord made a covenant with Abram, saying:
> "To your descendants I have given this land,
> From the river of Egypt to the great river, the river Euphrates."

The first part of the Abrahamic Covenant entails a specific, limited, earthly, and temporary promise relating that the nation of Israel, the type of the eternal Israel of God, will be confined to the land between two of the greatest rivers of the world: the Euphrates and the Nile.

However, notice what the Lord remarked to Abraham in Genesis 13:14–15:

> And the Lord said to Abram, after Lot had separated from him: "Lift your eyes now and look from the place where you are, northward, southward, eastward and westward; for the land which you see I give to you and your descendants *forever.*"

Furthermore, remark what the Lord related to Abraham in Genesis 17:7–8:

> And I will establish My covenant between Me and you and your descendants after you throughout their generations, for an *Everlasting* covenant, to be God to you and your descendants after you.
>
> Also I give to you and your descendants after you the land in which you are a stranger, all the land of Canaan, as an *Everlasting* possession; and I will be their God.

Please, take notice of the time frame involved here: *eternity!* The Bible indicates clearly that "the world is passing away" (1 John 2:17) and that "the heavens and the earth…are reserved for fire until the day of judgment and perdition of ungodly men" (2 Peter 3:7). As such, God could not make an eternal promise for that which is obviously "passing away."

Moreover, the Lord, through the writings of Apostle Paul, states in Romans 4:9–13 the following revealing declaration:

> Does this blessedness then come upon the circumcised only, or upon the uncircumcised also?
> For we say that faith was accounted to Abraham for righteousness.
> How then was it accounted? While he was circumcised, or uncircumcised? Not while circumcised, but while uncircumcised.
> And he received the sign of circumcision, a seal of the righteousness of the faith which he had while still uncircumcised, that he might be the father of all those who believe, though they are uncircumcised, that righteousness might be imputed to them also, and the father of circumcision to those who not are of the circumcision, but also who walk in the steps of the faith which our father Abraham had while still uncircumcised.
> For the promise that he would be heir of the world was not to Abraham or to his seed through the law, but through the righteousness of faith.

Please, notice that the Lord discloses that His full promise to Abraham was that he would become "the father of all those who believe, though they are uncircumcised" (verse 11), and not simply the "father of circumcision" to the "circumcised." Notice further that God articulates in verse 13 that Abraham would be "heir of the world," and not just heir of the restricted territories between the rivers Euphrates and Nile.

As a result, we can ascertain that the second part of God's Abrahamic Covenant promised that he would be the eternal father of all the believers in the new world (new heavens and new earth), which God will create after the destruction of this present evil and cursed world (Isaiah 65:17, Revelation 21:1).

Three generations later, Joseph, Abraham's great-grandson through Isaac and Jacob, after becoming the second in command to Pharaoh, the Egyptian king, invited his father, Jacob, and the other sixty-nine members of his family to migrate to Egypt, thereby avoiding the great seven-year famine that was spreading across the known world.

Over four hundred years later, Israel, now a mighty nation of nearly two million individuals, found herself enslaved and severely afflicted by the Egyptian king. The Lord God appointed Moses to rescue His people and bring them back to the Land of the Promise, the territories whose boundaries entail the Euphrates and Nile rivers.

Moses led Israel for forty years throughout the wilderness, and the Lord God, the Creator, Sustainer, Owner, and Judge of the entire universe, appointed Joshua as Moses's successor and as the leader that would conquer the land of Canaan from the ten nations (Kenites, Kenizzites, Kadmonites, Hittites, Perizites, Rephaims, Amorites, Canaanites, Girgashites, and Jebusites [Genesis 15:20–21]) as His judgment on their wickedness.

Established by God as the nation to occupy the land between the Nile and Euphrates rivers, Israel flourished and became a mighty and powerful nation. The new generation of Israelites that arose in the land nearly three hundred years later committed the same sins, the same atrocities that the ten nations whom they replaced had perpetrated.

As His judgment for the adulterous and idolatrous behavior of the nation, the Lord God, at first blush, divided Israel into two separate countries (Israel, the Northern Kingdom; and Judah, the Southern Kingdom). Then, He allowed the Northern Kingdom to fall under the rule of the Assyrian nation and carried into captivity.

Nearly one hundred years later, God brought judgment against the people of Judah as they were captured by the Babylonians and led captives into the land of the Chaldees. God prophesied Judah's demise through the prophet Jeremiah by issuing the following decree:

> And this whole land shall be a desolation, and an astonishment; and these nations shall serve the king of Babylon seventy years. And it shall come to pass, when seventy years are accomplished, that I will punish the king of Babylon, and that nation, saith the Lord, for their iniquity, and the land of the Chaldeans, and will make it perpetual desolations.

History reports that in 609 BC, Judah was conquered by the Babylonian Empire, thus ushering the start of the seventy-year captivity prophesied by God through the auspices of the prophet Jeremiah.

Daniel, one of the young Jewish captives taken into Babylon, became a top counselor and advisor to the Babylonian kings that reigned during the seventy-year captivity. As the end of the seventy years approached, Daniel started praying fervently for the Lord to fulfill His promise to end the Jewish demise. And the Lord boldly answered his request by revealing the following amazing prophecy:

> Seventy weeks [literally seventy sevens] are determined upon thy people and upon thy holy city, to finish the transgression, and to make an end of sins, and to make reconciliation for iniquity, and to bring in everlasting righteousness, to seal up the vision and prophecy, and to anoint the Most Holy.
>
> Know therefore and understand, that from the going forth of the command to restore and build Jerusalem unto the Messiah the Prince, shall be seven weeks [literally seven sevens], and threescore and two weeks [literally sixty-two sevens: one score equals twenty units]: The street shall be built again, and the wall, even in troublous times.
>
> And after threescore and two weeks [again literally sixty-two sevens] shall Messiah be cut off, but not for himself: and the people of the prince that shall come shall destroy the city and the sanctuary; and the end thereof shall be with a flood, and unto the end of the war desolations are determined.
>
> And he shall confirm the covenant with many for one week [literally one seven]: and in the midts of the week [literally of the seven] he shall cause the sacrifice and oblation to cease, and for the overspreading of abominations he

shall make it desolate, even until the consummation, and the determined shall
be poured upon the desolate.

There it is, ladies and gentlemen, the most significant, the most consequential, the greatest prophetic, the most comprehensive, the most far-reaching, the most beautiful piece of literature of all time. It is divine in its perspective, precise in its prophetic outlook, accurate in its historical relevance, and mysterious in its theological significance.

Seventy Sevens (many—if not most—biblical scholars too quickly opt for "week" and not "seven" as the exclusive translation of the Hebrew word *ve-sheva*; we will stick to the literal meaning of *seven*. The word *ve-sheva* equally translates as "seven" or as "week") are determined: what are the units and constraints of time involved here? Yes! It's true that part of the Seventy Sevens, when considered in terms of our common and normal 365.2422 units of days in a year, leads to the exact moment when Jesus Christ began His public ministry and the precise day of His death on the cross (We shall prove this shortly); however, the totality of "real-time value" that the Seventy Sevens entails has not been understood and explained by anyone.

What is the biblical precedence for a "time gap" that theologians and biblical scholars have advocated to explicate the full time schedule required by the Seventy Sevens? On what basis can they legitimately make the case that God has "stopped the prophetic clock" of the Seventy Sevens vis-à-vis the last seven of the Seventy Sevens? Time, ontologically, presupposes an ongoing activity.

Furthermore, even if God had stopped the prophetic clock of the Seventy Sevens at T = Sixty-Nine Sevens, whenever God would reactivate the last seven, someone could readjust the last seven a posteriori to make it fit—evenly or otherwise—in our normal time paradigm; and as such, the prophetic time clock would still not have "stopped," as our biblical scholars would have us believe!

Seventy Sevens are determined! Determined by whom? Who has the historical foresight and the chronological insight to make so daring a proposition? Who can control time to the point of allocating portions of it to precise future events? Are historical events coincidences, happenstances, or has time been precisely calibrated to accompany all the daily events occurring in our world?

The Bible asserts that the God who created the universe has predetermined and choreographed all the events happening throughout the entire universe: God, after all, knows the end from the beginning of all things.

Seventy Sevens are determined upon thy people and thy holy city. Who are those people, and what is that holy city? Most theologians and Bible scholars posit that the Jewish people and Jerusalem are involved here exclusively. Let's remember the twin promise of God to Abraham: the temporary and earthly promise materialized in the nation of Israel and the Jewish people as the types of the permanent and heavenly realities of the New Jerusalem and all God's children whose names were written in the Lamb's Book of Life from the foundation of the world.

In other words, when God alluded to Daniel concerning his "people" and his "holy city," He could have in view both realities, and not exclusively national Israel and the people of that nation. Why do so many theologians pontificate that the city and people in view *must uniquely* be the Jewish people and the present Jerusalem? Isn't Daniel also an inhabitant of the New Jerusalem of God? Are not Daniel's people also all the people of God saved by the blood of the Lamb of God slain from the foundation of the world?

Let's remember here that when Jesus proclaimed to the Jews of His days (John 2:19) that if they could "destroy this temple," He can "in three days…raise it up." The Jewish people and scholars mistakenly assumed that Jesus was opining on the elaborate Herod's temple that required forty-six years to build. Jesus was in fact referring to "the temple of His body" (John 2:21). Are the present biblical exegetes guilty of the same crime when they insist that Israel and the Jewish people *must* be the only entities at play in the Seventy Sevens of Daniel 9?

> Seventy Sevens are determined upon thy people and thy holy city, to finish the transgression, and to make an end of sin, and to make reconciliation for iniquity, and to bring in everlasting righteousness, and to seal up the vision and prophecy, and to anoint the Most Holy.

The six purposes of the revelation of the Seventy Sevens affirm beyond a shadow of doubt that not just the nation of Israel is in focus here. The complete annihilation of "the transgression and of sin," foreshadowed in the protevangelium (Genesis 3:15), could only refer to the sacrifice of Jesus on the cross at Calvary as "the Lamb of God who takes away the sin of the world" (John 1:29), and not the sin of national Israel.

The excessive cost of the "reconciliation for iniquity," the tremendous ransom payment warranted for the "sealing of the vision and prophecy, and the anointing of the most Holy," and the sacrificial offering susceptible of ushering in "everlasting righteousness" presuppose the salvation of the entire world, not just the redemption of the people and the territories between the Nile and Euphrates rivers; after all, the destruction of the present earth by fire (2 Peter 3:7) and "everlasting righteousness" entail sequential and not simultaneous occurrences.

Know therefore and understand! Those twin commands require every Bible student to pay particular attention to the ensuing proffers: the doubling of the command establishes its divine import and guarantees the imminent occurrence of all its propositions (Genesis 41:32).

> Know therefore and understand, that from the going forth of the commandment to restore and to build Jerusalem unto the Messiah the Prince shall be seven sevens, and threescore and two sevens: the street shall be built again, and the wall, even in troublous times.

We now are graciously given a specific time constraint: "the going forth of the command to restore and to build Jerusalem," as the initial time in consideration, and "unto the Messiah," as the final time. In other words, the SOVEREIGN and SUPREME GOD, the Master Choreographer of the atomic details of all the events in the history of the world, announces, somewhere between 605 BC and 530 BC through the prophet Daniel, to the world that His Messiah the Prince would appear on earth seven sevens and sixty-two sevens (one score equals twenty units), units of time from "the command to restore and to build Jerusalem."

A REQUIEM FOR EVOLUTION

At first blush, anyone with a slight modicum of mathematical prowess can realize that seven sevens and sixty-two sevens form the arithmetical equivalent of sixty-nine sevens. The sixty-nine-million-dollar question (pardon the pun): Why did the Lord God indicate to Daniel a time span of seven sevens and sixty-two sevens and not simply sixty-nine sevens? Why did the Maker of the universe differentiate the first seven sevens from the sixty-two sevens? Why didn't the King of kings simply assert that the time at play from the command to build Jerusalem to the introduction of Jesus embodies a time span of sixty-nine sevens? God, let's recall, does not parse His words (Psalm 12:6).

Since the God who spoke the universe into existence took the time to highlight the first seven sevens of the sixty-nine sevens, a genuine Bible student would automatically wonder where else in the Holy Scriptures are seven sevens highlighted? We read in Leviticus 25:8–10 the following interesting divine fiat concerning the Jubilee:

> And thou shall number seven Sabbaths of years unto thee, seven times seven years, and the space of the seven Sabbaths of years shall be unto thee forty nine years. Then shall thou cause the trumpet of the jubilee to sound on the tenth day of the seventh month, in the day of atonement shall ye make the trumpet sound throughout all your land. And ye shall hallow the fiftieth year, and proclaim liberty throughout all the land unto all the inhabitants thereof: it shall be a jubilee unto you; and ye shall return every man unto his possession, and ye shall return every man unto his family.

At least two quick inferences can be made here: First, God links the Jubilee with seven sevens. Second, God plainly asserts that the time unit in question with regard to the seven sevens is equal to forty-nine years (verse 8). Could the Lord God have endeavored to highlight the first seven sevens in Daniel 9:25 to make sure all biblical students of this magnificent prophecy "know and understand" that the first unit of time to consider when studying the Seventy Sevens of Daniel entails first of all a Jubilee year? Second of all, is not the Lord and Ruler of the universe relating that an actual period of forty-nine years of 365.2422 days (verse 8) should also be considered?

Let's review what the Holy Scriptures teach concerning the timings of the Jubilees. God related to Moses in Leviticus 25:1–7 the following directives:

> And the Lord spake unto Moses in Mount Sinai, saying, speak unto the children of Israel, and say to them, When ye come into the land which I give you, then shall the land keep a Sabbath unto the Lord. Six years thou shall sow thy field, and six years thou shall prune thy vineyard, and gather in the fruit thereof; but in the seventh year shall be a Sabbath of rest unto the land, a Sabbath for the Lord: thou shall neither sow thy field, nor prune thy vineyard. That which growth of its own accord of thy harvest thou shall not reap, neither gather the grapes of thy vine undressed: for it is a year of rest unto the land. And the Sabbath of the land shall be meat for you; for thee, and for thy servant, and for thy servant, and for thy maid, and for thy hired servant, and for thy stranger that sojourneth

> with thee. And for thy cattle, and for the beast that are in the land, shall all the increase thereof be meat. And thou shall number seven Sabbaths of years unto thee, seven times seven years; and the space of the seven Sabbaths of years shall be unto thee forty and nine years. Then thou shall cause the trumpet of the Jubilee to sound on the tenth day of the seventh month, in the day of atonement shall ye make the trumpet sound throughout all your land. And ye shall hallow the fiftieth year, and proclaim liberty throughout all the land unto all the inhabitants thereof: it shall be unto you; and ye shall return every man unto his possession, and ye shall return every man unto his family.

In other words, the children of Israel, upon their entrance into the Promised Land, were ordered by God through Moses to count seven sevens years or forty-nine years from their arrival in the land in 1407 BC in order to arrive at the Sabbath of the Jubilee, the year prior the fiftieth year, the actual Jubilee year. Thereafter, they would continue to celebrate the Feast of Jubilee every fifty years, proclaiming liberty throughout the entire land after hallowing the Sabbath of the Jubilee the year before.

Let's see, fifty years deducted from 1407 BC yields 1357 BC; and another fifty years removed from 1357 BC would give 1307 BC, thereby assuring that every year ending in 57 BC or 07 BC, and AD 44 or AD 94 as Jubilee years (Please, refer to Appendix 2 for tables of Jubilee years as we pick here 457 BC as the first Jubilee for the sake of our present study since 458 BC was the year that set in motion the beginning of the Seventy Sevens of Daniel 9, the year that the command to rebuild Jerusalem was given. Please also consider Appendix 1 for the background information ascetaining our correct understanding even though, as a matter of fact, the year 1357 BC constitutes the actual Jubilee 1).

Let's now consider what the Holy Scriptures declare concerning the timing of the start of the Seventy Sevens. The Word of God reveals (Daniel 9:25) that "from the going forth of the commandment to restore and to build Jerusalem unto the Messiah the Prince" shall be seven sevens and sixty-two sevens. In other words, the starting point of the Seventy Sevens must consider the "commandment to restore and to build Jerusalem." Most Bible commentaries mistakenly offer 445 BC as the only possible alternative, while the Word of God leaves us with three distinct choices: 445 BC, 537 BC, and 458 BC. Let's consider the Bible commentators' favorite starting point, 445 BC, and pinpoint the numerous valid arguments against it.

First of all, 445 BC does not relate in any particular way to the Jubilee years (See appendix 2) and does no justice to the differentiation that the Word of God succinctly makes in highlighting the first seven sevens from the sixty-two sevens.

Second of all, most Bible scholars do not seem to understand the import of one of the most important hints that God has given us to "know" and "understand" the full meaning of the Seventy Sevens: the marked delineation of the first seven sevens from the other sixty-two sevens. God is very meticulous, pithy, and deliberate in His choice of the precise wording and coding of data for effective and efficient information transfer (1 Timothy 3:16).

Third, the Word of God specifies that the beginning of the Seventy Sevens must begin with a "commandment" of the restoration and building of Jerusalem. Nehemiah chapter 2, the section of the Holy Writ dealing with the send-off of Nehemiah, the king's cupbearer, by King Axtaxerxes in 445 BC, does not mention any type of "commandment" by the king to his beloved servant for his journey. There was simply a request by Nehemiah (Daniel 2:5) and the king's immediate acceptance of the proposition of his beloved servant (verse 6).

Fourth, the biblical scholars advocating 445 BC as the starting point of the Seventy Sevens would have us multiply 360 days (the number of Jewish Calendar days in a year) by 483 sevens (the sixty-nine sevens [Daniel 9:25] multiplied by seven is equal to 483 sevens) to arrive at 173,880 days (Jewish Calendar days of 360 days per year), and then divide the 173,880 Jewish Calendar days by 365.242 Gregorian or Solar Calendar days per year. The result rounded to the nearest ten-thousandths would equal 476.0679! Multiplying the decimal 0.0679 by 365 Gregorian days would yield 24.7835 days. Subtracting 445 BC from the even 476 and accounting for the extra twenty-four days would yield the year AD 31 or 32 as the coming year of the Messiah!

That is arithmetical gymnastic of the first order: biblical scholars performing eisegetical flops in the name of exegetical flips. What is the biblical precedence that would allow anyone the right to multiply by Jewish Calendar days and then divide by Gregorian days? Moreover, there are actually 365.2422 solar days in a given year and not 365.242 to be arithmetically accurate to the ten-thousandths. Furthermore, multiplying the decimal 0.0679 by 365.2422 would yield 24.7994 days, which can only be rounded to 25 as a whole number and not 24.

Fifth, the obvious fallacy of the mathematical computations of the Bible scholars leaves them with the seeming logical option of advocating their famous "Prophetic Time Gap" as an explanation of the Seventy Sevens. Time, as we have previously submitted, entails an ongoing activity. As such, those Bible scholars are left stranded in the unenviable position of proposing the scientifically implausible stoppage of time as a cover for their weird prophetic interpretation—an uncomfortable situation when observed through the scientific lenses of Einstein's theory of relativity where the presence of time is essential.

Let's now pay heed to the second possible starting time: 537 BC. King Cyrus of Persia, in the first year of his reign, commanded Nehemiah and nearly fifty thousand Jews to return to the Promised Land to rebuild Jerusalem, the city of God, and the temple of the Lord. One of the most important criteria warranted by Daniel 9, a "command" was issued by King Cyrus; nonetheless, the year 537 BC bears no relationship to the first seven sevens of Daniel 9, does not fit with the Jubilee patterns (See appendix 2), and does not lead to the Messiah the Prince on a seventy sevens time increment.

458 BC entails the starting time that meets all the pertinent requirements of the prophecy of the Seventy Sevens. Ezra (chapter 7, verse 23) reports the following words of King Artaxerxes:

> Whatsoever is commanded by the God of heaven, let it be diligently done for the house of the God of heaven: for why should there be wrath against the realm of the king and his sons?

First, an all-important "command" had been issued by the God of Heaven vis-à-vis the rebuilding of "the house of God," and the king is readdressing the order of the King of all kings by making God's command His own.

Second, 458 BC relates to the Jubilee years pretty remarkably: it falls one year before the 457 BC Jubilee (See appendixes 1 and 2), and would allow the migrating Jews plenty of time to arrive in Jerusalem, celebrate the Sabbath Jubilee in 458 BC, and make all the preparations for the observance of the upcoming Jubilee the following year.

Third, 458 BC explicates clearly the reason God had to differentiate the first seven sevens from the rest of the sixty-two sevens (Daniel 9:25): God was providing a significant clue to anyone willing to "know" and "understand" the full meaning of the Seventy Sevens prophecy to consider and isolate a Jubilee interval of fifty years as the first important time marker in the second avenue leading to the Second Coming of our Lord and Savior Jesus Christ, considering that the first avenue leads from the starting time of 458 BC directly to the crucifixion of our Lord and Savior at the cross in AD 33.

Fourth, 458 BC does not elicit the cessation of time, an unfathomable concept bereft of biblical precedence and barren of scientific support.

Fifth, 458 BC mysteriously leads to both the First and Second Comings of Jesus Christ, both the judgment of Christ at the Cross and the judgment of the world at the end of time, both the payment of sin by the Lamb of God who takes away the sin of the world and the destruction of the wicked as payment for their sin, quintessential prerequisites for any system daring to shed light on the full spectrum of the Seventy Sevens biblical prophecy.

Let's focus on the first avenue of the Seventy Sevens linking 458 BC to the year of crucifixion of Jesus Christ. Daniel 9:25, let's recall, makes the following significant revelations:

> Seventy Sevens are determined upon thy people and upon thy holy city, to finish the transgression, and to make an end of sins, and to make reconciliation for iniquity, and to bring in everlasting righteousness, and to seal up the vision and prophecy, and to anoint the most holy.

When was reconciliation made for iniquity? When were the sins of the people of God ended? When was the transgression of God's people finished? Of course at the cross on Calvary! Daniel 9:25 removes all doubts that the primary focus of the Seventy Sevens Prophecy entails the people of God whom the Lord Jesus came to save from their sins (Matthew 1:21). When was the ransom paid? Again at the cross on Calvary!

God is hereby proclaiming to anyone who would listen that He had established a specific time table linking His "commandment" for the restoration of Jerusalem, the city of God, and the rebuilding of the House of God to the time that He "purchased" His people "with His own blood" (Acts 20:28).

When was that payment made? How can we know without a shadow of doubt the year that Jesus was crucified? Daniel 9:25 provides the answer: Seventy sevens! In that realm, solar days of 365.2422 days are the units of time at play here. Let's see, 70 years multiplied by 7 yields 490 years; and 458 BC (the starting time in Ezra chapter 7) subtracted from the 490 years of the Seventy Sevens is equal to 32 plus 1 (to account for the year 0) would yield AD 33, as the year that Jesus was crucified at the cross on Calvary! Incredible! The first avenue of the Seventy Sevens emphatically predicts that from God's command to restore Jerusalem and rebuild the temple to the crucifixion of Jesus at the cross, a period of 490 years, leaves the year AD 33 as the exact year that Jesus hung on the cross to pay for the sins of His people.

Is there any other way one can ascertain the accuracy of that date? Can we arrive at the same year by another alternative? Luke 3:1 relates the following:

> Now in the FIFTEENTH year of the reign of Tiberius Caesar, Pontius Pilate being governor of Judea, and Herod being tetrarch of Galilee, and his brother Philip tetrarch of Ituraea and of the region of Trachonitis, and Lysanias the tetrarch of Abilene, Annas and Caiaphas being high priests, the word of God came unto John the son of Zacharias in the wilderness.

The Holy Scriptures hereby relay the exact timing of the start of John the Baptist ministry in those two critically important verses. John, we are reminded, ushered his repentance campaign during the fifteenth year of the reign of Tiberius Caesar. Why would God lay down this historical time marker? Why was the start of John the Baptist's ministry so important an event that it prompted God to lay down this crucial time marker?

Very reliable historical sources (*Encyclopaedia Britannica*: http://www.britannica.com/biography/Tiberius and *Tiberius the Politician* by Barbara Levick: https://en.wikipedia.org/wiki/Tiberius#Levick) report that Tiberius Caesar acquired absolute power in AD 14. As a result, God is indicating that John the Baptist began his public ministry in the year AD 29 (AD 15 + AD 14) as the "forerunner" who would introduce the Messiah Jesus to the nation of Israel and the world.

From AD 29, the starting time of John the Baptist's ministry, how can we determine the timing of the crucifixion of Jesus Christ? Reading the Gospel of John, one can infer that Jesus's public ministry, while affected by five Passovers, actually intersperses four distinct Passovers, the last three are prominently displayed in the Gospel of John.

The AD 29 Passover (See appendix 4), the first of the five at play here, occurred the same year John the Baptist began his public ministry of baptismal repentance. The forerunner had actually arrived on the premises: the Bridegroom would not be far behind.

The second Passover that coincided with Jesus's public ministry is not featured in the Gospel of John. It occurred before the first recorded public miracle of Jesus at Cana of Galilee. Since it is not featured in the Gospel of John, we will not dwell on it.

The third Passover occurred early in Jesus's ministry, a short while after His first public miracle, turning water into wine at Cana of Galilee (John 2:13 and 23). Is God's reference to the Passover here simply a coincidence? Why did God "inspire" (2 Timothy 3:16) the apostle John to reference on two occasions in the second chapter of his Gospel (verses 13 and 23) the Jewish Passover Feast? Is it as a time marker susceptible of shedding light on the timing of Jesus's public ministry?

The fourth Passover (John 6:4) took place at the height of Jesus's public ministry. Crowds were following him as they saw him perform incredible acts, miraculous actions that they had never seen before; and right before the upcoming Passover, Jesus would feed over five thousand, asserting Himself as the real Passover Lamb of God that they should eat for eternal life (John 6:31–39).

The fifth Passover (John 11:55, 12:1, 13:1, 18:28, 18:39, 19:14), the last Passover that occurred during Jesus's ministry, fulfilled all the types of the Passover Feast. As Jewish priests throughout the nation of Israel were killing Passover lambs to atone for the sins of the people, Jesus, the real Lamb of God who would take away the sin of the world (John 1:29), was being crucified as the concretization of all the Old Testament sacrifices for the atonement of sin.

As a result, Jesus's public ministry, one can accurately deduct, began after the AD 29 Passover and before the AD 30 Passover, continued during the AD 31, the AD 32 Passovers, and ended at the AD 33 Passover when Christ hung on the cross at Calvary.

Moreover, in his remarkable *Handbook of Biblical Chronology*, Jack Finegan justifiably argues that Jesus could not have been crucified in AD 32 as is advocated by many biblical scholars. Only AD 30 and AD 33, relates Jack Finegan, could be possible years for the Passover during which Jesus Christ was born according to the meticulous timings of the celebration of the Jewish Passover Feast and the Full Moon.

Therefore, the Seventy Sevens, the ministry of John the Baptist, and the timing of the Jewish celebration of the Passover in relation to the Full Moon constitute three powerful arguments that make the case for AD 33 as the actual year that Jesus Christ was crucified as the Passover Lamb of God who takes away the sin of the world.

Let's now consider the second avenue linking the Seventy Sevens to the end of the world. Again, let's reconsider verses 25, 26, and 27 of Daniel 9:

> Know therefore and understand, that from the going forth of the commandment to restore and to build Jerusalem unto the Messiah the Prince, shall be seven sevens, and threescore and two sevens: the street shall be built again, and the wall even in troublous times. And after threescore and two sevens shall Messiah be cut off, but not for himself: and the people of the Prince that shall come shall destroy the city and the sanctuary; and the end therefore shall be with a flood, and unto the end of the war desolations are determined. And he shall confirm the covenant with many for one seven: and the midst of the seven he shall cause the sacrifice and the oblation to cease, and for the overspreading of abominations he shall make it desolate, even until the consummation, and that determined shall be poured upon the desolate.

Again, the differentiation of the first sevens from the sixty-two sevens (verse 25) warrants the consideration of a Jubilee year as the starting point. In that realm, from the command for the rebuilding of the temple and the city in 458 BC to the end of the sixty-two sevens, one must consider first and foremost a Jubilee interval of fifty years. As a result, from 458 BC, the Jubilee interval mandated by Daniel 9 sets apart the years 457 to 407 BC as the actual years in view.

The sixty-two sevens quite naturally follow the Jubilee interval of fifty years; as a result, a period of 434 years would follow the Jubilee interval, thus leaving no choice but to subtract 406 BC (let's remember that we have to consider 457 to 407 as a distinct and isolated period of time) from 434 years (the following sixty-two sevens), and the result, AD 28 must be increased by 1 to account for the absence of year 0 to arrive at the familiar AD 29 as the year Jesus Christ began His public ministry: indeed from the command in 458 BC to "restore and build Jerusalem and the Messiah the Prince" entails a timetable of 50 years and 434 years!

Verse 26 of Daniel 9 relates that "after threescore and two weeks shall Messiah be cut off, but not for himself," but for the salvation of His people He had come to save (Matthew 1:21). In other words, verse 26 forecasts the death of Jesus in AD 33, after the 434-year interval, after AD 29, as we have proved by four distinct arguments.

Verse 26 continues, "And the people of the prince that shall come shall destroy the city and the sanctuary." Again, many scholars have posited here that the prince is a reference to the Antichrist! Where in Daniel 9 did we see the word *prince*? "That should be pretty easy…the preceding verse," you might quickly and somewhat sarcastically ad-lib, "identifies the Messiah as the Prince that shall come and whose people that will come will destroy the city and the sanctuary!"

Where in the world did so many bright biblical scholars find the justification to pontificate that the prince in reference in Daniel 9 must allude to a certain Antichrist that shall come to destroy the city and the sanctuary? Did not Jesus warn the Jewish people (John 2:19–21) that if they "destroy this temple, and in three days [He] will raise it up?" While Jesus meant His body, the Jewish scholars thought, unfortunately, that He had in view Herod's temple, which took forty-six years to build. The same rules might apply here as well: Why could not the sanctuary (part of the temple structure) and the city (please read Revelation 21 carefully: the Holy City entails an organism embodying both Christ and His people) not represent Christ here that would be killed not for His sins but for those of His people (Genesis 3:15 and Matthew 1:21)?

Daniel 9:27 states:

> And He shall confirm the covenant with many for one seven: and in the midst of the seven he shall cause the sacrifice and the oblation to cease, and for the overspreading of abominations he shall make it desolate, even until the consummation, and that determined shall be poured upon the desolate.

Again erudite biblical pundits affirm that the "he" must relate to the Antichrist who will come to sign a treaty with Israel: that is a classical case of biblical eisegesis in the clearest sense of the word—importing a foreign and inappropriate variable into the immediate context of a biblical passage.

So far in our analysis of the Seventy Sevens, we have arrived at sixty-nine sevens: there remains yet one more seven, the last seven as referenced in verse 27. Christ, by His death on the cross in the middle ("the midst," according to Daniel 9:27) of the last seven (three and a half years after AD 29 brings us to AD 33 when Jesus was sacrificed as the Lamb of God), confirmed by the shedding of His blood (Hebrews 9:16–20, 10:29; 1 Corinthians 11:25), the covenant of salvation for His people.

Christ, by dying on the cross in "the midst" of the last seven, more specifically three and a half years after the start of His public ministry (3 ½ years from AD 29 brings us to AD 33), renders useless the Old Testament sacrificial system of animal sacrifice ("the sacrifice and oblation") for the removal of all the sins of His people (Hebrews 9:11–15).

Therefore, using the Solar or Gregorian time system of 365.2422 days a year, the first seven sevens, the sixty-two sevens and half of the last seven were tagged as leading indicators of specific time intervals ushering the start of the ministry of Jesus as well as the crucifixion of the "Messiah the Prince" as an atonement for the sins of the people He had come to save.

What about the last 3 ½ sevens? What are the significant events highlighted in verse 27 that did not materialize 3 ½ years after the middle ("the midst") of the last seven? Let's review the words of verse 27:

> And He shall confirm the covenant with many for one seven: and in the midst of the seven he shall cause the sacrifice and the oblation to cease, and for the overspreading of abominations he shall make it desolate, even until the consummation, and that determined shall be poured upon the desolate.

The ominous phrases "overspreading of abominations," "until the consummation," "and that determined shall be poured upon the desolate" evoke the most supreme epic moment in the history of the world when sin will reach its nexus, "the overspreading of abominations" will be at critical mass, the time of "the consummation" will be manifest, and fire and brimstone, "that determined," for the wickedness of the world "shall be poured upon the desolate."

How then do we reconcile the interval of time from the judgment of Christ to Judgment Day, the end of the world, to a 3 ½ time interval? Since the fifty years of the 457 BC Jubilee, the start of Jesus's public ministry and the crucifixion fit particularly well on a Solar or Gregorian time continuum of 50 years, 434 years, and 3 ½ years respectively, how does the last 3 ½ relate to that continuum? Let's examine scriptural references dealing with a time increment of 3 ½.

We read in 1 Kings 17:1 the following:

> And Elijah the Tishbite, who was of the inhabitants of Gildead, said unto Ahab, As the Lord God of Israel liveth, before whom I stand, there shall not be dew nor rain these years, but according to my word.

1 Kings 18:1 relates:

> And it came to pass after many days, that the word of the Lord came to Elijah in the third year, saying, Go shew thyself unto Ahab; and AI will send rain upon the earth.

Commenting on the absence of rain eluded by the two previous verses, James 5:17 states:

> Elias was a man subject to like passions as we are, and he prayed earnestly that it might not rain: and it rained not on the earth by the space of three years and six months.

We read from Daniel 7:23 to 26 the following:

> Thus he said, the fourth beast shall be the fourth kingdom upon earth, which shall be diverse from al kingdoms, and shall devour the whole earth, and shall tread it down, and break it in pieces. And the ten horns out of his kingdom are ten kings that shall arise: and another shall rise after them; and he shall be diverse from the first, and he shall subdue three kings. And he shall speak great words against the most High, and shall wear out the saints of the most High, and think to change times and laws: and they shall given into his hand until a time and times and the dividing of time. But the judgment shall sit, and they shall take away his dominion, to consume and to destroy it unto the end.

Daniel 12:5 to 7 elucidates:

> Then I Daniel looked, and, behold, there stood other two, the one on this side of the bank of the river, and the other on that side of the bank of the river. And one said to the man clothed in linen, which was upon the waters of the river, How long shall it be to the end of these wonders? And I heard the man clothed in linen, which was upon the waters of the river, when he held up his right hand and his left hand unto heaven, and sware by him that liveth for ever that it should be for a time, times, and an half; and when he shall have accomplished to scatter the power of the holy people, all these things shall be finished.

Revelation 12:6 reveals the following:

> And the woman fled into the wilderness, where she hath a place prepared of God, that they should feed her there a thousand two hundred and sixty days.

We read further in Revelation 12:13 to 14 the following:

> And when the dragon saw that he was cast unto the earth, he persecuted the woman which brought forth the man child. And to the woman were given two wings of a great eagle, that she might fly into the wilderness, into her place, where she is nourished for a time, and times, and half a time, from the face of the serpent.

Concerning the "dragon," the "man child," and the "woman," of the preceding verses, it is biblically correct to identify the "dragon" as Satan (Revelation 20:2), the "man child" as Jesus (Isaiah 9:6, Matthew 1:18), and the "woman" as national Israel as a type of all God's people representing the Old and New Testament saints (Genesis 3:15, 2:21–22; Galatians 4:4).

Revelation 11:2 follows:

> But the court which is without the temple leave out, and measure it not; for it is given unto the Gentiles: and the holy city shall they tread under foot for forty two months (or 3 years and 6 months).

Revelation 11:3 adds:

> And I will give power unto my two witnesses, and they shall prophesy a thousand two hundred and threescore days, clothed in sackcloth.

Finally, Revelation 13:4 and 5 relates the timing of the ruling of the beast (See appendix 5 for a formal breakdown of the period of time of 3 ½ in the Holy Scriptures):

> And they worshipped the dragon which gave power unto the beast; and they worshipped the beast, saying, Who is like unto the beast? Who is able to make war with him? And there was given unto him to continue forth and two months.

Thus far we have perused over ten biblical passages—the first three (1 Kings 17:1, 18:1 and James 5:17) dealing with a period of time of 3 ½ years during which there was no rain due to the divine command issued by the prophet Elijah against King Ahab and his kingdom (Israel): a severe drought ensued that lasted 3 ½ years according to the prayer of the mighty prophet Elijah (1 Kings 17 and 18). We argue here that the 3 ½ years of drought of Elijah constitutes a type of the period of time of 3 ½ presented in the books of Daniel and Revelation.

The fourth passage (Daniel 7:24 through 26) spoke of a great king who will "speak great words against the most High" and will incredibly "wear out the saints of the most High" for a period of "time, times and the dividing of time."

When Daniel in the fifth passage (Daniel 12:5 to 7) questioned the "man in white linen, which was upon the waters of the river" concerning the length of time remaining for "the end of these wonders" that would precede the end of the world, the "man in white linen" swore "by Him that liveth for ever" that it would take a "time, times and an half."

Revelation 12:6 and 13 to 14, the sixth and seventh passages commenting on a period of time of 3 ½ declares that the "woman" who normally represents God's people across time and, in this particular context, identifies with the New Testament saints, that is, the invisible church of God, "fled into the wilderness," to a "place prepared by God," and is "fed" there during a period of 1,260 days.

Revelation 12:13 to 14 maintains that the woman who had flown to the wilderness was "nourished" for a period of "a time, times and half a time."

We must conclude here that the 3 ½ period of time that the woman is "nourished" or "fed" constitutes the same period of time: one verse states 1,260 days (Revelation 12:6), while the second relates a period of "a time, times and half a time."

The eighth passage (Revelation 11:2) speaks of the Holy City "treaded under foot" for forty months. The Holy City identifies with God's people, the woman in Revelation 12, persecuted for the same period of time: forty-two months can be identified as 1,260 (Revelation 12:6) as well as "time, times and half a time" (Revelation 12:14), or a period of 3 ½.

The ninth passage (Revelation 11:3) describes "two witnesses" that "shall prophecy" for a period of "one thousand two hundred and sixty days." We suspect, the same length of time (3 ½) being at play here—that God has taken liberty to describe the same event in distinct figurative ways. The church is quite often identified in the Holy Scriptures as two or three (Matthew 11:2, 18:16, 19, 20).

The tenth passage (Revelation 13:4–5) reveals a beast who is worshipped for a period of forty-two months! Here again the same time interval, 3 ½, is in view. This time, we hear that the beast is worshipped by his people for a period of 3 ½. Interesting!

The detailed analysis of the greatest piece of literary work in the history of the world has uncovered two avenues to Judgment Day: the first ended in AD 33 when Jesus Christ endured the wrath of God on behalf of His people He came to save; the second ends in Judgment Day when God will pour out His wrath on all His foes—Satan, the fallen angels, the "dogs, and sorcerers, and whoremongers, and murderers, and idolaters and whosoever loveth and maketh a lie," and all the individuals whose sins have not been paid for (Matthew 25:41; Revelation 22:15; John 16:9–11, 9:41; 1 John 3:9).

History attests that Jesus Christ began His public ministry in AD 29 and was crucified in AD 33, exactly in the middle of the last seven of the Seventy Sevens, thus corroborating the extraordinary accuracy of the prophecy of the Seventy Sevens of Daniel 9. We could not, however, account for the last 3 ½ sevens of the Seventy Sevens.

We began to wonder whether the Holy Scriptures hid somewhere in its sacred pages the master key to unlock the mystery of the last 3 ½ sevens, when suddenly we began to notice the application of our mysterious number in various epic biblical settings. We expected that! Our analysis of the Seventy Sevens—assuming that the Word of God is consistent and truthful—predicted the biblical association of the time interval from the Cross to the end of the world to the mysterious 3 ½, the residue of the delineation of the Sixty-Nine Sevens from the Seventy Sevens.

We learn of the divine command to Elijah to pray for a period of drought throughout the land of Israel for a period of 3 ½ years. We now believe that drought and the famine that ensued constituted a harbinger of the spiritual famine that would materialize in succeeding periods of 3 ½ highlighted in the rest of the Holy Scriptures.

We learn from the three Passovers of the Gospel of John as well as from the rest of the teachings of the four Gospels that Jesus ministered publicly on earth for a period of 3 ½ years! The spiritual famine that prevailed in Israel and in the entire world during Jesus's public ministry—He "came to His own and His own received Him not," and "He was in the world, and the world was made by Him, and the world knew Him not" (John 1:11 and 10)—was quite pronounced: the patterns of a drought occurring during an interval of time of 3 ½ are quite noticeable.

We learn from Daniel 7:24 through 26 of a king who will "speak great words against the most High" and who will "wear out the saints of the most High" during a period of "time and times and the dividing of time," a nuanced albeit magnificent way of expressing the same time interval of 3 ½. Here again, spiritual dearth and an interval of time of 3 ½ are at play.

We learn from Daniel 12:5 through 7 of a specific time that would mark the "end of these wonders" when "all these things shall be finished," and when "the power of the holy people" would be finally scattered, a time coming at the behest of a time interval of "times, times, and an half," again the pattern of spiritual dearth and an interval of time of 3 ½ are prominently featured.

We learn from Revelation 12:6 of a "woman" who "fled into the wilderness where she had a place prepared of God." She would stay in that sheltered and shielded place where she would be fed for a period of 1,260 days. The pattern of spiritual famine and a time interval of 3 ½ remains true.

We learn from Revelation 12:13 through 14 of the same woman being "nourished for a time, and times and half a time, from the face of the serpent." We may quite quickly and correctly identify the 1,260 days of Revelation 12:6 with the time, times, and half a time of Revelation 12:14; and again, the pattern of spiritual famine (it would take an act of God to feed and nourish her) and a period of time of 3 ½ holds true.

We learn from Revelation 11:3 of two witnesses "clothed in sackcloth" who would "prophecy for a thousand two hundred and sixty days." Are the two witnesses the "reincarnation" of Moses and Elijah? Absolutely not! Two or three typify the spiritual common denominator of the church who was commanded by her Lord in His Great Commission to "go" and "teach all nations baptizing them in the name of the Father, and of the Son, and of the Holy Ghost." We believe that the two witnesses represent the same entity of Revelation 12:6 and 12:14, the woman who has been commanded to preach the Gospel to a world spiritually famished for a time interval of 3 ½.

We learn from Revelation 11:2 that the Gentiles would "tread under foot" the Holy City for a period of forty-two months, in correspondence to the time of the preaching of the Gospel by the two witnesses. God has chosen a different way to express the same time interval: forty-two months are the equivalent of 3 ½ years! Again, a period of intense spiritual famine holds sway during a time interval of 3 ½.

We learn from Revelation 13:4 and 5 of a beast who would be worshipped for a period of forty-two months: a beast being worshipped represents the height of spiritual idolatry taking place during an interval of time of 3 ½.

We learn from Daniel 9:27 of the "overspreading of abomination" occurring in a period of time of 3 ½. Incredibly, the pattern remains true in all the aforementioned cases.

Finally, Jesus's 3 ½ year ministry entails yet another 3 ½ time sequence befitting the patterns of the prior biblical references.

As a result, we can boldly proclaim that the Bible, the Word of the Living God, declares the time from the crucifixion of Jesus Christ to the end of the world to be identified as a period of time of 3 ½ (See table 5). God is hereby indicating in various forms and settings the same pattern of spiritual apostasy taking place in a time frame of 3 ½.

How long is that period of 3 ½? No ONE KNOWS BUT GOD! Nevertheless, when the end shall come, the last 3 ½ will match perfectly and evenly the prior sixty-nine sevens to form a complete Seventy Sevens. Glory to God in the highest!

When was Jesus born, and how many years did He spend on the earth?

It is very disturbing to hear prominent preachers, pastors, theological professors, and biblical scholars posit that Jesus started His public ministry at thirty years of age and died on the cross at thirty-three. Laymen, Bible students, members of congregations, and students accept at face value their pontification without searching the Holy Scriptures to verify the truth of their assertion (Acts 17:10 and 11).

What is the genesis of such a misguided teaching? How can so many brilliant minds continue to propagate so false a biblical precept? Luke 3:23 provides a plausible answer. It declares:

> And Jesus himself began to be ABOUT thirty years of age, being (as was supposed) the son of Joseph, which was the son of Heli.

On the surface, this passage seems to indicate that Jesus was thirty at the start of His public ministry. However, the omission by so many experts of one very important variable from the equation of a normal understanding of the issue provides the answer as to why so many excellent biblical expositors have erred quite dramatically on a topic teeming with simplicity.

The crucial variable whose omission has led so many astray? The word *about*! There it is! "Jesus," proclaims the Holy Scriptures, "was *about* thirty" when He started publicly preaching. He was *not* thirty! The Greek word transliterated *hocei* was deliberately, carefully, and purposefully inserted by God, the real Author of the Holy Scriptures, to painstakingly warn the serious Bible student that Jesus was *not* thirty years old when He commenced His public ministry.

How old then was Jesus at the start of His ministry? And how old was He at the time of His death on the cross of Calvary? It remains clear that the timing of His birth plays a prominent role in the solution of those two questions.

Most if not all Bible dictionaries, Bible commentaries, search engines, and books relevant to the time of the birth of Jesus indicate that Herod the Great, the first Herod, who ordered the massacre of the children of Bethlehem—young boys of two years and younger—died in 4 BC.

Since Herod the Great killed the young boys of two years and under according to the report from the magi who had seen the mysterious star two years earlier, one must conclude that Jesus was born at least 6 BC.

Moreover, the same aforementioned sources relate that Jesus died in AD 33; as a result, Jesus must have been at least thirty eight years old (6 BC + AD 33 = AD 39 − 1 [no year 0] = 38) when He died.

Looking at the Jubilee calendars (See appendix 2), 6 BC is indeed very close to 7 BC, a Jubilee year. We then suspect that Jesus in all likelihood was born on a Jubilee year, and 7 BC fits in quite nicely with that proposition.

Let's reconfigure our operation: 7 BC added to AD 33 yields AD 40, minus 1 (to account for the absence of year 0), would yield thirty-nine or thirty-eight as the probable age of Jesus when He died, and subtracting the 3 ½ years of His public ministry and accounting for the actual month of the time of His birth, He was thirty-three or thirty-four or thirty-five when He started His public ministry: He was in fact *about* thirty (Luke 3:23) when He started His public ministry and not *exactly* thirty!

Raising a Few Questions on the Nature of the Antichrist

Who is the real Antichrist? Will a leader appear on the world's scene that will "sign a peace treaty with Israel for seven years," and then proceed to violate the terms of his agreement with the Jews after three and a half years? Is the Roman papacy the Antichrist as a great number of Protestant Reformers (Martin Luther, John Calvin, John Knox as a few examples) conjectured? Will a charismatic political ruler succeed in rebuilding the Jewish temple in Jerusalem and then turn against the Jews and take complete control of the world's political, financial, and religious institutions?

Let's examine the issue with the transparent lenses of the Holy Scriptures. First John 4:3 relates the following:

> And every spirit that confesseth not that Jesus Christ is come in the flesh is not of God: and this is that *spirit* of antichrist, whereof ye have heard that it should come; and even now already is in the world.

The Kings James Translation, which is arguably the most reliable translation in existence, has not been faithful in articulating the salient points of the preceding verse. It italicizes the second *spirit* to indicate the addition of a word not present in the original Greek. The *Interlinear Hebrew Greek English* holds the following verbatim rendition:

> And every spirit which not confesses Jesus Christ in (the) flesh having come, of God not is; and this is the antichrist which you heard that is coming, and now in the world is already.

The latter translation presents a more grammatically correct translation than the former. The grammatical error in the *Interlinear Hebrew Greek English* translation consists in ignoring the grammatically correct genitive case in the clause "and this is the antichrist, which you heard that is coming," in lieu of the grammatically correct albeit stylistically poor "and this is the of the antichrist, which you heard that he is coming."

We are then grammatically justified to offer the following presentation of the verse:

> And every spirit which does not confess that Jesus Christ has come in the flesh is not of God; and this is of the antichrist, which you heard that is coming, and now is already in the world.

The Word of God nearly two thousand years ago proclaimed that the "spirit which does not confess that Jesus Christ has come in the flesh is of the antichrist." The Bible thus presupposes that the Antichrist was already working in the world in biblical time in the hearts and minds of the critics of Jesus who maintained that Jesus Christ had not taken human flesh. The same Antichrist is still operating in the psyche of the present and future opponents of the Gospel who preach the same heresy.

Since the Holy Scriptures identify the character present in biblical time as the same agent that will come, it then becomes impossible to categorize the Antichrist as a particular human being. Satan, Lucifer, the Dragon, the Old Serpent befits the title of Antichrist perfectly.

Second Thessalonians 2:3 and 4 states:

> Let no man deceive you by any means: for that day shall not come, except there come a falling away first, and that man of sin be revealed, the son of perdition; who opposeth and exalteth himself above all that is called God, or that is worshipped; so that he as God sitteth in the temple of God, shewing himself that he is God.

The Word of God offers additional insights in the character of the Antichrist. He is identified as "that man of sin" and as "the son of perdition" who mounts a frontal assault on God as he is "worshipped" as God and "sits in the temple of God, showing himself that he is God." Who historically fits that template completely? Lucifer of course! Isaiah 14 (verses 12 to 17) makes the point clearly; however, why is he called a "man" of sin and a "son" of perdition?

The Bible considers the kings of Babylon and Tyrus as types of Satan. (Quotes from Ezekiel 28, Revelation 18, and appropriate quotes for Babylon.)

And 2 Corinthians 11:14 and 15 reveals:

> And no marvel; for Satan himself is transformed into an angel of light. Therefore it is no great thing if his ministers also be transformed as the ministers of righteousness; whose end shall be according to their works.

The Word of God boldly proclaims that near the end of the world, Satan will be "transformed into an angel of light," and "his ministers" will be operating as "ministers of righteousness" attempting to destroy "the elect" if that was possible.

Where can Satan, incredibly described in the Word of God as "the angel of light," and his emissaries, shockingly identified in the Word of God as "the ministers of righteousness," find the elects of God for the application of their deceptive, destructive, and deadly teaching? Of course, mainly in the churches!

Is it now surprising that so many frontline organizations (the Episcopal Church, the Anglican Communion, the Association of Welcoming and Affirming Baptists, the United Church of Christ, the Evangelical Lutheran Church, the Moravian Church, the Old Catholic Church, the Presbyterian

Church (USA), the Affirming Pentecostal Church International, and many other frontline denominations) are accepting homosexuality for their laity and increasingly advocating it for their clergy?

The "mystery of iniquity" (2 Thessalonians 2:7) has been active in the local churches since the time of the apostles: the apostle John related the words of Jesus to the church of Pergamos (Revelation 2:13): "I know thy works, and where thou dwellest, even where Satan's seat is." Let's focus on the plain words of Jesus: the Church of Pergamos found its locus exactly where Satan is sitting, or ruling (Revelation 13:2). In other words, Satan has "occupied" the church of Pergamos by establishing his rule inside the church (Remember the parable of the wheat and tares of Matthew 13:24–30).

We are reminded here to review the following prophecy of Jesus in Matthew 24 concerning "the abomination of desolation" that should "stand in the holy place." And mindful that many Bible readers, students, pastors, and scholars would miss the mark on that point, Matthew, the disciple of Christ who wrote, under the inspiration of the Holy Spirit, the book that bears his name solemnly warns his readers in Matthew 24:15, "Whoso readeth, let him understand."

The misguided proposition that the passage in view refers to the Antichrist desecrating the rebuilt Jewish temple reminisces of John 2:19 where the Lord Jesus dared the Jews to "destroy this temple, and in three days [He] will raise it up." Of course, Jesus was referring to "the temple of His body," and not Herod's temple that took "forty six years" to build.

I am afraid that the advocates of the new temple may be guilty of the same theological fallacy: it could well be that Jesus, in Matthew 24, was referring to Satan increasingly taking control of the local churches—does anyone remember the church of Pergamos?

Moreover, the church of Thyatira was reprimanded by Jesus for allowing "Jezebel, which calleth herself a prophetess, to teach and to seduce [His] servants to commit fornication, and to eat things sacrificed to idols." Again, one church is scolded for allowing false teaching in its midst: the "mystery of iniquity" carries on.

In Matthew 24, Jesus used Daniel 9:27 as a backdrop for prophesying that the "abomination of desolation" will be manifest before the end-time, thus echoing Daniel's prophecy of the Seventy Sevens.

A Pithy Look at Heaven

What is heaven like? Where do spirit-filled, born-again, and saved individuals go when they pass away? Who will inhabit the New Heavens and the New Earth that God will create at the end of the world? What is the fate of the present earth and the present heavens?

Incredibly, the entire scientific literature is silent about those very important questions. The world of philosophy does not opine on topics it considers outside the realm of rational thought. Both ancient and modern cultures and religions abound in their portrayal of the afterlife.

The Assyrians believed that after death, everyone descended into the "Great Billow." The Babylonians theorized that humans were transported into the "House of Dust," a grim, bleak, and dark underworld where "the spirits of men eat dust and crawled on their bellies."

The Egyptians maintained that humans were endowed with a life-force (ka), which left the body at the time of death for the Osiris, "a lush and pleasant land in the underworld."

A REQUIEM FOR EVOLUTION

The Persians argued that the souls of dead people had to cross a bridge called Chinvat: "Good souls found the bridge to be a wide and comfortable beam leading to heaven," while bad souls experienced the bridge as "a razor-sharp blade from which they fell headlong into hell."

The Greeks thought that heaven consisted of an "underworld, deep beneath the earth, where Hades, the brother of Zeus and Poseidon, and his wife, Persephone, reigned over countless drifting crowds of shadowy figures—the 'shades' of all those who had died."

The Romans held the notion that heaven or Olympus was simply the province of the gods, and that everyone else's destination entailed the Elysian Fields or a restful and blissful existence in Hades located right over the Styx River.

The Chinese interpretation of the afterlife hails from a mixture of two religions: Taoism and Mayahana Buddhism. They maintained that after death, "one's spirit is taken by messengers to the gods of walls and moats, Ch'eng Huang." The virtuous souls are then led to one of the Buddhist paradises, "the dwelling place of the Taoist immortals, or the tenth court of hell for immediate rebirth." The sinful souls, after forty-nine days, "descend to hell, located at the base of the mythical Mount Meru" for a "fixed period of punishment." Afterward, "the souls in hell drink an elixir of oblivion in preparation for their next reincarnation."

Muslims consider heaven as a "paradise…where they will enjoy spiritual and physical pleasures forever." Judgment Day is viewed as "passing over hell on a narrow bridge in order to enter Paradise," and all the souls who fall, "weighted by their bad deeds, will remain in Hell forever," in order to suffer "spiritual and physical torment eternity."

What then do the Holy Scriptures teach about heaven? According to the Word of God, where do spirit-filled, born-again, and saved individuals go when they die? The Bible relates that God, in the not too distant future, will create New Heavens and a New Earth (Isaiah 65:17 and 2 Peter 3:13): is that really so? What does the Holy Writ prophesy concerning the present heavens and earth?

"These are," say the Holy Scriptures, "the generations of the Heavens and of the earth when they were created, in the day that the Lord God made the Earth and the Heavens." In that regard, the question "What is heaven like?" is not appropriate. God in fact did create many heavens. What are those heavens like? Who inhabit them?

The Word of God appears silent about the specific nature of those heavenly places and beings. Nonetheless, the Holy Scriptures reveal the following points in Ephesians 3:8–11:

> Unto me [Paul], who am less the least of the saints, is this grace given, that I should preach among the gentiles the unsearchable riches of Christ; and to make all men see what is the fellowship of the mystery, which from the beginning of the world hath been hid in God, who created all things by Jesus Christ; to the intent that now unto the principalities and powers in heavenly places might be known by the church the manifold wisdom of God, according to the eternal purpose which he purposed in Christ our Lord.

The Bible makes mention in those verses of "principalities and powers in heavenly places." Who are those principalities and powers? What kinds of creatures are they? Moreover, Colossians 1 verse 16 reveals the following:

> For by Him [Christ] were all things created…whether they be thrones, or dominions, or principalities, or powers, all things were created by him and for him.

To the "principalities and powers in heavenly places," we must add "thrones" and "dominions." We must remember that God hails from eternity past; as such, He must have created a multitude of creatures before the advent of time. (We must recall that Genesis does not chronicle the creation of the angels, the cherubim, the seraphim, the thrones, and the dominions) We will in all likelihood be overwhelmed in heaven at the sight of all the various types of creatures that inhabit God's universe.

Nehemiah 9 verse 6 offers a very insightful depiction of God's creative and sustaining powers:

> You alone are the Lord; You have made heaven, The heaven of heavens, with all their host, The earth and everything on it, The seas and all that is in them, And You preserve them all. The host of heaven worships You.

The terms "heavenly places" and "heaven of heavens" suggest a plurality of heavens. After all, God is depicted throughout the pages of the Holy Scriptures as the Lord of Hosts (1 Samuel 15:2, 1 Chronicles 17:24, Psalm 24:10, Jeremiah 25:27, Isaiah 48:2, Amos 3:13, Zechariah 1:3, Malachi 1:4, 6, 8, 9, to cite those few references). Who exactly are those hosts? When were they created? What do they look like? They, in all likelihood, must also inhabit the heavenly places mentioned earlier.

In Isaiah 66:1, God proclaims that "the heaven is my throne, and the earth my footstool." Please, take note of the singular nature of this heaven, the throne of the Living God. In 2 Corinthians 12:2–4, the Holy Scriptures recount Apostle Paul's vision of this heaven:

> I know a man in Christ who fourteen years ago—whether in the body I do not know, or whether out of the body I do not know—such a one was caught to the third heaven. And I know such a man—whether in the body or out of the body I do not know, God knows—how he was caught up into Paradise and heard inexpressible words, which it is not lawful for a man to utter.

The Word of God vividly equates the "Third Heaven" with the Paradise of God where the throne of God finds its locus. We recall here the conversation of Jesus with the two criminals that were crucified with Him:

> Then one of the criminals who were hanged blasphemed Him, saying, "If you are the Christ, save Yourself and us." But the other, answering, rebuked him, saying, "Do you not even fear God, seeing you are under the same condemnation? And we indeed justly, for we receive the due rewards of our deeds; but this Man has

done nothing wrong." Then he said to Jesus, "Lord, remember me when You come into Your kingdom." And Jesus said to him, "Assuredly, I say to you, today you will be with Me in Paradise."

The Third Heaven, also called the Paradise of God or Abraham's Bosom (Luke 16:22, 23:43; 2 Corinthians 12:4; Revelation 2:7) is then the place where all the spirit-filled, born-again, and saved individuals go when they expire. After all, the Bible indicates that "to be absent from the body" for a child of God is "to be present with the Lord" (2 Corinthians 5:8) in the Third Heaven, the Paradise of God, where the throne of God resides.

In Isaiah chapter 6, God opens the curtains of the Third Heaven in order to allow the prophet Isaiah to pen the following words:

> In the year that King Uzziah died, I saw the Lord sitting on a throne, high and lifted up, and the train of His robe filled the temple. Above it stood seraphim; each one had six wings: with two he covered his face, with two he covered his feet, and with two he flew. And one cried to another and said: "Holy, holy, holy is the Lord of hosts; The whole earth is full of His glory!" And the posts of the door where shaken by the voice of him who cried out, and the house was filled with smoke.

The Lord God also granted to Apostle John a similar albeit more complete view of the Third Heaven, the Paradise of God in Revelation chapter 4:

> After this, I [John] looked and saw a door that opened into heaven. Then the voice that had spoken to me at first and that sounded like a trumpet said, "Come up here! I will show you what must happen next." Right then the Spirit took control of me, and there in heaven I saw a throne and someone sitting on it. The one who was sitting there sparkled like precious stones of jasper and carnelian. A rainbow that looked like an emerald surrounded the throne.
>
> Twenty-four other thrones were in a circle around that throne. And on each of these thrones there was an elder dressed in white clothes and wearing a gold crown. Flashes of lightning and roars of thunder came out from the throne in the center of the circle. Seven torches, which are the seven spirits of God, were burning in front of the throne. Also in front of the throne was something that looked like a glass sea, clear as crystal.
>
> Around the throne in the center were four living creatures covered front and back with eyes. The first creature was like a lion, the second one was like a bull, the third one had the face of a human, and the fourth one was like a flying eagle. Each of the four living creatures had six wings, and their bodies were covered with eyes. Day and night they never stopped singing, "Holy, holy, holy is the Lord, the all-powerful God, who was and is and is coming!"

> The living creatures kept praising, honoring, and thanking the One who sits on the throne and who lives forever and ever. At the same time the twenty-four elders knelt down before the One sitting on the throne. And as they worshiped the One who lives forever, they placed their crowns in front of the thrones and said, "Our Lord and God, You are worthy to receive glory, honor and power. You created all things, and by your decision they are and were created."

A sequel to that vision prompted the apostle John to write the following:

> After this, I saw a large crowd with more people than could be counted. They were from every race, tribe, nation, and language, and they stood before the throne and before the Lamb. They wore white robes and held palm branches in their hands, as they shouted, "Our God, who sits upon the throne, has the power to save his people and so does the Lamb."
>
> The angels who stood around the throne knelt in front of it with their faces to the ground. The elders and the four living creatures knelt there with them. Then they all worshiped God and said, "Amen! Praise, glory, wisdom, thanks, honor, power, and strength belong to our God forever and ever! Amen!"

The Word of God declares that the present earth, the heavens that we can see with our naked eyes and with a telescope (the planets, stars, galaxies, quasars, pulsars, nebulae, black holes), the heavens that we cannot see, as well as the Third Heaven will be destroyed with fire at the end of the world when God will create New Heavens and a New Earth. "For behold," declares the Lord of Hosts, "I create New Heavens and a New Earth: and the former shall not be remembered, nor come into mind." That verse, along with many others (Isaiah 66:22, 2 Peter 3:13, and Revelation 21:1), vehemently contradicts the theory put forth by Randy Alcorn (I would recommend albeit reluctantly the reading of his book *Heaven*), Anthony Hoekema, Herman Bavinck, and many other writers positing that the New Heavens and the New Earth that Gold will create consist primarily in the restoration of the present heavens and earth. "Eye has not seen," contravene the Holy Scriptures, "nor ear heard, nor have entered into the hearts of man the things which God has prepared for those who love Him."

Mr. Alcorn and his cohorts counteract with the unbiblical principle of "continuity" while formulating the following arguments:

> God could just destroy his original creation and put it all behind him. But he won't do that. Upon creating the heavens and the earth, he called them "very good." Never once has he renounced his claim on what he made. He isn't going to abandon his creation. He's going to restore it. We won't go to Heaven and leave Earth behind. Rather, God will bring Heaven and Earth together into the same dimension, with no wall of separation, no armed angels to guard Heaven's perfection from sinful mankind (Genesis 3:24).

Well, their line of reasoning, as was indicated earlier, flies in the face of many Bible verses. For example, God the Father, in Hebrews 1:10–12, addresses God the Son in the following terms:

> You, Lord, in the beginning laid the foundation of the earth, And the heavens are the work of Your hands. They will perish, buy You remain; And they will grow old like a garment; Like a cloak You will fold them up, And they will be changed. But You are the same, And Your years will not fail.

God the Son, for His part, makes the following bold assertion contrasting the present universe with His words: "Heaven and earth will pass away, but My words will by no means pass away."

Finally, we sincerely believe that Mr. Alcorn and his like-minded friends do not represent the scoffers that the Holy Scriptures addressed in 2 Peter chapter 3:

> Above all, you must understand that in the last days scoffers will come, scoffing and following their own evil desires. They will say, "Where is this 'coming' he promised? Ever since our ancestors died, everything goes on as it has since the beginning of creation." But they deliberately forget that long ago by God's word the heavens came into being and the earth was formed out of water and by water. By these waters also the world of that time was deluged and destroyed. By the same word the present heavens and earth are reserved for fire, being kept for the day of judgment and destruction of the ungodly.

What then are the role and nature of the New Jerusalem, the city so prominently displayed and depicted in the book of Revelation? God, through the auspices of the apostle John, writes:

> Now I saw a new heaven and a new earth, for the first heaven and the first earth had passed away. Also there was no more sea. Then I, John, saw the holy city, the New Jerusalem, coming down out of heaven from God, prepared as a bride adorned for her husband. And I heard a loud voice from heaven saying, "Behold, the tabernacle of God is with men, and He will dwell with them, and they shall be His people. God Himself will be with them and be their God. And God will wipe away every tear from their eyes; there shall be no more death, nor sorrow, nor crying. There shall be no more pain, for the former things had passed away." Then He who sat on the throne said, "Behold, I make all things new." And He said to me, "Write, for these words are true and faithful."

The apostle John "saw" the New Jerusalem "coming down from God, out of heaven," quite probably into the New Earth, since "the tabernacle of God [will] be with men," and "He will dwell with them, and they shall be His people."

God delineates the exact configurations of the New Jerusalem (Revelation 21:15 to 17) "according to the measure of a man," for "the length and the breadth and the height of it are equal." The dimensions? Twelve thousand furlongs or stadia by twelve thousand furlongs or stadia by twelve thousand furlongs or stadia: the equivalence of 1,400 miles or 2,200 kilometers by 1,400 miles or 2,200 kilometers by 1,400 miles or 2,200 kilometers.

The surface area of the New Jerusalem entails 1,960,000 square miles or 4,480,000 square kilometers; and its volume: 2,744,000,000 cubic miles or 10,648,000,000 cubic kilometers.

Concerning the surface area of the New Jerusalem, Randy Alcorn makes the following observations:

> This is forty times bigger than England and fifteen thousand times bigger than London. It's ten times as big as France or Germany and far larger than India. But remember, that's just the ground level. Given the dimensions of a 1,400-mile cube, if the city consisted of different levels (we don't know this), and if each story were a generous twelve feet high, the city could have over 600,000 stories. If they were on different levels, billions of people could occupy the New Jerusalem, with many square miles per person.

The Lord God revealed to the apostle John in his vision on the island of Patmos in the South Aegean Sea off the coasts of Greece that the foundations of the wall surrounding the New Jerusalem "were garnished with all manner of precious stones" (Standard Full-Color Bible) and that the city's twelve gates (three on the north side, three on the south side, three on the east side, and three on the west side) were guarded by twelve angels. The structure of the city is that of "pure gold," and it had no temple, no sun, no moon, and no night "for the glory of God gave the city light" (Easy-to-Read Version).

The apostle John concludes His description of the New Jerusalem with the following words:

> And he [the angel] showed me a pure river of water of life, clear as crystal, proceeding from the throne of God and of the Lamb. In the middle of its street, and on either side of the river, was the tree of life, which bore 12 fruits, each tree yielding its fruit every month. The leaves of the tree were for the healing of the nations. And there shall be no more curse, but the throne of God and of the lamb shall be in it, and His servants shall serve Him. They shall see His face, and His name shall be on their foreheads. There shall be no night there: They need no lamp nor light of the sun, for the Lord gives them light. And they shall reign forever and ever.

A Bird's-Eye View of Hell

Hell does not exist in a vacuum. It is the direct, logical, righteous, and perfect consequence of sin, the violation of the sacred law of God, and a frontal assault against the holy nature of the

Creator, Maker, Owner, Ruler, Sustainer, and Judge of the universe (1 John 3:4, Romans 4:15, Matthew 7:23, 13:41, Psalm 18:30, 19:7, 51:4).

God has created all things according to His good pleasure and for His glory (Revelation 4:11): His divine sovereignty requires Him to set the rules of engagement in His universe and to establish the consequences of falling short of His high standards of holiness and perfection (Romans 3:23, Matthew 5:48).

In His divine sovereignty, God has decreed that throughout the universe He has created, the SOUL WHO SINS SHALL DIE (Ezekiel 18:20). This, ladies and gentlemen, entails the starting point for an accurate understanding of the nature of hell: DEATH awaits the sinner, for God has so decreed by His own divine prerogatives (Please, see chapter 10 for a more detailed discussion of the types of death facing the sinner).

The sinner *dies* spiritually first, and then physically and psychologically (Genesis 2:17, James 1:15, 1 Corinthians 15:56). The outright rebellion against the holy and righteous commands of God engenders the prompt and immediate spiritual *death* of the perpetrator.

Lucifer, the first sinner in God's universe (1 John 3:8), was found guilty of murder (John 8:44, Deuteronomy 5:17, and Exodus 20:13), lying (John 8:44, Exodus 20:16, Deuteronomy 5:20), and pride (Isaiah 14:13 and 14). He and his cohorts of fallen angels who disobeyed the command of God by leaving their "positions of authority," thereby forfeiting their "proper dwelling" (Jude 6), *died* spiritually and are now awaiting complete destruction in hell after Judgment Day (Jude 6, Matthew 25:41).

Sinful mankind, from Adam and Eve to the last human born right before the end of this world, must confront physical *death* in this life and spiritual and psychological *death* in hell after Judgment Day (Hebrews 9:27). The only alternative to that bleak predicament focuses on the salvation of the soul by the faith of Jesus Christ (Not faith in Jesus Christ surprisingly. Please, again see chapter 10: faith in Jesus Christ follows the faith of Jesus Christ in the life of a believer) ushering in the rapture of the believer after the Second Coming of our Lord and Savior Jesus Christ (1 Thessalonians 4:16 and 17, 1 Corinthians 15:51 to 57).

What then is the fate of an individual after she passes away? It all depends whether she is born again (John 3:3), that is born of the Spirit (John 3:5, Romans 8:9), or not. If she is anointed with the Holy Spirit, the believer is instantly carried by angels into the presence of the Lord Jesus Christ in the Third Heaven, also called Paradise or Abraham's Bosom (Luke 16:22, 23:43; 2 Corinthians 5:8, 12:4; and Philippians 1:23).

All the individuals without the Holy Spirit face a dire situation when they *die*. Their soul descends into Sheol (the Hebrew word used in the Old Testament in Deuteronomy 32:22; Job 2:9, 7:9; Isaiah 14:9 and 10, 11, and 15; Psalm 6:5, 49:14; and many other Old Testament passages), also called Hades (the Greek word used in the New Testament in Matthew 11:23, 16:18; Luke 10:15; Revelation 1:18, 6:8, 20:13 and 14; and many other New Testament passages), the grave (the English word used for the Hebrew word *Sheol* in such Old Testament passages as Psalms 6:5, 30:3, 31:17; Proverbs 1:12, 30:16; Ecclesiastes 9:10; Isaiah 14:11; and the English word used for the Greek word *Hades* in such New Testament passages such as Matthew 16:18, Revelation 1:18, and many other New Testament verses), and hell (the English word used in Luke 16:23, Acts 2:27 and 31, and many other New Testament passages).

Therefore, the soul of unsaved mankind leaves this earth for Sheol, also called Hades, or the grave, or hell, a place of darkness (Matthew 25:30, 2 Peter 2:4 and 17), torment (Luke 16:24 and 25), and degrees of punishment (Luke 12:47 and 48) in order to await Judgment Day.

After Judgment Day, all the individuals without the Holy Spirit, namely unsaved and unregenerate mankind, will be thrown into the lake of fire, appropriately called Gehenna (Matthew 5:22, 29, 30, 10:28, 18:9, 23:15; Mark 9:43, 45, 47; Luke 12:5; James 3:6). The lake of fire (also called hell in such passages as Matthew 5:22, 29, 30, 10:28, 11:23, 18:9, 23:33; Mark 9:43, 45, 47) is typified by the Valley of the Son of Hinnom (Joshua 15:8, 18:16), a valley near Jerusalem "used as a burying place for criminals and for burning garbage."

It is significant that the Holy Scriptures call the lake of fire the Second Death (Revelation 20:14 and 21:8): individuals thrown into the lake of fire simply *die*! If physical *death* entails the cessation of the physical senses of seeing, hearing, smelling, touching, and tasting, spiritual *death* warrants the termination of the three spiritual senses of conscience, fellowship, and intuition (Deuteronomy 2:30, Psalm 51:10, John 13:21, Mark 2:8, Acts 18:5, Luke 1:47, and Romans 8:16; please, read chapter 10 for a more detailed analysis of the three senses of the human spirit).

Concerning God's judgment of Sodom and Gomorrah, the Holy Scriptures make the following insightful observation:

> Even as Sodom and Gomorrha and the cities about them in like manner, giving themselves over to fornication, and going after strange flesh, are set forth for an example suffering the vengeance of eternal fire.

God, in His Holy Scriptures, declares that Sodom, Gomorrah, and the surrounding cities suffered "the vengeance of ETERNAL FIRE." If the fire that devoured Sodom, Gomorrah, and the surrounding cities was of "ETERNAL" duration, would not such a fire be still burning somewhere in the Middle East? Indeed and in truth, all those cities were burned up and totally consumed by God, who is a consuming fire (Deuteronomy 4:24 and Hebrews 12:29). Satan, the fallen angels, and every individual whose name was not written in the Lamb's Book of Life will likewise endure the "vengeance of *eternal fire.*

What about Revelation 20:10 where God seems to indicate a fire of eternal duration? Revelation 20:10 reads as follows:

> And the devil that deceived them was cast into the lake of fire and brimstone, where the beast and the false prophet are, and shall be tormented day and night for ever and ever.

The Word of God clearly declares that the Devil, the Beast and the False Prophet, "shall be tormented day and night for ever and ever" in the lake of fire. The Holy Scriptures acknowledge three times (Mark 9:44, 46, and 48) that the "worm" of every individual thrown into the lake of fire "does not DIE," and the eternal fire in the Gehenna "is not quenched." Why did God choose the word *worm* in association with the eternal punishment of the wicked thrown into the lake of fire?

Let's remember that worms evolve from the decay of a *dead* corpse. Likewise, spirituals worms will be generated by the *dead* and decaying spiritual corpses in the lake of fire. Those spiritual worms will not "die," and the eternal fire burning them will "not quench." The Word of God in the book of Job (chapter 21, verse 26) relates that "worms shall cover" all the *dead* corpses of the individuals thrown into the lake of fire: this, ladies and gentlemen, is indeed the dreadful Second Death!

Why do the Holy Scriptures mention three times (Psalm 16:10, Acts 2:27, and Acts 2:31) that the soul of Jesus "was not left in hell?" Did Jesus go to hell when He died? The Spirit of Jesus went to Paradise, also called Abraham's Bosom (Luke 23:43, 16:22) when He passed away at the cross on Calvary. The word *hell* chosen for the Greek word *Hades* surmises that the Holy Scriptures sometimes use the term *Hades* to identify both the grave, or Sheol, and Paradise, also called Abraham's Bosom.

Chapter 9

All to the Praise and Glory of God

Thou art worthy, O LORD, to receive glory and honour and power for thou hast created all things, and for thy pleasure they are and were created (Revelation 4:11).

To make all men see what the fellowship of the mystery, which from the beginning of the world hath been hid in God, who created all things by Jesus Christ:
    To the intent that now unto the principalities and powers in heavenly places might be known by the Church the manifold wisdom of God,
    According to the eternal purpose which He purposed in Christ Jesus our Lord (Ephesians 3:9–10).

Thousands…millions…billions…trillions of years (as calibrated by our finite time system of 365.2422 days a year) before the creation of the point of singularity, the moment that heralded the beginning of space, energy, and time, when the four known natural forces—gravity, electromagnetism, strong nuclear and weak nuclear—were mysteriously constrained into a giant super-force inside a point with a density in the millions of millimeters of mercury and a temperature in the millions of degrees Celsius, God was! God is! And God will always be!

What preceded the creation of the point of singularity? What set in motion the imprisonment of the four natural forces inside a tiny minuscule point? What force caused the explosion of the point of singularity into the production of the known universe? Why has the point of singularity evolved into the space, time, and energy configurations characteristic of our present universe?

The laws of physics and logic warrant unquestionably the existence of a creator for the universe. Newton's first law of motion, the principle of inertia, asserts that "the vis insita, or inner force of matter, is a power of resisting by which every body, as much as in it lies, endeavours to preserve its present state, whether it be of rest or of moving uniformly forward in a straight line." In layman's terms, "an object at rest stays at rest and an object in motion stays in motion with the same speed and in the same direction unless acted upon by an unbalanced force."

What is the "unbalanced force" that "acted" upon the inertia of the point of singularity, initiated the big bang, the cosmic explosion of the universe, and caused the transformative separation of the four natural forces?

Newton's law of inertia warrants the intervention of a powerful supernatural *force* outside the realms of our present four natural forces as the agent responsible for disturbing the "inertia," or, in more understandable terms, the "rest" of the point of singularity and initiated the big bang "explosion" of the universe and the continued expansion of our present cosmos: the grandiose manifestation of the laws of science and the magnificent intervention of the supernatural are not mutually exclusive after all.

Moreover, the laws of logic also argue categorically for the existence of a creator for the universe. Theologians and philosophers used to stand firmly behind the First Cause argument to make the case for God as the original Creator. If indeed everything has a cause, they would surmise as a premise, then tracing back everything for its a priori cause would eventually lead to God as the logical First Cause. Therefore, they would conclude that God must be the First Cause of everything!

This apparently valid syllogism installing God as the First Cause of everything does not logically keep God as the First Cause: God must also have a First Cause, since it was assumed that everything has a First Cause.

Furthermore, looking for the First Cause of everything would lead to an infinite series of First Causes—a logical impossibility and absurdity! Since the world exists and the First Cause argument leads us nowhere, there *must* be something or someone *self-existent* and *eternal* that accounts for the existence of everything! "The only possible alternative to this," affirms Dr. RC Sproul, "is that something comes into being without a cause or is self-created."

Self-creation violates the first primary law of logic—the law of noncontradiction. Someone or something must possess an a priori existence in order to self-create: obviously, someone cannot exist and not exist at the same time.

The other option—"Something comes into being without a cause"—leads mercilessly to another dead end: "Indeed," argues R. C. Sproul, "if it comes into being without any cause, it cannot even be its own cause." The assertion that someone or something is his or its own cause is in fact a logical absurdity: "It has no cause," concludes R. C. Sproul, and "it cannot be an effect."

Therefore, since the world exists and the First Cause, the No-Cause, and the Self-Creation premises cannot account for the existence of anything, there *must*, as was argued earlier, be someone or something *self-existent* and *eternal* accountable for the existence of everything; in other words, logic requires that "something, somehow, somewhere at some time has the power of *being intrinsically*," and is the raison d'etre of all things.

Pretty much all the scientists and philosophers came to the same conclusion at the dawn of the last century, before the big bang held sway throughout the scientific and philosophical communities; in fact, the most renowned scientists and *hommes sages* du jour rightfully, or so it seemed, posited that the universe itself was the *self-existent* and *eternal* entity accountable for the creation of everything! Bertrand Russell, a philosopher, mathematician, historian, and logician of the first kind, presented that argument in one of his famous sentences: "If there can be anything without a cause, it may just as well be the world as God."

As a result, there remained but only two competing theories for the self-existing entity responsible for the existence of the universe—the universe itself according to the Steady State naturalist scientists and philosophers, or God, as advocated by the Holy Scriptures, the theistic scientists, and the philosophers and theologians making the sensible and intuitive case that the universe is a manifestation of the handiwork of God.

If it can be demonstrated that the universe had a beginning and could not be self-existent, God would then be crowned as the sole entity liable for the creation of the universe. Bertrand Russell tragically erred by erecting his origin argument along the following lines:

> Either the world had a beginning, or it did not. If it did not, it did not need a cause (God). If it did, we can ask, "Who caused God?"
> But if God had a cause, he is not God. In either case, we do not arrive at a first uncaused cause (God).

Sir Bertrand Russell was trapped by his own misguided enthymeme—the *unexpressed* premise "if everything has a cause" would logically lead to the valid and yet unsound and erroneous conclusion that God does not exist!

The first law of thermodynamics, the law of energy conservation, states that, "energy cannot be created nor destroyed." The second law, the law of energy decay, postulates: "in a 'closed system,' the amount of usable energy in the universe is decreasing." Those two laws indicate clearly that the universe is "running out of usable energy."

Roy Peacock, a brilliant scientific writer and a scholar in the field of thermodynamics, comments on the impact of the second law on the structure of the universe:

> The Second Law of thermodynamics is probably the most powerful piece of legislation in the physical world. It ultimately describes every process we have ever discovered: It is the final Court of Appeal in any dispute relating to action and

procedures, whether they are generated or man inspired. It draws the conclusion that in our universe there is an overall reduction in order, a loss of available energy that is measured as an increase in entropy. So the available stock of order is being exhausted. Akin to the dying battery of a flashlight, useful energy is being dissipated into entropy after which none remains for use…For us to live in a universe in which the Second Law of thermodynamics holds, then, it must be a universe that has a starting point, a creation.

It is significant to note that from the two main cosmological models that claimed to provide a clear explanation of the past of the universe—the big bang theory, which assumed a beginning and a continued expansion of the universe, and the steady state theory, which postulated that the universe "has existed eternally in a state of constant density," and that "space has been expanding eternally"—the big bang theory has overwhelmingly won the hearts and minds of most cosmologists as a result of the "discovery of the background radiation in 1965, which was predicted by the Big Bang Theory." Let us remember that the big bang theory presupposes a beginning for the entire cosmos: God, therefore, must be by default or design the Creator of the entire universe!

Moreover, as the *Self-Existent* and *Eternal Being*, GODS (the Holy Scriptures denote specifically the plural Hebraic ELOHIM in Genesis 1:1), He created (the singular "Bara" is clearly identified here; the Bible indeed is its own grammar!) the heavens and the earth.

What then was God doing before the creation of Genesis? Of course, He was not "spending his time preparing hell for people who ask questions like this!" He was busy creating, sustaining, maintaining, fellowshipping with the principalities (Romans 8:28, Ephesians 3:10, 6:12), powers (Ephesians 3:10, Colossians 1:16, 2:15), thrones (Colossians 1:16), dominions (Colossians 1:16), worlds (Hebrews 1:2, 11:3), angels (Psalms 68:17, 104:4, 148:2), seraphim (Isaiah 6:6), cherubim (1 Samuel 4:4, 1 Chronicles 13:6), Lucifer (Isaiah 14:12–17), and Himself (Genesis 1:26, Ephesians 1:11).

If we may use the present universe filled with billions and billions of galaxies and stars as patterns, God in all likelihood must have created billions and billions of worlds populated by all kinds of creatures before He embarked on the creation of the present universe: the creation story of Genesis presupposes the a priori creation of the morning stars and the sons of God who "shouted for joy" (Job 38:7) at the sight of God creating the present universe.

God must have looked at all the worlds, all the principalities, all the dominions, all the powers, all the thrones, and all the wonderful and marvelous creatures that He had made, and He must have felt that all His handiworks were indeed "very good." Perfection reigned supremely everywhere. All of God's creatures lived in perfect bliss and had a perfect knowledge of their creator and of the world around them. Genuine agape love summarized every interaction, every act of fellowship, and every conversation between God and His creatures and among the creatures themselves.

It was God's good pleasure to reveal Himself to all His marvelous creatures in all of His glory and majesty by exhibiting *all* His divine attributes, thereby receiving true worship, remarkable fellowship, and constant praise and adoration. Let's consider a few of the attributes that God wanted to exhibit to His creatures in His quest to elicit from them perfect adoration.

God is *sovereign*. He "has made everything beautiful in His time" (Ecclesiastes 3:11), and He rules and reigns over all the works His hands have made (Revelation 11:15, Zechariah 6:13, Revelation 12:5). God had from eternity past had ruled and reigned over the loving, joyful, peaceful, good, gentle, meek, kind, obedient, and blessed creatures He had brought into existence; could He also rule and reign over the loveless, sorrowful, restless, bad, unkind, proud, disobedient, and cursed entities some of His creatures became as sin made its appearance in God's universe? God's *sovereignty*, in that regard, was not perfectly exhibited before the Fall of Adam and Eve.

God was known and is still known by His creatures as *self-existent*. They recognized that He had *Being* intrinsically woven in His nature. Even though God had "fearfully and wonderfully" (Psalm 139:14) made them, He Himself was not created, nor was He self-created: He has always existed, exists now, and will forevermore exist. God's creatures worship and praise Him for their own existence (Psalm 148, Hebrews 7:3).

God was and is even now reverenced as *self-sufficient*. All His creatures depend on Him for their daily sustenance (2 Corinthians 3:5; 2 Corinthians 9:8). "Open your mouth wide," God has declared to all His creatures, "and I will fill it" (Psalm 81:10). "Be anxious for nothing," God recommends all His creatures, "but in everything by prayer and supplication, with thanksgiving, let your requests be made known to God; and [My] peace, which surpasses all understanding, will guard your hearts and minds through Christ Jesus."

God has revealed Himself to His created beings as *eternal*. He is from eternity past to eternity future: He "inhabits eternity" (Isaiah 57:15). The angels, the archangels, the seraphim, the cherubim, the principalities, the powers, Lucifer, and all the hosts of the worlds that God has made were all created in eternity past, and were designed for an "eternal excellency" (Isaiah 60:15). They were living in constant fellowship with God, the Eternal Life (1 John 5:20) who had brought them into existence out of nothing (Revelation 5:13), and were promised His constant divine providence (Hebrews 5:13), and an eternity of divine relationship and fellowship.

In all His dealings with His creatures, God has always identified Himself as *omnipotent*. He has unlimited and infinite power to accomplish whatever He wishes: "With God," declares Jesus, "all things are possible" (Matthew 19:26). He is the *Almighty*, the God who revealed to Mary that "with God nothing shall be impossible" (Luke 1:17), and the EL SHADAI who declared to Abraham that there is nothing "too hard for the Lord" (Genesis 18:14).

God has demonstrated to His created beings that He is *omniscient*. He is *all-knowing*: nothing escapes His attention. He has *perfect knowledge* of all His creatures (Hebrews 4:13, Psalm 139) and *perfect knowledge* of all things. In Hebrews 4:13, God makes the following ominous assertion:

> Neither is there any creature that is not manifest in his sight: but all things are
> naked and opened unto the eyes of him with whom we have to do.

The manifestations of God throughout the worlds He has created clearly exhibit the undeniable notion that He is *omnipresent*. He is everywhere present. He is always in contact with the center, the surface, the circumference or the perimeter, and the volume of all the marvelous worlds and the wonderful works that His handy hands have made, both visible and invisible (Psalm 149, Psalm 46:1); and He incredibly *fills* both heaven and earth (Jeremiah 23:24).

The grandeur of God's marvelous creations prove beyond a shadow of doubt that He is *infinite*. He has an infinite mind that guarantees a complete understanding of all things (Psalm 147:5). He views from the end the beginning of all things and considers the beginning of everything as a fait accompli (Revelation 21:6, Revelation 22:13).

God is *triune*. He has revealed Himself to His creatures as the *Father*, the *Son*, and the *Spirit*. The plural ELOHIM in Genesis 1:1 presupposes the trinity of the Godhead acting as *one* in creating—the singular is referenced to indicate the *three* acting as *one*: whenever any *one* is active, the other *two* "is" also active and completely involved as well—planning, maintaining, sustaining, and ruling the present cosmos and the world to come (Matthew 28:19, Genesis 1:1, Deuteronomy 6:4, 2 Corinthians 13:14).

God is *good*. He is gracious to all. He has made all creatures and all things "fearfully and wonderfully" and has placed them in their rightful position; and He has provided the proper environment for them to shine and reflect His glorious majesty (Matthew 19:17, Jeremiah 33:11). In that regard, Jesus opines, "There is none good but one, that is, God." Before the creation of time and the introduction of sin, God had not shown to His creatures that He was also equally *good* to the fallen, the sinful, the lowly, the prodigal, the godless, the rebellious, and the wicked! God's *goodness* was "limited" to the godly, the perfect, the sinless, the sanctified, and the obedient: God's *goodness* was not fully and perfectly distributed!

God is *immutable*. He cannot change! "I am the Lord, and I change not," He has proclaimed. And Jesus Christ is "the same yesterday, and today, and forever" (Hebrews 13:8). "Heaven and earth shall pass away, but my words shall not pass away," Jesus boldly asserted to His followers in His marvelous Olivet Discourse (Matthew 24:35).

God is *transcendent*. He is beyond all of His creations! Having formed our present universe with its present specifications of energy, time, and space, God supersedes them all! He is simultaneously present in all the worlds He has created; and the earth, the heaven, and the heaven of heavens cannot contain Him (1 Kings 8:27, 2 Chronicles 6:18, Jeremiah 23:24).

God is *truthful*. He is the *Truth*! The prophet Samuel acknowledged that God's words were tried words (2 Samuel 22:31). David also affirmed that God's words were "pure words, as tried in a furnace of earth, purified seven times" (Psalm 12:6).

God is *wise*. "There is no wisdom," cry the Holy Scriptures, "or understanding or counsel against the Lord!" (Proverbs 21:30). God had prepared His divine economy before He created this present universe (Ephesians 1:4), and His Redeeming Lamb was "slain from the foundation of the world" (Revelation 13:8).

God is *joyful*. David exclaimed that in God's "presence is fullness of joy," and at His right hand there are "pleasures for evermore" (Psalm 16:11). God is willing and able to bring all His loved ones "before the presence of His glory with great joy" (Jude 24). In fact, "there is," says Jesus, "joy in the presence of the angels over one sinner that repents."

God is *graceful*. Noah, Moses, and the apostle Paul found grace in God's sight (Genesis 6:8, Exodus 33:13, 2 Corinthians 12:9). Jesus was full of "grace and truth" (John 1:14). God's last promise in the Holy Scriptures to His people is that His grace be with them all (Revelation 22:21).

God is *peaceful*. He is the God of peace (1 Thessalonians 5:23, Philippians 4:9). Peace comes from God (1 Timothy 1:2, 2 Timothy 1:2, Titus 1:4, Philemon 3). "Peace I leave with you," says Jesus to all His followers, "my peace I give to you," and continues the Son, "not as the world gives do I give to you." All the Scriptures were given to us that in our Lord and Savior Jesus we might have complete peace (John 16:33).

God is *kind*. He is "kind to the unthankful and to the evil" (Luke 6:35). In eternity past, He had shown His kindness to His obedient creatures unshackled by the unholy bounds of sin. Would God be equally kind to disobedient, rebellious, ungrateful, unthankful, unholy, and evil creatures? God, quite naturally, knew that He would; nonetheless, He had not yet revealed to anyone the fullest extent of His kindness. As such, before the advent of time, God's kindness was not exhibited in its fullest dimension.

God is *gentle*. His gentleness always makes His people great (2 Samuel 22:36, Psalm 18:35). Gentleness is one of the fruits manifesting the presence of the Holy Spirit in the lives of God's children (Galatians 5:22).

God is *temperate*. He has ordered His creatures to add temperance to the knowledge He has given them (2 Peter 1:6) in their pursuit of godliness. The words of the following song concerning God's temperance are apropos here:

> Unresting, unhasting and silent as night,
> Nor wanting, nor wasting, thou rulest in might;
> Thy justice like mountains high soaring above
> Thy clouds which are fountains of goodness and love.

God is *love* (1 John 4:16). Love is the essence of His being and of His nature (1 John 4:8); and love is of God (1 John 4:7). "For God so loved the world," the Holy Scriptures proclaim, "that He gave His only begotten Son, that whoever believes in Him should not perish but have everlasting life." Continue the Holy Scriptures: "But God demonstrates His love toward us, in that while we were yet sinners, Christ died for us." "Greater love," Jesus states, "has no man than this, than to lay down one's life for his friends." "By this," relates the Word of God, "we know love, because He laid down His life for us." Therefore, "we also ought to lay down our lives for the brethren." Jesus opines on the two great commandments:

> You shall love the Lord your God with all your heart, with all your soul, and with all your mind.
> This is the first and great commandment. And the second is like it: "You shall love your neighbor as yourself.
> On these two great commandments hang all the Law and the Prophets.

God is *Spirit*, and all His creatures who worship Him must do so in spirit and in truth (John 4:24). "The Spirit Himself," say the Scriptures, "bear witness with our spirit that we are the children of God." As "children of God," we are "heirs of God and joint heirs with Christ."

God is "*light* and in Him is no darkness at all." He dwells in "unapproachable light" (1 Timothy 6:16). He is known as the "Father of *Lights*" who grants "every good and every perfect gift" to all His beloved children (James 1:17). Before the beginning of time, all of God's creatures lived in the light of the presence of God: darkness was not yet, and an alternative to light entailed an unfathomable conjecture. Would darkness extinguish light? How could anyone live in a world filled with darkness? How would light interact with darkness? What was stronger: light or darkness? God, quite naturally, knew the answers to all those questions; however, He had to bring all His creatures to a point where they could answer those questions for themselves.

God is *merciful*. Mercy always belongs to the Lord our God (Daniel 9:9); however, before the introduction of time and the subsequent fall of man, God had not yet demonstrated to His creatures that He can show mercy to the fallen, the sinful, the unholy, the unlovable. In fact, the concept of mercy was an unknown idea throughout the worlds the Lord God had made: everyone was "fearfully and wonderfully" made and enjoyed uninterrupted fellowship with God; and they lived in perfect harmony with their fellow creatures and reverenced the Creator for the wonderful works His hands had made.

How would God react to the fallen, the sinner, the unholy? How would God deal with outright rebellion to His authority? How would He respond to sin? Such questions never entered the heart of God's creatures. God, nonetheless, had other ideas.

God is *meek*. Jesus describes Himself as "meek and lowly in heart" (Matthew 11:29). "Blessed are the meek, for they shall inherit the earth," declares Jesus. King David extolled that the meek will also "delight themselves in the abundance of peace" in the restored earth that they will inherit. Moses, a man who had spent considerable time in the presence of God, was described as "very meek, above all the men which were upon the face of the earth."

God is *faithful*. He renews His faithfulness to His creatures every day (Psalm 92:2), and His faithfulness is known to all generations (Psalm 89:9, Psalm 119:90). God's has established His faithfulness in all the worlds that He created (Psalm 89:2), and all His words are true and *faithful sayings* (Revelation 22:6, 21:5).

Jesus is called the *Faithful Witness* (Revelation 1:5), the *Faithful* and *True Witness* (Revelation 3:14), the *Faithful* (Revelation 19:11). God was always *faithful* to all His creatures in eternity past: would He be *faithful* to a fallen world? Would He remain *faithful* in carrying out His eternal plan in the face of blatant rebellion from some of His creatures? Would His words still ring true when seemingly contradicted by the rants and ravings of raging rulers of darkness? Time would tell.

God is *holy*. He is *holy, holy, holy*! He requires that all His creatures be also *holy* (Deuteronomy 7:6, 14:12; Leviticus 11:44, 45). No one is like our God, glorious in *holiness* (Exodus 15:11). All God's creatures should praise the beauty of His *holiness* (2 Chronicles 20:21) as He sits upon the throne of His *holiness* (Psalm 47:8). God has spoken in His *holiness* (Psalm 108:7), and He swears by His *holiness* to judge His enemies and to deliver His people from their hands (Amos 4:2, Luke 1:75). The four living creatures dwelling around the throne of God did not "rest day and night, saying '*Holy, Holy, Holy, LORD God Almighty*, who was, and is, and is to come.'"

God is *perfect*. He is complete in everything and is found wanting in nothing whatsoever, and He requires all creatures to be likewise (Matthew 5:48). God is quite naturally *perfect* in all His attributes; however, He desires that all His creatures experience a *perfect* measure of all of them.

God's perfection is the factor common to all His attributes: God is *perfectly sovereign, perfectly holy, perfectly righteous, perfectly loving, perfectly wise, perfectly merciful*. In other words, His *perfection* modifies completely all the attributes that He possesses.

For example, God's strength was manifest abundantly in the life of the apostle Paul after his conversion: He was then commissioned by the Holy Spirit to embark on an international missionary journey that paved the way for the propagation of the Gospel throughout the world. He then received from the Lord, as a confirmation of the importance of his ministry and as an attestation of his spiritual maturity, an "abundance of…revelations" (2 Corinthians 12:9) that could render any mortal "exalted above measure."

As a result, the exemplary and legendary apostle was given a "thorn in the flesh, the messenger of Satan to buffet [him]." The greatest missionary, pastor, theologian, biblical apologist, expositor, and writer requested three times that the Lord should remove his "thorn in the flesh." The Lord, however, responded, "My grace is sufficient for thee: for my strength is made perfect in weakness."

In other words, Paul had experienced God's strength throughout his ministry; nonetheless, the Lord needed him to be weak in order to receive a *perfect* dose of His strength. God looks for ways to dispense upon His called-out ones a *perfect* measure of His wonderful divine attributes in order to confirm them in the image of His Son, our Lord and Savior Jesus Christ.

God is *righteous* (Ezra 9:15). He loves *righteousness* and *judgment* (Psalm 45:7, 72:2). He judges the world and makes war with *righteousness* (Psalm 96:13, Revelation 19:11). All the Gentiles shall see the *righteousness* of God, and all the kings shall see His glory (Isaiah 62:2). God has coupled *righteousness* and *love* as the two most telltale attributes characteristic of His godliness: "In this the children of God and the children of the devil are manifest: Whoever does not practice *Righteousness* is not of God, nor is he who does not *Love* his brother." Jesus exclaims, "Therefore by [those] fruits you will know them." *Righteousness* is exhibited in the Scriptures as the key characteristic of the new heavens and the new earth that the old creation moans and groans for: "Nevertheless," declares the Word of God, "we, according to His promise, look for new heavens and a new earth in which *Righteousness* dwells." In His word, the Lord establishes *righteousness* as the harbinger of *joy* and *gladness* of heart (Psalm 32:11, 58:10, 64:10, 68:3, 107:42), and He has promised to make sure that the righteous "shine forth as the sun in the kingdom of their Father" (Matthew 13:43).

God is *patient*. He is the God of *patience* and *consolation* who wants all His children to be likewise in accordance to the teachings of His Firstborn Son, our Lord and Savior Jesus Christ (Romans 15:5). He waits, waits, and waits for His children to "humble themselves, and pray, and seek [His] face, and turn from their wicked ways" so that He can "heal" them (2 Chronicles 7:14); and He is the God who requests that His children be "sound in faith, in love, in *Patience* (Titus 2:2).

God is *long-suffering* from eternity past; however, His faithful creatures had never seen Him patiently endure the outright rebellion of His fallen creatures. In order "*to show His wrath and to make His power known*," He has up to now "endured with much *Longsuffering* the vessels of wrath prepared for destruction." He is not "slack concerning His promise"; nevertheless, He is "longsuffering toward us, not willing that any should perish but that all should come to repentance." Let us recall the fruit (the singularity of the noun in the New Testament belies the quantity and variety of its attributes) of the Spirit is *love, joy, peace, longsuffering, gentleness, goodness, faith, meekness, temperance.*

God is *impartial*. He is fair to all. His *impartiality* is based on His righteous and His loving and faithful dealings with all His created beings. The Jewish disciple of Jesus, Peter, was summoned by the Holy Spirit of God to Caesarea to preach the Gospel, God's good news of salvation to mankind, to a centurion of the Italian regiment named Cornelius and his entire household. Mindful of the separatist demands of his strict Judaist upbringing, which made no provision for any religious or racial intermingling between a Jew and a gentile, Peter was quite naturally inclined to recluse himself; however, the Lord showed him a vision that "what God has cleansed, [Peter] must not call common" (Acts 10:15). After meeting the gentile Cornelius and his household, Peter, finally realizing that the Lord does not allow racial favoritism, boldly exclaimed:

> In truth I perceive that God shows no *Partiality*.
> In every nation whoever fears Him and works righteousness is accepted of Him.

Commenting on God's *impartiality* in Old Testament times, Jesus makes the following remarkable observation:

> But I tell you truly, many widows were in Israel in the days of Elijah, when the heavens were shut up three years and six months, and there was a great famine throughout the land; but to none of them was Elijah sent except to Zarepath, in the region of Sidon, to a woman who was a widow.
> And many lepers were in Israel in the time of Elisha the prophet, and none of them was cleansed except Naaman the Syrian.

God's people, His sons of peace whom He chose before the foundation of the world, consist of all the Jews and gentiles whom He predestinated as heirs with Christ of the New Heavens and the New Earth that He will create at the end of this world.

Jesus chose to heal the centurion's servant of paralysis (Matthew 8:5, Luke 7:1) to demonstrate that He cares for the master as well as the servant. He restored to life the ruler's daughter in order to reveal that He is concerned with the young as well as the old (Matthew 9:18–23, Mark 5:22, 35, Luke 8:40, 49). He exorcised a Devil-possessed, blind and dumb man to illustrate that He does not disregard spiritual oppression and mental deficiency (Matthew 9:32). He cured the hemorrhaging woman to exhibit His concern for an unclean woman (Matthew 9:20, Mark 5:25, Luke 8:43). He renewed a man's withered hand to show His love for the handicapped (Matthew 12:9, Mark 3:1, Luke 6:6). He gave sight to two blind men to exemplify His love for the blind (Matthew 20:30, Mark 10:46, Luke 18:35). He cleansed the ten lepers to affirm His passion for the cast out, the homeless, and the downtrodden (Luke 17:11). He quickened the nobleman's son to authenticate that He values the upper, middle, and lower classes equally (John 4:46). God brought salvation to the household of the short in stature Zacchaeus (Luke 19), while picking the tall and physically imposing Saul as Israel's first king. He rescued from destruction the pagan prostitute Rahab (Joshua 2 and 6) and put her in Christ's lineage, while preserving the Virgin Mary (Matthew and Luke 1) as the mother of Jesus. God enlisted the Moabatess Ruth in the Israeli family (Ruth 1–4), the Jewish Hannah as the mother of Judge Samson (Judges 13:24), the barren Sarah as the mother of Isaac and the Jewish people (Genesis 11, 12, 16), the fruitful Leah (Genesis 29) as the prominent mother of the twelve tribes. Jesus was introduced as an infant to the octogenarian prophetess Anna who had lived with only one husband seven years from her virginity (Luke 2:36); and later in His ministry, He introduced Himself to a Samaritan woman who had had five husbands and was living with a man who was not her husband (John 4). God's kingdom is made of individuals of all nations, people, tongues, kindred (Revelation 7:9), tribes, races, classes, and every possible and conceivable types of demographic (the entire Holy Scriptures are referenced here). God revealed to the great prophet Samuel His modus operandi in His consideration of people in the following verse (1 Samuel 16:7): "Do not look [on] appearance…For the Lord does not see as man sees; for man looks at the outward appearance, but the Lord looks at the heart."

God is a *consuming fire* who devours sin, iniquity, unrighteousness, and anything unholy in all the worlds He has made (Hebrews 12:29). It is interesting to note that the Holy Scriptures *directly* (remember that word please!) assign to God only *four* nominal attributes: He is *Love* (1 John 4:16), He is *Spirit* (John 4:24), He is *Light* (1 John 1:5), and He is a *Consuming Fire* (Deuteronomy 4:24, Hebrews 12:29).

God *is*! Attributing adequately and completely qualities to a God who is *eternal*, *immortal*, *self-existent*, *almighty*, *all-knowing*, and *infinite* entails an impossible endeavor beyond the capabilities of any mortal! Not even *eternity* is sufficient to reveal God in all of His splendor, majesty, glory, and power. God, nonetheless, chose time as a valuable interlude between eternity past and eternity future for at least two basic reasons. First, God opted to reveal His attributes hitherto unknown to His creatures. Second, the Almighty willed to display in a more perfect way His attributes already familiar with His creatures.

God was from eternity past *merciful*; however, none of His wonderful creatures had ever experienced His mercy: there was no sin at all in all the worlds that God had amazingly created. Moreover, God's *perfection* warranted that His *mercy* be displayed in a *perfect* manner.

God was from eternity past a *consuming fire*. His *perfect wisdom*, nonetheless, required that His *righteous* judgment be manifest to all His creatures. Furthermore, His *holiness* warranted that He display to *all* His *perfect* remedy for unrighteousness and *wickedness*: Eternal destruction by His *consuming fire*!

God was *love* from eternity past; however, before the sacrifice of His Son on Calvary, no one had known the depth of His great love. By shedding His own blood (Acts 20:28) as the redeeming penalty for the sins of His people (Matthew 1:21), God demonstrated His *perfect love* to all His creatures: "Greater love has no one than this, than to lay down one's life for his friends," Jesus would declare.

God was *long-suffering* from eternity past; however, He opted to create and "endure" the rebellion and disobedience of the appointed "vessels of wrath prepared for destruction" in order to "make His *Power* known" and to "show His *Wrath*" as a *consuming fire* (Romans 9:22).

God was *meek* from eternity past. He, nonetheless, had never demonstrated to His creatures the depth of His meekness. In the person of our Lord and Savior Jesus Christ, God was in the fullness of time "made a little lower than the angels for the suffering of death" (Hebrews 2:9). He was "seen by angels" (1 Timothy 3:16) in the flesh and ministered by them (Mark 1:13) after fasting forty days and nights in the wilderness in the company of wild beasts and being tempted by the Devil.

God's *perfection* demands that His attributes be *fully* and *perfectly* displayed and experienced. The *perfect* exhibition of His attributes manifests the complete effulgence of His glory. Like the brilliant radiance of a rainbow, God's glory shines brilliantly when His attributes are on full display.

As such, a falling away was needed; an opponent with his own kingdom and the *perfect* set of opposite *values* and *attributes* exhibited by God had to initiate a frontal assault on God, His kingdom, and on all the *attributes* of His personhood.

The leader of the rebellion, like God, should be able to rule over a great company of God's creatures (a third of the angels and a majority of the human race would suffice here!) and should be allotted the proper time and space to establish and implement the rules of engagement of his kingdom.

The revolutionary leader and his associates should be given the power susceptible to "steal" members of God's kingdom and be given the opportunity to "kill" its leaders and members. They should have the right to "destroy" the kingdom of God, and…oh!…God Himself at first blush—the final checkmate of the Triune God would entail the complete elimination of Godliness and Godlikeness all across the universe!

All of God's creatures should be allowed to witness the quality of life in the kingdom of the revolutionary leader: A life of unrestrained *Godlessness*, complete *Unrighteousness*, and passionate *Hatred* could, at least in the theoretical mind of a valiant and quick-witted opponent, overcome the goody, goody, goody, loving, loving, loving, meek, meek, meek, meek, and apparently weak lifestyle of God and the members of His household. War should be declared on the *Peaceful* Godhead and on all the members of His family to disquiet their tranquility and make them question the raison d'etre of God Himself, His Way and His Truth. Would *evil* triumph over *good*? Would *hatred* overcome *love*? Would *unrighteousness* overwhelm *righteousness*? Would *wickedness* overtake *holiness*?

The answers to all those questions were quite obvious to the *Almighty* from eternity past; however, God, in His *perfect wisdom* and *absolute sovereignty*, opted to exhibit His *divine attributes* in a way hitherto unknown to all His creatures. And so, in the fullness of time, God "left [Lucifer and a third of the angels]," in order to "try [them]," so that "He might know all that was in [their] heart" (2 Chronicles 32:31, Deuteronomy 8:2).

Almost instantly, Lucifer began to reason within himself along the following lines:

> I will ascend into heaven,
> I will exalt my throne above the stars of God;
> I will also sit on the mount of the Congregation
> On the farthest sides of the North;
> I will ascend above the heights of the clouds,
> I will be like the Most High.

There…there…there…it started! Sin wrapped in swaddling covers of pride lying deep within the confines of Lucifer's heart. The seeds of an epic revolution susceptible of overthrowing God and His kingdom were germinating in the fertile soil of Lucifer's mind: God was preparing the perfect opponent that would challenge all the *attributes* of His character, declare war against His reign over the worlds He had created, and expose to the witnessing eyes of all His creatures the dire consequences of a kingdom where God is absent, where *hatred* rules, where *unrighteousness* is the modus operandi, where *pride* stands tall, where *holiness* is mocked, where *love* is ridiculed, where *meekness* is considered *weakness*, where *gratitude* is treated as *cowardice*, where *peace* is identified as *boredom*.

To formalize His kingdom, Lucifer was allowed to attract "a third of the stars of heaven" (Revelation 12:4) and to fight against the Most High. In that light, the Bible solemnly notes:

> And war broke out in heaven: Michael and his angels fought with the dragon; and the dragon and his angels fought, but they did not prevail, nor was a place found for them in heaven any longer.
>
> So the great dragon was cast out, that serpent of old, called the Devil and Satan, who deceives the whole world; he was cast to the earth, and his angels were with him.

Lucifer, who became Satan, the Dragon, the Great Dragon, the Devil, was permitted by God to rule with his cohorts of fallen angels over his kingdom of darkness and over the earth as a spectacle to the hosts of heaven and the inhabitants of the earth of the dire consequences of Satanic reign.

The whole world can now formally testify that Satan's kingdom is characterized by viruses, death, sorrow, crying, pain (Revelation 21:4), theft, murder, suicide, destruction (John 10:10), wars and rumors of wars (Matthew 24:6), corruption and violence (Genesis 6:11), wickedness and evil (Genesis 6:4), adultery, fornication, uncleanness, lewdness, idolatry, sorcery, hatred, contention, jealousy, outburst of wrath, selfish ambition, dissention, heresy, envy (Galatians 5:19), selfishness, covetousness, boasting, pride, blasphemy, disobedience, ingratitude, wickedness, hatred, truce breaking, lying, incontinence, strife, mocking, treason, godlessness (2 Timothy 3:2–5), lust of the flesh, lust of the eyes, pride of life (1 John 2:15–16), curses, confusion, rebuke, perdition, plagues, diseases, illnesses, defeat, enmity, phobias, madness, blindness, slavery, humiliation, famine, hunger, nakedness, natural disasters, plagues (Deuteronomy 28), terrorism, racism, secularism, aging, poverty, epidemics, earthquakes, hurricanes, typhoons, pornography, prostitution, drunkenness, cheating, hypocrisy, materialism, witchcraft, juvenile delinquency, child prostitution, kidnapping, extortion, futility, foolishness, darkness, vile passions, dishonor, hatred of God, debased mind, maliciousness, evil-mindedness, whispering, lack of discernment, backbiting, untrustworthiness, grudge, sexual immorality (Romans 1), crime, prejudice, discrimination, injustice, greed, bestiality, laziness, gluttonies, oppression, depression, recession, inflation, unemployment, economic crashes, plagues, curses, accidents, and all the other evils and ills manifest in our present world.

In the midst of that dark cacophony of doom and gloom, God's attributes shine even brighter than before: His *long-suffering* of the "vessels of wrath fitted for destruction" (Romans 9:22) is supercharging His *righteousness*, the underpinning of His kingdom and the real *peace* that it produces, to contrast sharply with the constant turmoil prominently featured in every country of the world, in every family, in the lives of most—if not all—of the citizens who now inhabit planet earth.

Lives are now being continually destroyed all over the world by the *unrighteousness* that undergird most—if not all—of the interactions of the citizens of the world. In fact, Satan himself, the prince of this world (John 12:31, 14:30, 16:11), the thief, killer, and destroyer-in-chief (John 10:10) "walks about like a roaring lion, seeking whom he may devour" (1 Peter 5:8).

The *love* of God, a prominent part of the essence of His nature, characterized in His Word by the Golden Rule—"Whatever you want men to do to you, do also to them" (Matthew 7:12) and "You shall love your neighbor as yourself" (James 2:8)—and well-articulated and demonstrated by Jesus in offering His life as a ransom for His friends: "Greater love has no one than this, than to lay down one's life for his friends" (John 15:13), proclaims Jesus to the entire universe in the face of the greed, selfishness, and self-righteousness en vogue in the hearts and minds of men and women living in a fallen world.

The *beauty* of the *holiness* of God stands in sharp contrast to the petty, ugly, mundane, dangerous, destructive, evil tendencies, inclinations, and activities that profligate the Satanic world system. The *holiness, justice,* and *righteousness* of God demand that He destroy all the works of the Devil and his demonic cohorts (1 John 3:8).

The Holy Scriptures declare that the entire creation "groans and labors with birth pangs" (Romans 8:22) awaiting its deliverance from the futility and the "bondage of corruption" of Satan's kingdom into "the glorious liberty of the children of God" when all of God's sons shall be revealed (Romans 8:19–22) to inherit the New Heavens and the New Earth that God has promised them (Revelation 21:1–2, Isaiah 65:17, 66:22).

The verdict has been rendered. The debate is over: "There is no wisdom nor understanding nor counsel against the Lord" (Proverbs 21:30). Time, that faint, fair, fickle, and factious interlude between eternity past and eternity future that God created as a little experiment to contrast to all His creatures His *perfect attributes* with the opposite set of attributes—or, for that matter, any other conceivable sets of attributes!—clearly and vividly demonstrates beyond a shadow of doubt the temerity, the arrogance, the ungratefulness, the foolishness, and the wickedness of any "high thing that exalts itself against the knowledge of God" (2 Corinthians 10:5). It also serves notice to any other creature in eternity future—should God decide once more to remove His presence and His grace—to argue for a Godless governance and existence.

Moreover, the manifestation of evil in time does not directly glorify God. It is not fair to proclaim that God takes pleasure in World War I, World War II, the terrorist attacks on 9/11, or any of the gory characteristics of evil identified earlier: God does not take pleasure in the death of the wicked (Ezekiel 33:11). God's *perfect attributes* shine brighter and purer in the midst of the greatest catastrophe that evil could muster: "where sin abounded, *Grace* abounded much more" (Romans 5:20). *Sin* had to appear for *grace* to unveil and exhibit *all* its brilliant features and kaleidoscopic contours.

To God be all the glory, the honor, the power, the majesty, and the victory forever and ever!

Chapter 10

The Bible Unveils God's Salvation Program for Mankind

Jesus answered and said unto them, *This is the work of God, that you believe* on him whom he has sent. (John 6:29)

For unto you it is *given* in the behalf of Christ, not only to *believe* on him, but also to *suffer* for his sake. (Philippians 1:29)

Ye have *not chosen me*, but *I have chosen you* and ordained you, that ye should go and bring forth fruit, and that your fruit should remain. (John 15:16)

No man can come to me, except the Father which has sent me draw him. (John 6:44)

The following words of Jesus, "For God so loved the world that He gave His only begotten Son, that whoever believes in Him should not perish but have everlasting life," arguably represent the most famous pronouncement ever uttered by anyone in the annals of history. They are more well-known than Martin Luther King's love resolution: "I have decided to stick with love. Hate is too great a burden to bear!" More people have quoted the most famous verse of the Bible than Fred R. Bernard's aphorism that "a picture is worth a thousand words." Harry S. Truman's political maxim of courage in the face of adversity, "If you can't stand the heat, get out of the kitchen," does not come close. Sun-Tzu's dictum to "keep your friends close and your enemies closer," and Howard Ruff's adage that "it wasn't raining when Noah built the Ark," do not hold a candle to John 3:16.

Jesus's summary statement of the Gospel—God's "good tidings of great joy…to all people" that were announced with felicitous pomp and magnificent fanfare by the heavenly choir of angels—represents the apotheosis of all of Scripture, the most singularly important, significant, and consequential words ever spoken by anyone under the sun.

Salvation, the unique expression that best characterizes John 3:16, exhibits the preeminent storyline of the most famous book of all time, the Bible. Salvation presupposes a rescue from a situation most undesirable: death, in this case, spiritual then physical.

The curtain slowly opened on the first act of the epic history of mankind to reveal Adam and Eve, God's original perfect couple, enjoying sweet paradise. God had created Adam from "the dust of the ground," had wonderfully and fearfully "breathed into his nostrils the breath of life," thereby producing "a living soul," and had "made" (the same Hebrew word God will use in commanding Noah in Genesis 6:14 to "make," or, one might argue, "build" an ark, thus anticipating the church to be "built" as the Bride of Christ; even as Eve was conceived when God "caused a deed sleep to fall on Adam," and pierced the side of his flesh, the church was then also constructed when God caused Christ, the "last Adam," to fall asleep and pierced his side as well!) the woman Eve and brought her to Adam as his wife and "help meet for him."

God's ominous command in Genesis 2:17 to the blissful pair, though straightforward and simple in its articulation, is nonetheless unquestionably the least understood in the entire Holy Writ. The misguided interpretation of that solitary proclamation alone has not only helped produce a wave of religious sects, but also has engendered a great deal of imbroglio in the Christian brotherhood.

Let me bravely and boldly articulate that the genesis of the enormous confusion that the word *salvation* elicits both within and without the Christian community stems from a careless and blatant disregard of the teaching of Genesis 2:17. In that realm, Adam and Eve were the forerunners of a great company of rebels.

In Genesis 2:17, the Almighty God issued the following command to Adam and Eve:

> But of the tree of the knowledge of good and evil, thou shalt not eat of it: for in the day that thou eatest thereof thou shalt surely die.

Let us review God's foreboding edict to Adam and Eve in layman's terms, "You must never eat of the tree of the knowledge of good and evil, for the *day* that you eat of it, *you will surely die*!" Let us remember that God does not play fiddle with His warnings. Numbers 23:19 remarks:

> God is not a man, that He should lie, nor a son of man, that He should repent. Has He said, and will He not do? Or has He spoken, and will He not make it good?

God had forewarned the aboriginal inhabitants of planet Earth that they would face *the death penalty* the day they would disobey Him and eat of the tree of the knowledge of good and evil. One must unequivocally determine the precise meaning of God's ominous statement before ascertaining its profound consequences and wonder with bated breath the type of death God had in mind.

Did God imply only physical death? It is historically accurate that Adam and Eve did not die physically the same day that they ate of the tree of the knowledge of good and evil. The Bible relates that Adam would survive to the ripe old age of 930 years! God did not relate in the Scriptures the timing of Eve's physical death. God's pronouncement of physical death on the fallen pair did eventually come to fruition.

Did the Almighty have in mind only psychological death? The Bible reveals that Adam and Eve were able to converse with God after their disobedience. Adam would argue to God that Eve was the one responsible for his disobedience, while Eve would make the point that she was beguiled by the serpent. We thus may correctly affirm that Adam and Eve did not die psychologically the exact day of their disobedience.

We may therefore justifiably conclude that God's declaration of *death* was fourfold: spiritual as a start (the loss of the presence of God, Genesis 3:8, the absence of fellowship with the Almighty, Genesis 3:10, the short-circuiting of the energy that the Holy Spirit provides, Romans 8:11, and finally the incapacitation of the human spirit, Psalm 51:10), then physical (both Adam—Genesis 5:5—and Eve would experience physical death), and then psychological (physical death always elicits the loss of consciousness, hence psychological death), and finally spiritual again (anyone who does not experience regeneration, that is, the second birth, will have to confront the Second Death in the lake of fire appropriately surnamed hell [John 3:3, 16; Revelation 20:14 and 15]), thus completing the perfect cycle of death—the Second Death representing the complete destruction of the soul in hell, (again Revelation 20:15), the eternal separation from the presence of God, who makes the following ominous assertion in Revelation 20:14: "And death and hell were cast into the lake of fire. This is the second death."

What does spiritual death entail? What did God have in mind when He warned Adam and Eve that they would "*die*" the day they would eat of the tree of knowledge of good and evil? Let's examine the behavior of the fallen pair after their mortal act of disobedience.

The Bible declares that "[t]he eyes of both of them were opened, and they knew that they were naked; and they sewed fig leaves together and made themselves coverings." Subsequently, they "[h]id themselves from the presence of the Lord God among the trees of the garden."

Their *free will* to turn to God, to initiate any meaningful interaction with the Almighty, and to have a genuine relationship with the Creator, who had so "fearfully and wonderfully" made them and had placed them in a perfect environment, was *permanently lost*: they were categorically and irrevocably *dead spiritually*, unless and until the God to whom nothing is impossible could resurrect or quicken or give life to their *dead spirits*, thereby guaranteeing them a new spiritual birth so that for all practical purposes they would be *born again*!

The Bible identifies the *spiritually dead* as able to carry multiple activities physically and psychologically, but not spiritually:

> They ate, they drank, they married wives, they were given in marriage, until the day that Noah entered the ark, and the flood came and destroyed them all. Likewise as it was also in the days of Lot: They ate, they drank, they bought, they sold, they planted, they built; but the day that Lot went out of Sodom it rained fire and brimstone from heaven and destroyed them all.

"Let the dead bury their own dead," Jesus would proclaim in Luke 9:60. The natural tendency of the *spiritually dead* is to become and remain very much occupied in the material, physical, romantic, financial, social, cultural, philosophical, and intellectual realms of life, while exhibiting simultaneously no vital sign of any kind of authentic and godly spirituality whatsoever: the *spiritually dead* will always run away and hide from the presence of God, and to appease their conscience of any godly remorse, they will "cover" (Genesis 3:7) themselves with "philosophy and vain deceit, after the tradition of men, after the rudiments of the world, and not after Christ," for they are matter-of-factly *spiritually dead*.

Watchman Nee, the preeminent Chinese Christian, illustrates the point:

> The life of an unregenerated person almost entirely is governed by the soul.
>
> He may be living in fear, curiosity, joy, pride, pity, pleasure, delight, wonder, shame, love, remorse, elation.
>
> Or he may be full of ideas, imaginations, superstitions, doubts, suppositions, inquiries, inductions, deductions, analyses, introspections.
>
> Or he may be moved-by the desire for power, wealth, social recognition, freedom, position, fame, praise, knowledge-into making many daring decisions, into personally arbitrating, into voicing stubborn opinions, or even undergoing patient endurance. All these and other like things are merely manifestations of the soul's three main functions of emotion, mind and will.

Furthermore, the *spiritually dead* individuals are naturally inclined to pay particular "heed to deceiving spirits and doctrines of demons" and will, left alone, never be "able to come to the knowledge of the truth."

Looking through the corridors of time, the Lord God took inventory of all the children of men "to see if there are any who understand, who seek God." The verdict of the Supreme Judge:

> There is none righteous, no, not one: there is none who understands, there is none who seeks after God.
>
> They have all turned aside; they have together become unprofitable; there is none who does good, no, not one.

They are all in fact *dead*! Thy are *dead* to any king of fellowship with the Holy God of the Bible. They are *dead* to any sort of relationship with the mighty Creator of the entire universe. They are *dead* in the very nexus of their beings and are therefore incapable of any meaningful spiritual activity vis-à-vis the *Lord God* Almighty: man's *free will*, the freedom that had enabled him to choose whom to obey, God or Satan, was forever lost when he foolishly sold his God-given birthright to Lucifer for a bowl of the fruit of the knowledge of good and evil.

A *spiritually dead* person has *no saving faith*! A *spiritually dead* individual cannot *accept* the redemption of Christ. A *spiritually dead* soul cannot and will not *receive* the message of the Gospel, for he/she is *spiritually dead*!

What then can the *spiritually dead* do to be saved? *Nothing*! *Nothing*! *Nothing*! He/she is and remains *spiritually dead* until a *Living Force* can energize him/her spiritually; otherwise, he/she was not really *spiritually dead*! How then can anybody be saved? Voila! The Savior, the *Lord God* thunders from heaven (Romans 10:17): "So then faith comes by hearing, and hearing by the word of God!"

Let us carefully outline the three main elements succinctly presented here in the salvation sequence: *Faith*, then *hearing*, and finally, *the Word of God*. Most Bible readers, students, and sadly many pastors, theologians, and biblical scholars commit the obvious mistake of making *faith* the starting point of the salvation sequence: actually *it is the last*! The real, applicable, and saving sequence follows: *the Word of God* first and foremost, then *hearing*, and finally *faith*.

A *spiritually dead* human being does not and could not possibly have saving faith! *The Word of God* must first be preached or presented to him/her. Second, *the Word of God* must cause him/her to *hear*: let us remember that the *spiritually dead* has no godly spiritual senses operational in as much as the *physically dead*'s five senses are totally inactive.

A *physically dead* human being cannot see, hear, smell, touch, or taste anything pertaining to this material and physical world. Likewise, a *spiritually dead* person cannot "in spirit and in truth" (John 4:24) worship God, nor can he/she initiate any meaningful fellowship with the Holy God of the Bible: he/she is totally incapable of exercising his/her three spiritual senses—conscience, intuition, and communion—for meaningful fellowship with Almighty God.

In his critically acclaimed masterpiece, *The Spiritual Man*, Watchman Nee makes the following insightful comments with regard to man's spiritual senses:

> According to the teaching of the Bible and the experience of believers, the human spirit can be said to comprise three parts; or, to put it another way, one can say, it has three main functions. These are conscience, intuition and communion.

Brother Watchman Nee then painstakingly outlines the biblical support for his remarkable observation:

A) The Function of Conscience in Man's Spirit
    "The Lord your God *hardened* his spirit" Deut. 2.30
    "Saves the *crushed* in spirit" Ps. 34.18
    "Put a new and *right* spirit within me" Ps. 51.10
    "When Jesus had thus spoken, he was *troubled* in spirit" John 13.21
    "His sprit was *provoked* within him as he saw that the city was full of idols" Acts 17.16

"It is the Spirit Himself bearing *witness* with our spirit that we are *children* of God" Rom. 8.16

"I am present in spirit, and as if present, I have already *pronounced judgment*" 1 Cor. 5.3

"I had no *rest* in my spirit" 2 Cor. 2.13 AV

"For God did not give us the spirit of *timidity*" 2 Tim. 1.7

B) The Function of Intuition in Man's Spirit
"The spirit indeed is *willing*" Matt. 26.41
"Jesus *perceiving* in his spirit" Mark 2.8
"He *sighed* deeply in his spirit" Mark 8.12
"He was deeply *moved* in spirit" John 11.33
"Paul was *pressed* in the spirit" Acts 18.5AV
"Being *fervent* in spirit" Acts 18.25
"I am going *to* Jerusalem, *bound* in the spirit" Acts 20.22
"What person *knows* a man's thoughts except the spirit of the man which is in him" 1 Cor. 2.11
"They *refreshed* my spirit as well as yours" 1 Cor. 16.18
"His spirit was *refreshed* by you all" 2 Cor. 7.13AV

C) The Function of Communion in Man's Spirit
"My sprit *rejoices* in God my Savior" Luke 1.47
"The true worshipers will *worship* the Father in spirit and truth" John 4.23
"Whom I *serve* with my spirit" Rom.1.9
"We *serve*…in the new life of the spirit" Rom. 7.6
"You have received the spirit of sonship when we *cry* Abba Father" Rom. 8.15
"The Spirit himself bearing witness *with* our spirit" Rom. 8.16
"He who is *united* to the Lord becomes one spirit with him" 1 Cor. 6.17
"I will *sing* with the spirit" 1 Cor. 14.15
"If you *bless* with the spirit" 1 Cor. 14.16
"In the spirit he *carried me away*" Rev. 21.10

Cut off from the Life of God or the Holy Spirit, the conscience of a *spiritually dead* man's spirit cannot and will not lead him to a life of fellowship with God. We read the sad but true account of Judas Iscariot in Matthew 27:3–5:

> Then Judas, which had betrayed him, when he saw that [Jesus] was condemned, repented himself, and brought again the thirty pieces of silver to the chief priests and elders, saying I have sinned in that I have betrayed innocent blood. And they said, What is that to us? See thou to that. And he cast down the pieces of silver in the temple, and departed, and went and hanged himself.

Without the regenerative assistance of the Holy Spirit, the intuition of a *spiritually dead* individual's spirit cannot be "instructed in the way of the Lord" (Acts 18:25) and will not receive "the spirit of wisdom and revelation in the knowledge of [Jesus]" (Ephesians 1:17).

Devoid of the presence of the life of God, the communion of a spiritually dead person's spirit "rejoices [not] in God" (Luke 1:47) and absolutely cannot "worship [God]…in truth" (John 4:24).

This is where the rubber meets the road, the quintessence of the entire salvation mystery. It is significant that the Word of God nowhere uses the active verbs *receive* and *accept* in the aforementioned salvation sequence. *The Word of God* must have "quickened" or "made…alive" (Ephesians 2:1, 5; Colossians 2:13) the *spiritually dead* in order for saving *faith* to be realized.

The psalmist, under the auspices of the Holy Spirit, proclaims in Psalm 119:50 that God's "word hath quickened me." *The Word of God* is in fact "quick and powerful" (Hebrew 4:12) to enable the *spiritually dead* to *hear*, and thereby *receive* and *accept* saving *faith*.

St. Augustine, one of the greatest biblical expositors of all time, expresses the same sentiment:

> Now if faith is simply of free will, and is not given by God, why do we pray for those who will not believe, that they may believe?
>
> This would be absolutely useless to do, unless we believe, with perfect propriety, that Almighty God is able to turn to beliefs wills that are perverse and opposed to faith.

Charles Spurgeon, arguably the best prolific preacher of all time, opines:

> Is not the sinner by nature dead in sin? And if God requires him to make himself alive, and then afterward he will do the rest for him, then verily, my friends, we are not so much obliged to God as we had thought; for if he require so much as that of us, and we can do it, we can do the rest without his assistance.

If God is in fact the "author and finisher of…faith" (Hebrews 12:2), could there be "unrighteousness with God" (Romans 9:14) in granting merciful faith (Romans 9:15) to some and not activating the hearing of others (Romans 9:18)? God categorically answers, "I will have mercy on whom I will have mercy, and I will have compassion on whom I will have compassion."

It logically follows that the apostle Paul, under the directives of the Holy Spirit, would make the same conclusion: "Therefore God has mercy on whom He wants to have mercy, and He hardens whom He wants to harden."

Following the same drift, Dr. D. James Kennedy opines:

> Again and again we see that people are predestined (elected) to salvation—but nowhere do we see that anyone is ever predestined to condemnation of Hell.
>
> When we think of God as unfairly, arbitrarily electing people to Heaven or Hell, it is as if we have a mental picture of a row of people sitting on a fence, and God passes down the line and points at each one, "It's Hell for you, Heaven for

you, Hell, Hell, Hell, Heaven, Hell…" Now, that would be unfair—and absolutely capricious! But that's not the kind of God that we serve.

Dr. R. C. Sproul, considering the apparent albeit untrue appearance of injustice and unfairness on the part of God in granting mercy on whom He wills and in hardening the hearts of others, makes the following insightful observation:

> If God chooses sovereignly to bestow His grace on some sinners and withhold His grace from some other sinners, is there any violation of justice in this? If we look at those who do not receive this gift, do they receive something they do not deserve? Of course not! If God allows these sinners to perish, is He treating them unjustly? Of course not! One group receives grace; the other receives justice: No one receives injustice!

If the sovereignty of God is so prominently featured in the salvation process, why then does God still "find fault" (Romans 9:19) with the *spiritually dead* since his/her lack of faith (Hebrews 11:6) makes it "impossible to please Him?"

"On the contrary," retort the Holy Scriptures, "who are you, o man, who answers back to God?" Indeed, the potter has the prerogative "over the clay, to make from the same lump one vessel for honorable use and another for common use."

It then becomes quite clear why the Holy Scriptures insist that individuals can only be saved by the FAITH OF JESUS CHRIST!" In Galatians 2:16, we read from the Word of God:

> Knowing that a man is not justified by the works of the law, but by the faith of Jesus Christ, even we have believed in Jesus Christ, that we might be justified by the faith of Christ, and not by the works of the law: for by the works of the law shall no flesh be justified.

The New International Version, the American Standard Bible, the Interlinear Bible, and various other prominent translations of the Bible err majestically in opting to translate the terms "faith of Jesus Christ" for "faith in Jesus Christ," thus tragically opening the door for the biblically incorrect notion of human participation and intervention in the divine act of salvation.

God, in His sovereign wisdom, chose the Greek genitive case *of* and rejected the locative case *in*, in describing the "author" of the word *faith* in prominent display in this important verse. The translators, by inserting the little word *in* instead of the grammatically correct *of*, have made it possible to attribute saving faith to the *spiritually dead*!

The Holy Scriptures further relate in Galatians 2:20 that those that are spiritually raised from the dead and are made spiritually alive owe their existence to the "faith of the Son of God." Again, the genitive case (of the Son of God as opposed to in the Son of God) was selected to describe the originator of the faith in view here.

Writing, under the auspices of the Holy Spirit, to the "foolish" Galatian Christians "bewitched" by the false teaching of the Judaisers who were advocating the observance of the works of the law for salvation, the apostle Paul wondered, "Did you receive the Spirit by the works of the law, or by the *Hearing* of *Faith*?"

Paul quickly answers:

> But the scripture hath concluded all under sin, that the promise by faith of Jesus Christ might be given to them that believe.

Here again, the genitive case is used to affirm that the faith of "them that believe" is none other than the "faith of Jesus Christ." We may then conclude that the faith that God utilizes to save the heathen (Galatians 3:8) is also the "faith of Jesus Christ."

It is interesting to note the Word of God maintains (Ephesians 3:12) that "we have boldness and access with confidence by the faith of Him." The "Him" of verse 12 modifies the Jesus Christ our Lord (of verse 11) who has granted us the right to "come boldly to the throne of grace, that we may obtain mercy and find grace to help in time of need." Once more, the saving faith that pleases God is the "faith of Jesus."

The Holy Scriptures continue in Colossians 2:12.

> Buried with him in baptism, wherein also ye are risen with him through the faith of the operation of God, who hath raised him from the dead.

The faith that frees the *spiritually dead* from the claws of death is "of the operation of God," and not of man! Such a marvelous revelation prompted the apostle Paul to write:

> Yea doubtless, and I count all things but loss for the excellency of the knowledge of Christ Jesus my Lord for whom I have suffered the loss of all things, and do count them but dung that I may win Christ, and be found in him, not having mine own righteousness, which is of the law, but that which is through the faith of Christ, the righteousness which is of God by faith.

Indeed, the faith that has raised countless of *spiritually dead* from the power of spiritual death, the "*Common Faith*" (Titus 1:4) of all believers spanning the Old and New Testaments, "*the Faith of the Saints*" (Revelation 13:10) of God throughout the history of the world, "*the Faith of God's Elect*" (Titus 1:1), the bride of Christ, "*the Faith of the Gospel*" (Philippians 1:27) of Jesus Christ, "*the Faith of Abraham*" (Romans 4:16), which can only be identified as "*the Faith of Our Lord Jesus Christ*" (James 2:1 and Revelation 14:12). He is called (Revelation 3:14, 19:11) the *faithful*.

We all must be keenly aware that the word *faith* in Greek (*pistis*) is a derivative of the active verb *believe* (*pisteuo*); in that light, the Bible lists *faith* as a by-product of *work*. In 1 Thessalonians 1:3, the apostle Paul remarks to the saints in Thessalonica the following:

> Remembering without ceasing your work of faith, and labor, and labor of love, and patience of hope in our Lord Jesus Christ, in the sight of God and our Father.

In 2 Thessalonians 1:11, the beloved apostle continues:

> Wherefore also we pray always for you, that our God would count you worthy of this calling, and fulfill all the good pleasure of his goodness, and the work of faith with power.

We must pay particular attention to the important phrase "*work of faith*" mentioned in both verses. Faith is indeed the residue of work. We are saved by works after all, the wonderful works of our Lord and Savior Jesus Christ who performed all the works of the law of God. Since faith is a work, it then becomes amazingly clear that our individual faith could not possibly save us.

The Bible forcefully proclaims:

> For by grace are ye saved through faith; and that not of yourselves: it is the gift of God: Not of works, lest any man should boast.
> For we are his workmanship, created in Christ Jesus unto good works, which God hath before ordained that we should walk in them.

We are indeed saved by faith, the *faith of Jesus Christ*. It is interesting that the Word of God declares that saving faith is a *gift of God*! It is not the result of our "*work of faith*," we would then have plenty of ground to boast in the sight of Almighty God.

What about the numerous biblical references where it is grammatically correct to accept the translation "faith in Jesus Christ?" Let us examine all of them.

In Galatians 3 verse 26, the Word of God declares, "For ye are all the children of God by faith in Christ Jesus." The Word of God clearly uses the locative case (*in* or *at*) here. The original statement even makes use of the Greek preposition *en* (our English *in*), thereby guaranteeing the correct translation of "faith in Christ."

In Ephesians 1:15, we read, "Wherefore I also, after I heard of your faith in the Lord Jesus, and love unto all the saints." Again, the preposition *in* warrants the locative case to justify the translation: "faith in the Lord."

Colossians 1:3–4 states:

> We give thanks to God and the Father of our Lord Jesus Christ, praying always for you, since we heard of your faith in Christ Jesus, and of the love which ye have to all the saints.

The Greek *in* and the locative case are displayed here as well to indicate the correct translation is "faith in Christ Jesus."

The apostle Paul relates to Timothy, his beloved disciple the following:

> And from a child thou hast known the holy scriptures, which are able to make thee wise unto salvation through faith which is in Christ Jesus. (2 Timothy 3:15)

Both the Greek preposition *in* and the locative case are used to affirm the correct translation: "faith in Christ Jesus."

The Word of God in Acts 24:24 reveals:

> And after certain days, when Felix came with his wife Drusilla, which was a Jewess, he sent for Paul, and heard him concerning the faith in Christ.

Here, the literal translation "concerning the into Christ faith" is properly rendered "concerning the faith in Christ." The Greek preposition *eis* (into) is better translated as the English preposition *in*.

In his prominent discourse to King Agrippa (Acts 26:18), Paul argued to the king that the Lord Jesus Himself, concerning the gentiles, had given him (Paul the Apostle) the following commands:

> To open their eyes, and to turn them from darkness to light, and from the power of Satan unto God, that they may receive forgiveness of sins, and inheritance among them which are sanctified by faith that is in me.

Again, the Word of God uses the preposition *eis*, our English *in*, with the accusative case *eme* to justify the correct translation "faith that is in me."

In Colossians 2:5, Paul, while exhorting the Christians at Colosse to continue to grow in their knowledge of our Lord Jesus, commended them for their consistency of their "faith in Christ." The Word of God again uses the Greek preposition *eis* to indicate our English *in* in the proper translation of "faith in Christ."

We can correctly argue that the Holy Scriptures do differentiate between the phrases "faith of Jesus Christ" and "faith in Jesus Christ" by the use of the preposition *in* with either the locative (*in* or *at*) or the accusative case (our English direct complement) to designate the latter and the genitive case to indicate the former.

As a result, the translation by so many prominent versions of the Bible of "faith in Jesus," or "faith in Jesus Christ," or "faith in Christ," or "faith in Christ Jesus" when the genitive case clearly and correctly warrants "faith of Jesus," or "faith of Jesus Christ," or "faith of Christ," or "faith of Christ Jesus" is truly grammatically inexcusable. It has opened the door for the theologically incorrect teaching that human intervention plays a role in the salvation process.

If we are saved by our "faith in Jesus Christ," saving faith then must stem from our personal assent, or acceptance, or reception, or belief in Jesus Christ, a truly spiritual impossibility, since we are spiritually dead!

We are saved by the "*faith of Jesus Christ!*" That faith, acquired through the "*hearing*" of the "*Word of God*" is apprehended and becomes our own personal "*faith in Jesus Christ*."

In all the preceding cases where an iteration of "faith in Jesus Christ" is mentioned, the Word of God assumes an a priory reception of "faith of Jesus Christ" by the individual or the parties involved.

The contextualized setting of Galatians 3:26 illustrates the point brilliantly. After identifying the recipients of his letter as his "brethren" (verse 11 of chapter 1) who had received "the promise by faith of Jesus Christ" (verse 22), the apostle then reminded them of their glorious status of "children of God by faith in Christ Jesus (verse 26). Their faith *in* Christ Jesus was the residue of the faith *of* Jesus Christ, which had been given to them earlier.

Paul "gave thanks" (Ephesians 1:16) to God for the faith of the Ephesians "in the Lord Jesus" (verse 15) after calling them "saints" (verse 1) who were "faithful" (verse 1) as a result of the faith of Jesus Christ, which had been granted to them.

The apostle Paul, after calling the Colossians "saints," and "faithful brethren" (Colossians 1:1*)*, gave "thanks to God and the Father of our Lord Jesus Christ" (verse 3) for their "faith *in* Christ Jesus" (verse 4), the gift they had received when they were spiritually made alive.

In 2 Timothy 3:15, Apostle Paul gave Timothy, his young apprentice, the following words of advice:

> But continue thou in the things which thou hast learned and hast been assured of, knowing of whom thou hast learned them; and that from a child thou hast known the holy scriptures, which are able to make thee wise unto salvation through faith which is in Christ Jesus.

We need to remark that the venerable apostle acknowledges that the Holy Scriptures, which are "able to make [Timothy] wise unto salvation through faith which is in Christ Jesus," were presented and preached to the young Timothy. The faith that Timothy had in Jesus Christ was the consequence of that preaching.

In Acts 24:24, the Bible relates that Felix heard Paul "concerning the faith in Christ." The faithful apostle preached the Word of God to both Felix and his wife. Did they *hear* the Word of God? Physically, they did; however, were they able to *hear* spiritually? The Word of God is silent, and so are we.

What about the verses where Jesus seems to indicate salvation based on the personal faith of the individual? "Thy faith hath saved thee" (Luke 7:50), Jesus would proclaim to the woman who anointed His feet with the alabaster box of ointment.

"Thy faith has saved thee" (Luke 18:42), Jesus would declare to the blind man who had requested that He should heal him of blindness? "Thy faith hath made thee whole," Jesus would utter to various individuals in Matthew 9:22, Mark 5:34, Mark 10:52, Luke 8:48, 17:19.

The Word of God answers in Ephesians 2:8 and 9:

> For by grace are ye saved through faith; and that not of yourselves: it is the gift of
> God; not of works, lest any man should boast.

The different individuals to whom those comments were addressed had all previously received the faith of Jesus Christ, which has now become their suggestive faith in Jesus Christ. When the Holy Scriptures assert (Habakkuk 2:4 and Hebrews 10:38*)* that "the just shall live by faith," we must recognize that the individual that "shall live by faith" has already been declared "just" by the faith of Jesus he had already received: he will most assuredly live by his faith in Jesus Christ.

Let us also recall that faith is a consequence of the presence of the Holy Spirit: Galatians 5:22, where faith is listed as the seventh "fruit" of the Holy Spirit, makes the case succinctly clear. The corollary must also be true: where the Holy Spirit is absent, as it is in the life of the unbeliever, faith will be absent also!

Moreover, when the Jews asked Jesus what they should do to that [they] might work the works of God (John 6:28). Our Savior answered thusly in verse 29b: "This is the WORK of God, that you believe in Him whom He sent." In other words, Jesus plainly related to His questioners that to *believe* in Him (Jesus) is a *work* that *only* God can accomplish: man is thus saved not by his *work* of believing in Jesus but by the *work* of God causing him to hear first and foremost the *Word* of God and then to *believe* in His Son Jesus Christ.

What about the numerous verses in the Scriptures attesting justification by faith (Romans 3:24, 28, 30, 5:1, 9:30)? The faith in view is undeniably the *common faith*, the *faith of the saints*, the *faith of God's elect*, the *faith of the Gospel*—all stemming from the *faith of our Lord Jesus Christ*.

The case is closed, the matter settled: salvation is indeed of the Lord and—of the Lord only! The critics who argue that human participation or involvement—one must *accept*, or *believe*, or *receive* the free gift that God has provided—make God a liar when He mysteriously linked *sin* with *spiritual death* (Genesis 2:17, Ezekiel 18:20, Deuteronomy 24:16, Romans 6:23).

In that light, they must explain what God had in mind when He clearly and categorically pronounced the death sentence on anyone found with sin. They must also attribute to the *spiritual dead* the ability to self-resurrect spiritually in order to *hear, understand, accept,* and *receive* the commands of God to believe in Jesus Christ for salvation (1 Corinthians 2:14, Acts 16:31, 1 Thessalonians 4:14).

Sadly, that perception of the doctrine of soteriology, where human participation and responsibility are prominently featured in the salvation process (the *spiritually dead* has to "sign the check" presented by God in order to "cash in" his salvation bargain!), has found its way in numerous Christian communities and has done a tremendous disservice to the clear teaching of the Word of God.

Charles R. Swindoll, one of the famous articulators of the Gospel in the world today, illustrates the point clearly:

> The standard of righteousness is belief in Jesus Christ.
> Whoever believes in Him will be square, plumb, and level with the cornerstone.

Continues our preeminent preacher with a global audience of nearly two thousand radio stations:

> Furthermore, everyone is responsible to meet the standard of the gospel—belief—because the good news is intended for everyone. Some theologians object to this because responding in faith to the gospel appears too much like a good deed. By their reasoning, if people have the ability to believe in Christ of their own free

will, then they can claim credit for their own salvation. Because we know that no one can be declared righteous except by the gracious act of God. It follows that his belief in Christ must not be freely and independently chosen, but compelled by the Holy Spirit. This doctrine (called 'irresistible grace' by theologians) is the result of reasoning that sounds logical, but finds no direct support in the Bible. If we continue this line of reasoning, you must conclude that only those who are compelled by the Holy Spirit have the ability to accept the gift of Christ's atonement.

The proposition that salvation can be "freely and independently chosen" by the *spiritually dead* without being "compelled by the Holy Spirit" enjoys the support of many in diverse Christian circles. Moreover, various biblical scholars posit the following interesting soteriology:

The New Testament speaks of salvation in three Greek tenses.
In the past, the believer has been saved from the penalty of sin (Eph. 2:8).
In the present, the believer is being saved from the power of sin (2 Cor. 2:15).
In the future, the believer will be saved from the presence of sin (Rom. 13:11, Matt. 5:10–12, Rev. 22:12).

So, you are a spiritually dead individual who has mysteriously and providentially come into contact with the *Word of God* through a simple conversation, a sermon, a message, an unusual event, or through the Holy Scriptures, and you ask, "What must I do to be saved?" The *Word of God* immediately and categorically commands you to "believe on the Lord Jesus, and you will be saved, you and your household."

If you were then given *"ears to hear"* the living *Word of God*, then you have now received the *faith of Jesus Christ*! You are now *born again*! You have been *regenerated*! Your human spirit has been *quickened* or *made alive*! The *Holy Spirit* has come to *indwell* your human spirit! The Triune God has come to make an *abode* in your spirit. You have become a *child of God*, a *son* of the *Living God*! The *Lord Jesus* will manifest Himself to you! You are now "an *heir of God*" through *Jesus Christ*! You have *eternal life*! You are now a member of the "*household of faith*." You are a *fellow citizen with the saints and of the household of God*! You are a *partaker* of the glory that shall be revealed. You have been *justified by faith*! You have *peace with God* through our *Lord and Savior Jesus Christ*! You are *blessed of God*! *All your sins* have been *washed away*! You have become a *new creature*! You have been freed from the *bondage of sin and of death*! Your name is now *written in heaven in the Book of the Lamb*! You are no longer under *condemnation*! But you have *crossed over from death to life*! You have been given *power to bear spiritual fruit that will glorify your Heavenly Father*! The *Holy Spirit* has enabled you to be a *witness of the Good News of forgiveness in Jesus Christ*! You have been *given the gift of righteousness by faith in Jesus*! You have been *united with Christ in His death and resurrection*! *All Things will work together for your good*! You have been *sanctified in Christ Jesus and have been called to be holy*! *The things that God has prepared for you are beyond human comprehension and imagination*! *All things—the world, and life and death, and the present and the future—are yours*! *Your body has now become a temple of the*

Holy Spirit! You are now not your own: you were bought with a great price, the blood of the Lamb of God! God, your Father of compassion, will comfort you in all your troubles! GOD *will always lead you in triumphal procession of Christ, and you will always spread to others the fragrance of His knowledge! As you behold Jesus, you are being transformed into His likeness with ever increasing glory! You have Christ in you as a treasure, and the all-surpassing power of God dwells in you! You have now become the righteousness of God! You have been rescued from the present evil age! It is no longer you who live, but Christ lives in you! You have been baptized into Christ and have put on Christ! You are Abraham's seed and heir according to the Promise! You will produce the fruit of the Spirit: love, joy, peace, patience, kindness, goodness faithfulness, gentleness, and self-control! You have been blessed in the heavenly realms with every spiritual blessing!* God has *chosen you* before the foundation of the world to be *holy* and *blameless* in His sight! *You* have been *saved* by grace through *God's gift* of *faith! You are God's workmanship created in Christ Jesus to do good works, which God has prepared in advance for you to do! God is able to do immeasurably more than you ask or can imagine according to His power at work in you!* Your identity in Christ was created to be like God in true righteousness and holiness! *You were once darkness, but now are light in the Lord! He who began a good work in you will carry it to completion until the day of Jesus Christ! God will work in you to do and to will according to His good purpose!* God will *meet all your needs* according to *His riches* in *Christ Jesus! Your Heavenly Father has qualified you to share in the inheritance of the saints in the Kingdom of Light!* God has *rescued you from darkness and brought you into the kingdom of His Beloved Son in whom you have redemption, the forgiveness of your sins!* You have been *reconciled to God through Christ's death* so that *you can be presented as holy in His sight without blemish and free from any kind of accusation!* Christ, *the mystery of God's riches, lives in you!* God has *made you alive with Christ and has forgiven all your sins! You have been raised with Christ, and your life is now hidden with Christ in God!* When Christ appears, *you will also appear with Him in glory! You are one of God's chosen people, and you are holy and dearly loved by Him! You have been rescued from the coming wrath!* You have been *called to be holy and blameless in the presence of God, your Father, when the Lord Jesus Christ returns with His holy ones! You will be with the Lord forever!* You have *received salvation through your Lord and Savior Jesus Christ!* God will *sanctify you completely* so that *your spirit and soul and body* will be *blameless* at the *coming of your Lord and Savior Jesus Christ!* God will *reward you* for *suffering for the sake of the Gospel!* God will *glorify Jesus Christ through you! You will share in the glory of your Lord and Savior Jesus Christ!* God has *richly provided everything for your enjoyment!* God has not given you a spirit of timidity, but *a spirit of power, a spirit of love, and a spirit of self-control!* God has *saved you* and has *called you to live a holy life!* God will guard what you have entrusted to Him for the day when *you will see Him in all of His glory! You will reign with your Lord Jesus Christ in His kingdom of glory!* You have been *equipped* for *every good work!* Jesus, who is now *interceding for you, will save you completely when He returns!* God has *called* and *saved you* to *give you the promised eternal inheritance! You have been given the faith to please God!* God, *your Heavenly Father, will give you every good and perfect gift! You will be blessed in all that you do!* God has *known* and *chosen you* according to His *wisdom* and *foreknowledge* that *you should obey the Lord Jesus Christ and be sanctified by the Holy Spirit!* God has given you *mercy, new birth, living hope, and an inheritance that can never perish! You have been redeemed by the precious blood of Jesus Christ and born again by the Living Word of God! You are part of a chosen people, a royal priesthood, a holy nation, a people belonging to God Himself! You must now die to sin and live for righteousness*! The wounds of Jesus have *healed you* and will *heal you completely*! God *cares so much for you that you should learn to cast all your cares upon Him and stop being anxious*! The God who has *called you to His eternal glory will restore you and make you strong, steadfast, and firm*! God has given you everything you need to have abundant life and live a godly life! You have *received great and precious promises so that you might participate in the divine nature and escape the corruption in the world*! You now have to make *your calling and election sure by growing in grace, faith, knowledge, goodness, perseverance, self-control, and brotherly love*! *You will live in the New Heaven and New Earth where righteousness dwells*! You must have *fellowship with all the brothers and sisters in the Church of Jesus Christ as His blood purifies you from all types of sins*! When you do sin, remember *you have been advocated to God the Father concerning your sins*! God has *lavished His great love on you by calling you His child, and you are His child indeed*! God has *given you eternal life, the life that is in His Son Jesus Christ*! *If you ask God anything according to His will, you can be sure He will hear you*! *You will be like Jesus, for you will see Him as He is*! The truth of the Gospel of Jesus will live in you forever! *Your faithfulness to the Gospel of Jesus should be to you a source of great joy*! *God has given you an abundance of His peace, mercy, love, and grace*! *The Lord will give you the power and ability to be holy and faithful and to pray in the Holy Spirit*! *The mercy of your Lord Jesus Christ has surely given you the eternal life that He has promised to you*! You will receive blessings upon blessings by reading and practicing the prophetic words of God! Christ has given you the right to sit on His throne! *You will reign with your Lord and Savior Jesus Christ forever and ever*! Since you have partaken in the First Resurrection, the Second Death has no power over you! God Himself will wipe all tears from your eyes, and you will experience no more death, no more crying, no more pain! You will eat of the Tree of Life and drink of the Water of Life, and God will give you a new name, and for eternity, He will call you His son!

Hallelujah! Praise the Lord!

Appendix I

How Do We Find the Jubilee Years?

The timing of the Exodus holds the key to the discovery of the Jubilee years. God had commanded the Israelites to celebrate the Jubilee Feast fifty years after their entrance into the Promised Land, one year after the Sabbath Jubilee (Leviticus 25:8–17).

As such, in order to determine the first Sabbath year and the first Jubilee year the children of Israel spent in the Promised Land, we must first identify the year of the Exodus of the children of Israel out of Egypt.

We start with 1 Kings 6:1 where we read the following:

> 6 And it came to pass in the four hundred and eightieth[a] year after the children of Israel had come out of the land of Egypt, in the fourth year of Solomon's reign over Israel, in the month of Ziv, which is the second month, that he began to build the house of the Lord.

The "he" here involves King Solomon, who began the construction of the first Jewish temple 480 years after the children of Israel had come out of Egypt. That same year Solomon began construction happened to coincide with the fourth year of King Solomon's reign in Israel! What year then was it when Solomon started building the temple? What year was his fourth year of reign—or for that matter, his first year of reign?

It turns out that the date of the division of Israel into two kingdoms after the death of King Solomon (1 Kings 11:41 to 1 Kings 12:24 and 2 Chronicles 9:29 to 2 Chronicles 11:4) is quite helpful in providing a needed bridge linking the 480 years of 1 Kings 6:1 with our modern calendar.

Edwin R. Thiele, a respected archeologist, author, and professor well-known for his great scholarly work, *The Mysterious Numbers of the Hebrew Kings*, affirms 931 BC as the year King Solomon died and the year that his kingdom was divided.

Since King Solomon reigned over the nation of Israel forty years (2 Chronicles 9:30 and 1 Kings 11:42), then going back forty years would yield 971 BC as the year King Solomon began to reign. As such, the fourth year of King Solomon's reign alluded to in 1 Kings 6:1 earlier would entail the 967 BC as the year in view in verse 1 of 1 Kings 6.

According to that verse, that year, 967 BC, is the 480th year after the children of Israel had left Egypt! Therefore, adding 967 to 480 would yield 1447 BC as the year of the great Exodus out of Egypt!

Since the children of Israel wandered in the wilderness for forty years (Joshua 5:6 and Numbers 32:13) after they had left the land of the Pharaohs, they must have arrived in the Promised Land in the year 1407 BC.

As such, the children of Israel were ordered by God to count fifty years from the year of their arrival for the first Jubilee year (Leviticus 25:8–12). Therefore, the year 1357 BC would then constitute the first Jubilee year; and the next Jubilee would be 1307 BC, and the years 1257, 1207, 1157, 1107, 1057, 1007, 957, 907, 857, 807, 757, 707, 657, 607, 557, and 507 would all constitute actual Jubilee years that the children of Israel actually celebrated. Appendix 2 and appendix 3 would entail the next Jubilee years in the pipeline.

As we have seen earlier, Jesus most likely came into this earth in a Jubilee year (7 BC). Could it be that His Second Coming will take place in one of the Jubilee years outlined in appendix 2?

Appendix II

The Jubilee Years (I)

Jubilee	Year (AD)
J1	457
J2	407
J3	357
J4	307
J5	257
J6	207
J7	157
J8	107
J9	57
J10	07 (AD)
J11	44
J12	94
J13	144
J14	194
J15	244
J16	294
J17	344
J18	394
J19	444
J20	494
J21	544
J22	594
J23	644

Jubilee	Year (AD)
J24	694
J25	744
J26	794
J27	844
J28	894
J29	944
J30	994

The Jubilee Years (II)

Jubilee	Year (AD)
J31	1044
J32	1094
J33	1144
J34	1194
J35	1244
J36	1294
J37	1344
J38	1394
J39	1444
J40	1544
J41	1594
J42	1644
J43	1694
J44	1744
J45	1794
J46	1844
J47	1894
J48	1994
J49	2044
J50	2094
J51	2144
J52	2194
J53	2244
J54	2294
J55	2344
J56	2394
J57	2444
J58	2494

Jubilee	Year (AD)
J59	2544
J60	2594

Appendix III

A Personal Account

One Sunday afternoon on a cold wintry day, as I laid in bed at the infamous Moseley Building in Nyack College, Nyack, New York, I began to focus on God as He was creating the universe. I could mentally see Him thunder His great voice as He began to call out of nothing one thing after another—the galaxies, the stars, our solar system, the earth, the animals, the birds, the sea creatures, and then man: the universe was unfolding right in front of my mental eyes.

I recall falling on my dorm bed at around 5:00 p.m., and by now it was nearly 6:15 p.m.; and aware that the doors of the cafeteria of Nyack College would be closed for dinner at 6:30 p.m., I quickly got up, crossed the snow-covered soccer field and headed for the school's cafeteria.

I finished eating dinner at around 6:50 p.m., and I was the lone student returning back to Moseley. I started to cross again the huge soccer field beholding the beauty of God's creation as the nearly foot of snow that had been deposited on the field hampered my steady progress.

Suddenly, I noticed a small whirlwind forming in the middle of the soccer field, and behold, it was moving speedily in my direction carrying with it a great deal of snow. The mechanism seemed to pick up speed as it moved toward me, and I stood for a few seconds, paralyzed by the amazing phenomenon unfolding right in my line of sight; and after a short while, I was covered with a small avalanche of snow!

I stood there speechless and began to muse on the meaning of all this. I retraced my thoughts of a few minutes earlier when I was lost gazing at the awesome power and grandeur of Almighty God. Then, out of the blue, the thought came to me that the spectacular show I had just witnessed was God's unusual way of saying, "Hi, Pierre!" I smiled, looked around content that no one else but God was looking at me, and I proceeded back to Moseley.

Appendix IV

The Passover Years

Passover AD 29	Passover AD 30	Passover AD 31	Passover AD 32	Passover AD 33
Same year John the Baptist began his public ministry.	Same year Jesus began His public ministry. This Passover is not mentioned in John's Gospel.	First Passover listed in John's Gospel (John 2:13, 23).	Second Passover indicated in John's Gospel (John 6:4).	Third Passover mentioned in John's Gospel (John 11:55, 12:1, 13:1, 18:28, 39, 19:14), the Passover when Jesus, the real Passover Lamb, was sacrificed at the cross on Calvary.

Appendix V

Periods of 3 ½ in the Scriptures

Jesus's public ministry on earth lasted a period of 3 ½ years according to the three Passovers of the Gospel of John.

1. 1 Kings 17:1, 18:1; James 5:17	Elijah prayed for no rain for 3 ½ years.
2. Daniel 7:23 to 26	The appearance of a king who will "speak great words against the Most High" and will "wear out the saints of the Most High during a period of "a time, times and the dividing of time," or a period of 3 ½.
3. Daniel 12:5–7	The length of time—"time, times and an half"—established to "scatter the power of the Holy People" and to arrive at "the ends of [the] wonders" taking place at the end of the world: a period of 3 ½.
4. Revelation 11:2	Holy City "treaded under foot for forty and two months," or 3 ½ years: another period of 3 ½.
5. Revelation 11:3	The two witnesses prophesy for one thousand sixty days or 3 ½ biblical years (360 days per year): another time interval of 3 ½.
6. Revelation 12:6 and 13–14	"Woman" (God's people across time and characterized here as the New Testament saints) is persecuted by Satan and is "nourished" and "fed" for a time, times and a half or a period of 3 ½.
7. Revelation 13:4–5	The beast is worshipped for a period of forty-two months or a period of 3 ½.
8. Daniel 9:27	After the crucifixion of Jesus in the middle of the last seven, a period of 3 ½ seven remains from Daniel's prophecy of the Seventy Sevens!
9. 3 ½ Solar years	A period of 1,278 days.
10. The Mystery of the 3 ½ Seven	3 ½ indicates the period of time from the Cross to the end of the world!

Appendix VI

Hermeneutical Analysis of the Word *Salt* in Colossians 4:6

Let's try to apply the biblical hermeneutical principles to learn the meaning of the word *salt* in Colossians 4:6, "Let your speech always be with grace, seasoned with salt, that you may know how you ought to answer each one." We wonder what the Lord is teaching here that our speech should be "seasoned with salt." This analysis will demonstrate once and for all the capacity of the true biblical hermeneutics to interpret the meaning of biblical passages and words.

We are children of God who have been granted His Holy Spirit and thus approach the study of this portion of the Holy Scripture with humility asking the Holy Spirit of God to enlighten our minds to the true meaning of this particular passage.

We stay away from biblical commentaries on the issue not because they are unreliable—most of them do provide practical biblical help on many issues—but because we trust that the Lord will guide us in the proper analysis of His word if we are faithful to the principles of Bible study as depicted in the Holy Scripture. We also refuse to rely on dictionaries to elicit the meaning of the word *salt* even though we are aware that salt is a preserving and flavoring agent: we want to allow the Word of God the complete freedom to guide us in our analysis.

Therefore, we begin to collect spiritual truths on the word salt by gathering all the biblical references pertaining to it. In that regard, we use the help of the *Young's Analytical Concordance of the Bible* because it locates the iterations of the word *salt* in close proximity (Actually we could have used the *Strong's Exhaustive Concordance of the Bible* as well, but it would have taken us a little bit of extra time).

Young's Concordance lists the word *salt* with its Hebrew transliteration *Melach* on page 832 along with the following references (please check the references with your own Bible): Genesis 14:3, 19:26; Leviticus 2:13; Numbers 18:19, 34:3, 12; Deuteronomy 3:17, 34:12; Joshua 3:16, 12:3, 15:2, 15:5, 18:19; Judges 9:45; 2 Samuel 8:13; 2 Kings 2:20, 21, 14:7; 1 Chronicles 18:12; 2 Chronicles 13:5, 25:11; Job 6:6; Psalm 60 (title); Ezekiel 43:24, 47:11; Zephaniah 2:9; Ezra 6:9, 7:22. As salt place and barren land, the word *salt*'s Hebrew transliteration is the word *Melechah* found in Jeremiah 17:6.

In the New Testament, the Greek transliteration of the word *salt* is *halas*, found in Matthew 5:13, Mark 9:50, Luke 14:34, and Colossians 4:6. The word *salt* is also identified by the Greek word *hals* found in Mark 9:49. The word *halukos* found in James 3:12 is also used for the word *salt*.

The adjective *salted*, again the Hebrew *Melach*, is found in Ezekiel 16:4; and in the New Testament, the adjective *salted* is represented by the word *halizomai* located in Matthew 5:13 and Mark 9:49. *Saltness* is transliterated by the Greek word *analos* found in Mark 9:50.

We have now gathered all the spiritual truths vis-à-vis the word *salt* found in the Holy Scriptures, and we are therefore ready to start comparing spiritual truths with spiritual.

Most of the references concerning the word *salt* in the Bible are neutral: they do not discriminate vis-à-vis the goodness or badness of the word; however, the following references stand out:

> Genesis 19 verse 26: "But his wife (Lot's wife) looked bad from behind him, and she became a pillar of salt."
>
> Leviticus 2 verse 13: "And every oblation of thy meat offering shalt thou season with salt; neither shalt thou suffer the salt of the covenant of thy God to be lacking from thy meat offering; with all thine offerings thou shalt offer salt."
>
> Numbers 18 verse 19: "All the heave offerings of the holy things, which the children of Israel offer unto the Lord, have I given thee, and thy sons and thy daughters with thee, by a statute for ever before: It is a covenant of salt before the Lord unto thee and to thy seed with thee."
>
> 2 Kings 2 verses 20, 21, and 22: "And [Elisha] said, Bring me a new cruse, and put salt therein. And they brought it to him. And he went forth unto the spring of the waters, and cast the salt in there, and said, Thus saith the Lord, I have healed these waters; there shall no be from thence any more death or barren land. So the waters were healed unto this day, according to the saying of Elisha which he spake."
>
> Job 6 verse 6: "Can that which is unsavoury [sic] be eaten without salt? Or is there any taste in the white of an egg?"
>
> Ezekiel 43 verses 22, 23, and 24: "And on the second day thou shalt offer a kid of the goats without blemish for a sin offering: and they shall cleanse the altar, as they did cleanse it with the bullock. When thou hast made an end of cleansing it, thou shalt offer a young bullock without blemish, and a ram out of the flock without blemish. And thou shalt offer them before the Lord, and the priests shall cast salt upon them, and they shall offer them up for a burnt offering unto the Lord."
>
> Ezra 6 verse 9: "And that which they have need of, both young bullocks, and rams, and lambs, for the burnt offerings of the God of heaven, wheat, salt, wine, and oil, according to the appointment of the priests which are at Jerusalem, let it be given them day by day without fail."
>
> Matthew 5 verse 13: "Ye are the salt of the earth: but if the salt have lost his savour, wherewith shall it be salted? It is thenceforth good for nothing, but to be cast out, and to be trodden under foot by men."
>
> Mark 9 verse 50: "Salt is good: but if the salt have lost his saltness, wherewith will ye season it? Have salt in yourselves, and have peace one with another."

> Luke 14 verse 34: "Salt is good: but if the salt have lost his savour, wherewith shall it be seasoned?"
>
> Colossians 4 verse 6: "Let your speech be always with grace, seasoned with salt, that ye may know how ye ought to answer every man."
>
> Mark 9 verse 49: "For every one shall be salted with fire, and every sacrifice shall be salted with salt."

At first blush, salt appears to be a great ingredient in the life of a believer: "Salt is good," says the Word of God in Mark 9:50 and Luke 14:34; and the Holy Scriptures command us to "have salt in [ourselves]" in Mark 9:50. However, the Bible indicates that salt could "lose it saltness," or "savor." What does that mean? Could salt actually lose its "saltness?" We think not: it would no longer be called salt in that regard. What then is it that makes salt a good ingredient in the life of a believer? Why would Jesus command His disciples and followers to "have salt" in themselves?

Jesus infers that His followers continually maintain the essence of their Christian experience—the presence of the Holy Spirit—in their lives. "Abide in Me, and I in you," Jesus orders all His followers in John 15 verse 4; and unless they obey, their fellowship with the Holy Spirit—their saltness—will come to an abrupt end, and their Christian light—the outward expression of their inward new life—would be quickly extinguished. "Ye are the light of the world," Jesus would continue right after telling His followers that they were the salt of the earth, thereby linking irrevocably the believer's inward saltness with her outward light (Matthew 5:13 and 14).

Yes! Salt is indeed a good thing for both culinary activities and spiritual fragrance and fervor; however, why did Lot's wife become a pillar of salt (Genesis 19 verse 26) after she had disobeyed the Lord's command not to look behind her? Why did God under the terms of the Old Testament (Mark 9:49 and Leviticus 2:13) request that "every sacrifice shall be salted with salt?" In the first instance, Lot's wife partook of God's judgment upon Sodom and Gomorrah; and in the second instance, all the sacrifices and the accompanying salts were burnt on the altar as God's judgment fell on the animals and the elements on the altar instead of upon the people guilty of perpetrating God's law.

The Word of God is thus the only document in the entire world that associates the word *judgment* with the word *salt*. There is no dictionary in the history of the world that has ever defined *salt* as "judgment," thereby making the point that the Bible is its own dictionary.

As a result, we can revisit Colossians 4:6 to ascertain God's teaching in that verse:

> Let your speech always be with grace, seasoned with salt, that you may know how you ought to answer each one.

Colossians 4:6 finds its locus in a chapter dealing with witnessing the Gospel of Christ (check out verse 4). Therefore, God is teaching that when we witness, we should always focus on both the grace of God in forgiving sin through the blood of Jesus Christ and on God's incoming judgment on those that refuse to believe the message of the Gospel. As followers of Jesus, we must learn to present to unbelievers the "whole counsel of God" (Acts 20:27) embodying salvation through belief in Jesus Christ and perdition through unbelief (John 3:16).

Citations

Chapter 2: The Requiem for Evolution

"Lord, I believe in you…Grant this through Christ our Lord. Amen," Pope Clement XI, the Universal Prayer, catholic.org/prayers/prayer.php?p=223.

"There cannot be…without a contriver," William Paley, *Natural Theology* (Boston: Gould and Lincoln, 1857), 10.

"Arrangement, disposition of parts…intelligence and mind," William Paley, *Natural Theology*, http://mind.ucsd.edu/syllabi/02-03/01w/readings/paley.html.

"DNA is like a computer…than any software created." Bill Gates, google.com/search?sourceid=navclient&ie=UTF-8&rlz=1T4TSHB_enUS331US331&q=bill+gates+dna+software.

"Lord, have mercy…and make this world hoary," *Basic Tests for the Roman Catholic Eucharist*, http://catholic-resources.org/ChurchDocs/Mass.htm.

"Day of Judgment" (Dies Irae), Thomas of Celano, http://en.wikipedia.org/wiki/Dies_Irae.

"Religion doesn't seem…between us that they shouldn't be"

"No, I don't know that…under God"

"I have never been an atheist…my state of mind"

"How is it that…the conventional faith"

"Would it not be too bold…world without end"

"Where is the promise…was erroneous"

"If it could be…absolutely break down"

"The cumulative…life enormously complex"

"Riddle…in an enigma," https://en.wiktionary.org/wiki/a_riddle_wrapped_up_in_an_enigma.

"Christians have their hymns…Atheists don't have no songs," Steve Martin, http://pacificvs.com/2010/05/28/atheists-dont-have-no-songs-video-and-lyrics/.

"Oh, give thanks to the Lord…For His mercy endures forever," Psalm 136, BibleGateway.com, Luke 15:10, New King James Version (NKJV), Thomas Nelson Inc., 1982.

"Alleluia…Amen," Michael W. Smith, Gamely, Douglas/Bizet, Georges, elyrics.net/read/m/michael-w.-smith-lyrics/agnus-dei-lyrics.html.

"Libera me…shall be shaken," angelfire.com/ri/cerat/LiberaMe.html,

"Heavenly Father…Amen," Billy Graham, snopes.com/politics/soapbox/prayernation.asp.

"As the Savior so taught us…Go now and overcome," http://re-worship.blogspot.com/2012/01/benediction-go-now-and-overcome.html

Chapter 3: The Living God

"And in Lystra…from sacrificing to them," BibleGateway.com, Acts 14:8–18, New King James Version (NKJV), Thomas Nelson, Inc., 1982.

"Yet man, this part of Thy creation…rest in Thee," Saint Augustine, *The Confession of Saint Augustine*, leaderu.com/cyber/books/augconfessions/bk1.html.

"For the wrath of God…and creeping things," biblegateway.com/passage/?search=Romans%201&version=NKJV.

"AGTCT…100," Stephen C. Meyer, *Signature in the Cell: DNA and the Evidence for Intelligent Design* (New York: HarperCollins Publishers, 2009), 23–24.

"This string of characters…in a living cell," Meyer, 104.

"This sequence…punctuation marks," Meyer, 104.

"The first words…the Information Interchange," Stephen Meyer, 105.

"Representations…in a living cell," Meyer, 105.

"Biological information," "specified information," "specified biological information," Meyer, 332, 333.

"Prebiotic simulation experiments," "realistic prebiotic conditions," "the desirable building blocks…amino acids," "undesirable by-products…amino acids," "creative power…selection," "the only known cause…information," "have not demonstrated…specified information," "conscious, rational…living state," Meyer, 337, 334, 335, 334, 334, 335, 341, 341, 341.

"Undirected material causes…of specified information," Meyer, 109.

"Conscious, rational…nonliving state," Meyer, 341.

"A single system…intelligent design," Michael J. Behe, *Darwin's Black Box* (New York: Free Press, 2006), 39.

"The cumulative results…enormously complex," Michael J. Behe, *Darwin's Black Box* (New York: Free Press, 2006), 4–5.

"Irreducibly complex," "the same mechanical elements…the stationary element," Michael J. Behe, *Darwin's Black Box* (New York: Free Press, 2006), 39, 70, 39.

"The elegant, coherent, functional systems…deliberate intelligent design," Michael Behe, *The Edge of Evolution: The Search for the Limits of Darwinism* (New York: Free Press, 2008), 166.

"Biology…the appearance of design," Richards Dawkins, "The Biblical View of Life's Origins Remains Dominant," *Evolution* (Greenhaven Press: Farmington Hills, 2005), 70.

"Protein molecules are the ultimate…to the human eye," Michael Denton, *Evolution: A Theory in Crisis* (Bethesda: Adler and Adler Publishers, Inc., 1986), 234.

"Molecular biology has shown…in the non-living world," Michael Denton, *Evolution: A Theory in Crisis* (Bethesda: Adler and Adler Publishers, Inc. 1996), 250.

"The heavens declare…shows His handiwork," BibleGateway.com, Psalm 19:1, New King James Version (NKJV), Thomas Nelson, Inc., 1982.

"We occupy the best overall place…the three major branches of astronomy," Guillermo Gonzalez and Jay W. Richards, *The Privileged Planet* (Washington DC: Regnery Publishing, Inc., 2004), 151.

"The fact that our atmosphere…by scientists," Guillermo Gonzalez and Jay Richards, *The Privileged Planet* (Washington DC: Regnery Publishing, Inc., 2004), x.

"Chance as a real force…once and for all," R. C. Sproul, *Not a Chance* (Grand Rapids: Baker Books, 2000), 214.

"Option 1…something that is self-existent" R. C. Sproul, *Not a Chance,* 159.

"The transcendental proof…moral absolutes," forananswer.org/Top_Ath/GreatDebate_v1.3.pdf.

"A 'presupposition' is not just…immunity to revision," http://theresurgence.com/2012/01/17/the-great-debate-does-god-exist.

"The presuppositional apologist…the impossibility of the contrary," Greg Bahnsen, *Presuppositional Apologetics,* http://theresurgence.com/2012/01/17/the-great-debate-does-god-exist.

"Sound foundation…moral values and duties," "moral values…grounded in God," "the greatest conceivable Being," "Perfectly Good," "Locus…of moral values," "God's own holy and loving nature…are measured," youtube.com/watch?v=yqaHXKLRKzg.

"You shall love…as yourself," BibleGateway.com, Luke 10:27, New King James Version (NKJV), Thomas Nelson, Inc., 1982.

"The position of the modern evolutionist…is illusory," *The God Debate II: Harris vs. Craig,* youtube.com/watch?v=yqaHXKLRKzg.

"There is at bottom…sole reason for being," *The God Debate II: Harris vs. Craig,* youtube.com/watch?v=yqaHXKLRKzg.

"Exalts itself…knowledge of God," "there is no wisdom…against the Lord," 2 Corinthians 10:5 and Proverbs 21:30, BibleGateway.com, Genesis 15:18, New King James Version (NKJV), Thomas Nelson, Inc., 1982.

Chapter 4: His Living Words

"Seventy weeks are determined…is poured on the desolate," biblegateway.com/passage/?search=daniel+9%3A+24-27&version=KJV.

"Verily, verily, verily, I say…the kingdom of God," biblegateway.com/passage/?search=john+3%3A+3&version=KJV.

"Except a man be born again…the kingdom of God," Ibid.

"For God so loved the world…have everlasting life," biblegateway.com/passage/?search=john+3%3A+16&version=NKJV.

"God is Spirit…and in truth," biblegateway.com/passage/?search=john+4%3A+24&version=NKJV.

"Know therefore and understand…even in troublesome times," biblegateway.com/passage/?search=daniel+9%3A+25&version=NKJV.

"Now learn this parable…pass away," biblegateway.com/passage/?search=Matthew+24%3A+32-35&version=NKJV.

"Seventy weeks are determined…to anoint the Most Holy," biblegateway.com/passage/?search=daniel+9%3A+24&version=NKJV.

"Because you have done this…and you shall bruise his heel," biblegateway.com/passage/?search=Genesis+3%3A14-15&version=NKJV.

"Then Moses called for the elders...to strike you," biblegateway.com/passage/?search=exodus+12%3A+21-+23&version=NKJV.

"My God, my God...forsaken me," "the Spirit of God...in my tongue," BibleGateway.com, Psalm 22:1 and 2 Samuel 23:2, New King James Version (NKJV), Thomas Nelson, Inc., 1982.

"The Spirit of the Lord...on my tongue," biblegateway.com/quicksearch/?quicksearch=the+Spirit+of+the+Lord+spoke+by+me+and+his+word+was+on+my+tongue&qs_version=NKJV.

"So Moses the servant of the Lord...vigor diminished," biblegateway.com/passage/?search=Deuteronomy34%3A+5-7&version=NKJV.

"Yet Michael the Archangel...rebuke you," biblegateway.com/passage/?search=jude+9&version=NKJV.

"For thus says the Lord...has sent Me," biblegateway.com/passage/?search=Zechariah+2%3A+8-9&version=NKJV.

"Then he showed me...rebuke you," biblegateway.com/passage/?search=Zechariah+2%3A+8-9&version=NKJV.

"I shall see him...the children of Sheth," Numbers 24:17, KJV, Standard Full-Color Bible (Ohio: Standard Publishing, 2007), 204.

"The kings of Tarshish...shall serve him," Psalm 72:10–11, KJV, Standard Full-Color Bible (Ohio: Standard Publishing, 2007), 706.

"But you...From everlasting," biblegateway.com/passage/?search=micah+5%3A+2&version=NKJV.

"Know therefore and understand...times," biblegateway.com/passage/?search=Daniel9%3A+25-27&version=NKJV.

Chapter 5: How to Study the Bible: A Poor Man's Biblical Hermeneutics

"In the beginning...and the Word was God," biblegateway.com/passage/?search=john+1&version=NKJV.

"But the natural man...they are spiritually discerned," biblegateway.com/passage/?search=1+Corinthians+2%3A+14&version=NKJV.

"Unless one is born again...the kingdom of God...That which is born of the flesh...of the Spirit is spirit," biblegateway.com/passage/?search=John+3&version=NKJV.

"Unless on is born of water and the Spirit...the kingdom of God," Ibid.

"That which is born of the flesh...of the Spirit is spirit," Ibid.

"To you it has been given...the kingdom of God," "Seeing they may see...their sins be forgiven them," BibleGateway.com, Mark 4:11 and 12, New King James Version (NKJV), Thomas Nelson, Inc., 1982.

"Seeing they may see...their sins be forgiven them," "Now we have received...freely given to us by God," BibleGateway.com, Mark 4:12 and 1 Corinthians 2:12, New King James Version (NKJV), Thomas Nelson, Inc., 1982.

"I thank you Father...revealed them to babes," biblegateway.com/passage/?search=Matthew+11%3A+25&version=NKJV.

"Now we have received...given to us by God...spiritual things with spiritual," BibleGateway.com, 1 Corinthians 2:12–13, New King James Version (NKJV), Thomas Nelson, Inc., 1982.

"What right have you…the salvation of God," BibleGateway.com, Psalm 50:16–23, New King James Version (NKJV), Thomas Nelson, Inc., 1982.

"These people draw near…the commandments of men," BibleGateway.com, Matthew 15:8–9, New King James Version (NKJV), Thomas Nelson, Inc., 1982.

"I thank You, Father…and have revealed them to babes," BibleGateway.com, New King James Version (NKJV), Thomas Nelson, Inc., 1982.

"The humble…teaches His way," BibleGateway.com, Psalm 25:9, New King James Version (NKJV), Thomas Nelson, Inc., 1982.

"Whom…teach knowledge," "Whom…to understand doctrine," Isaiah 28:9, Standard Full-Color Bible KJV (Ohio: Standard Publishing, 2007), 819.

"I'll turn conventional wisdom…the way of salvation," BibleGateway.com, 1 Corinthians 1:18–21, The Message, Thomas Nelson, Inc., 1982.

"And the Lord God formed man…a living soul," Genesis 2:7, Standard Full-Color Bible KJV (Ohio: Standard Publishing, 2007), 6.

"Suffer many things…the third day," biblegateway.com/passage/?search=Matthew+16%3A+21&version=KJV.

"Then he said to them…comprehend the Scriptures," biblegateway.com/passage/?search=luke+24%3A+44-45&version=NKJV.

"Your word…not sin against you," biblegateway.com/passage/?search=Psalms+119%3B+11&version=NKJV.

"This book of the law…great success," biblegateway.com/passage/?search=joshua+1%3A+8&version=NKJV.

"Be diligent…the word of truth," BibleGateway.com, 2 Timothy 2:15, New King James Version (NKJV), Thomas Nelson, Inc., 1982.

"All Scripture is God-breathed…for every good work," 2 Timothy 3:16, BibleGateway.com, New International Version (NIV), Thomas Nelson, Inc., 1982.

"But the natural man…they are spiritually discerned," 1 Corinthians 2:14, BibleGateway.com, New King James Version (NKJV), Thomas Nelson, Inc., 1982.

"And we the spirit of the world…with spiritual things spiritual things comparing," 1 Corinthians 2:12 and 13, BibleGateway.com, 1 Corinthians 2:12 and 13, Young's Literal Translation (YLT), Thomas Nelson, Inc., 1982.

"Whom shall [the Holy Spirit]…and there a little," Standard Full-Color Bible KJV (Ohio: Standard Publishing, 2007), 819.

"Tell me…but of the free," BibleGateway.com, Galatians 4:21–31, New King James Version (NKJV), Thomas Nelson, Inc., 1982.

"I will make you a great nation…the families of the earth shall be blessed," BibleGateway.com, Genesis 12:2–3, New King James Version (NKJV), Thomas Nelson, Inc., 1982.

"I loved Jacob…for the dragons of the wilderness," Standard Full-Color Bible KJV (Ohio: Standard Publishing, 2007), 1082.

"And even as they did not like…COVENANT BREAKERS," biblegateway.com/passage/?search=romans+1&version=KJV.

"Except a man be born…the kingdom of God," "That which is born of the flesh…of the Spirit is spirit," biblegateway.com/quicksearch/?quicksearch=except+a+man+be+born+again&qs_version=KJV.

"beginning at Moses…concerning Himself," "And their eyes were opened, and they knew Him," biblegateway.com/passage/?search=luke+24&version=KJV.

"Be diligent to present yourself…the word of truth," biblegateway.com/quicksearch/?quicksearch=be+diligent+to+present+yourself&qs_version=NKJV.

Chapter 6: A View of Time through the Prism of Biblical Chronology and Modern Dating Methods

"All scripture…in righteousness," biblegateway.com/passage/?search=2+Timothy3&version=NKJV.

"Every writing…in righteousness," biblegateway.com/passage/?search=2+Timothy3&version=YLT.

"For the prophecy…by the Holy Spirit," biblegateway.com/passage/?search=2+Peter1%3A+21&version=NKJV.

"And it came to pass…house of God," biblegateway.com/passage/?search=1+kings+6&version=KJV.

"Now the sojourn…from the land of Egypt," biblegateway.com/passage/?search=1+kings+6&version=KJV.

"And Solomon…Josiah his son," biblegateway.com/passage/?search=Matthew1%3A7-11&version=KJV. biblegateway.com/passage/?search=1+Chronicles3%3A10-14&version=NKJV.

"Most of the solid materials…of the crust of the earth," H. U. Sverdrup, Martin W. Johnson, and Richard H. Fleming, *The Oceans* (New York: Prentice Hall, Inc., 1942) p. 219.

"In more than 300 places…it needs further checking," Maurice Ewing, "New Discoveries on the Mid-Atlantic ridge," *National Geographic Magazine*, 1949, pp. 612–613.

"Every single element…no longer exist on Earth," "Nearly all the radioactive isotopes…no longer in existence," "coral generally grows…1 cm per year," Dr. Roger C. Weins, *Radiometric Dating: A Christian Perspective*, asa3.org/ASA/resources/Wiens2002.pdf.

Chapter 7: The Patterns of the Biblical Timetable

"Walked with God three hundred years," biblegateway.com/passage/?search=Genesis+5%3A+22&version=KJV.

"Made of one blood…and the bounds of their habitation," biblegateway.com/passage/?search=acts+17%3A+26&version=KJV.

"Know of a surety…with great substance," biblegateway.com/passage/?search=genesis+15%3A+13-14&version=KJV.

"But when the fullness of time…made under the law," biblegateway.com/passage/?search=Galatians4%3A4&version=KJV.

"Know certainly that your descendants…is not yet complete," Genesis 15:13–16, BibleGateway.com, Genesis 17:7–8, New King James Version (NKJV), Thomas Nelson, Inc., 1982.

"Now the sojourn of the children of Israel…went out from the land of Egypt," BibleGateway.com, Numbers 12:40 and 41, New King James Version (NKJV), Thomas Nelson, Inc., 1982.

"And it came to pass…to build the house of the Lord," BibleGateway.com, 1 Kings 6:1, New King James Version (NKJV), Thomas Nelson, Inc., 1982.

"Again the children of Israel…for forty years," biblegateway.com/passage/?search=judges+13%3A+1&version=KJV.

Chapter 8: An Attempt at Correcting Various Misunderstood Biblical Concepts

"One of the most famous examples…removed the highway's curse," Lisa Fritscher, "Hexako sioihexekontahexaphobia," phobias.about.com/od/phobiaslist/a/fear666.htm.

"Here is wisdom…His name is 666," BibleGateway.com, Revelation 13:18, New King James Version (NKJV), Thomas Nelson, Inc., 1982.

"Here is the wisdom…and its number [is] 666," Ibid.

"Now Ahaziah fell through…with him to the king," biblegateway.com/quicksearch/?quicksearch=now+Ahaziah+fell+through&qs_version=NKJV.

"And after this it came to pass…and paid tribute," BibleGateway.com, 2 Samuel 8:1–2, New King James Version (NKJV), Thomas Nelson, Inc., 1982.

"And it shall come to pass…one-third shall be left in it," BibleGateway.com, Zechariah 13:8, New King James Version (NKJV), Thomas Nelson, Inc., 1982.

"I will bring the one-third…The Lord is my God," BibleGateway.com, Zechariah 13:9, New King James Version (NKJV), Thomas Nelson, Inc., 1982.

"On the same day…the river Euphrates," BibleGateway.com, Genesis 15:18, New King James Version (NKJV), Thomas Nelson, Inc., 1982.

"And the Lord said to Abraham…your descendants FOREVER," biblegateway.com/passage/?search=genesis+13%3A+14-15&version=NKJV.

"And I will establish…and I will be their God," BibleGateway.com, Genesis 17:7–8, New King James Version (NKJV), Thomas Nelson, Inc., 1982.

"Does this blessedness then come…and I will be their God," biblegateway.com/quicksearch/?quicksearch=does+this+blessedness+then+come&qs_version=NKJV.

"And this whole land…perpetual desolations," biblegateway.com/passage/?search=jeremiah+25%3A+11-12&version=KJV.

"Seventy weeks…upon the desolate," KJV, Standard Full-Color Bible (Ohio: Standard Publishing, 2007), 1012.

"Know therefore and understand…even in troublesome times," biblegateway.com/passage/?search=Genesis41%3A32&version=KJV.

"And thou shall number…every man unto his family," biblegateway.com/passage/?search=Leviticus25%3A8-10&version=KJV.

"And the Lord spake…every man unto his family," biblegateway.com/passage/?search=Leviticus25%3A8-10&version=KJV.

"Whatsoever is commanded…of the king and his son," biblegateway.com/passage/?search=ezra+7%3A23&version=KJV.

"Seventy Sevens are determined…and to anoint the Most Holy," biblegateway.com/passage/?search=Daniel9%3A25&version=KJV.

"Now in the fifteenth year…Zacharias in the wilderness," biblegateway.com/passage/?search=Luke3%3A1&version=KJV.

"Know therefore and understand…be poured upon the desolate," biblegateway.com/passage/?search=daniel+9%3A+25-27&version=KJV.

"And He shall confirm the Covenant…poured upon the desolate," biblegateway.com/passage/?search=daniel+9%3A+27&version=KJV.

"And He shall confirm the Covenant…upon the desolate," Ibid.

"And Elijah the Tishbite…according to my word," biblegateway.com/passage/?search=1+Kings17%3A1&version=KJV.

"And it came to pass…upon the earth," biblegateway.com/passage/?search=1+Kings18%3A1&version=KJV.

"Elias was a man…three years and six months," biblegateway.com/passage/?search=James5%3A17&version=KJV.

"Thus he said…unto the end," biblegateway.com/passage/?search=daniel+7%3A+23-26&version=KJV.

"Then I Daniel looked…these things shall be finished," biblegateway.com/passage/?search=daniel+12%3A+5-7&version=KJV.

"And the woman fled…two hundred and sixty days," biblegateway.com/passage/?search=Revelation+12%3A+6&version=NKJV.

"And the dragon saw that…from the face of the serpent," biblegateway.com/passage/?search=Revelation+12%3A+13-14&version=NKJV.

"But the court…forty two months (or 3 years and 6 months)," biblegateway.com/passage/?search=Revelation+11%3A+2&version=KJV.

"And I will give power…clothed in sackcloth," biblegateway.com/passage/?search=Revelation+11%3A+3&version=KJV.

"And they worshipped…and two months," biblegateway.com/passage/?search=Revelation+13%3A+4-5&version=KJV.

"And Jesus Himself…which was the son of Heli," biblegateway.com/passage/?search=Revelation+13%3A+4-5&version=KJV.

"And every spirit that confesseth…now already in the world,"

"And every spirit…and now in the world already," biblegateway.com/passage/?search=1+John4%3A+3&version=KJV

"And every spirit…and now is already in the world," *The Interlinear Bible Hebrew-Greek-English* (London: 1984), 947.

"Let no man deceive you…that He is God," biblegateway.com/passage/?search=2+Thessalonians 2%3A3-4&version=NKJV.

"And no marvel…according to their works," biblegateway.com/passage/?search=2+Corinthians11%3A+14+-+15&version=NKJV.

"Great Billow," Jean Bottero, *Religion in Ancient Mesopotamia* (Chicago: University of Chicago Press, 2001).

"House of Dust," "the spirits of men...bellies," Paula Marie Stouton, helium.com/items/378814-examining-the-afterlife-in-early-babylonian-and-assyrian-religions.

"A lush...underworld," James P. Allen, *Middle Egyptian: An Introduction to the Language and Culture of Hieroglyphs* (Cambridge University Press, 2000) pp. 79–80.

"Good souls...to heaven," "a razor-sharp blade...into hell," mythencyclopedia.com/Pa-Pr/Persian-Mythology.html.

"Underworld...of all those who had died," metmuseum.org/toah/hd/dbag/hd_dbag.htm.

"One's spirit...of walls and moats," "the dwelling place...for immediate rebirth," "descend to hell....of the mythical Mount Meru," "the souls in hell...their next reincarnation," religionfacts.com/chinese_religion/beliefs/afterlife.htm.

"Paradise...pleasures forever," "passing over Hell...to enter Paradise," "weighted by their bad deeds...in Hell forever," "spiritual...eternity," religionfacts.com/islam/beliefs/afterlife.htm

"These are the generations...and the Heavens," KJV, Standard Full-Color Bible (Ohio: Standard Publishing, 2007), 6.

"Unto me...in Christ Jesus our Lord," KJV, Standard Full-Color Bible (Ohio: Standard Publishing, 2007), 1350.

"For by him...and for him," KJV, Standard Full-Color Bible (Ohio: Standard Publishing, 2007), 1363.

"You alone are the Lord...The host of heaven worships You," Nehemiah 9:6, BibleGateway.com, New King James Version (NKJV), Thomas Nelson, Inc., 1982.

"I know a man...for a man to utter," BibleGateway.com, 2 Corinthians 12:2 to 4, New King James Version (NKJV), Thomas Nelson, Inc., 1982.

"Then one of the criminals...you will be with Me in Paradise," Luke 23:39 to 43, BibleGateway.com, New King James Version (NKJV), Thomas Nelson, Inc., 1982.

"In the year that King Uzziah died...and the house was filled with smoke," Isaiah 6:1 to 4, BibleGateway.com, New King James Version (NKJV), Thomas Nelson, Inc., 1982.

"After this, I looked and saw...and by your decision they are and were created," BibleGateway.com, Revelation 4:1 to 11, Contemporary English Version (CEV), Thomas Nelson, Inc., 1982.

"After this, I saw a large crowd...forever and ever! Amen!" Revelation 7:9 to 12, BibleGateway.com, Revelation 7:9 to 12 (CEV), Thomas Nelson, Inc., 1982.

"For behold...nor come into mind," KJV, Standard Full-Color Bible (Ohio: Standard Publishing, 2007), 855.

"Eye has not seen...for those who love Him."

"God could just destroy...from sinful mankind" (Genesis 3:24), Randy Alcorn, *Heaven* (Carol Stream: Tyndale House Publishers, Inc., 2004), 88.

"You, Lord, in the beginning...Your years will not fail," Hebrews 1:10 to 12, BibleGateway.com, New King James Version (NKJV), Thomas Nelson, Inc., 1982.

"Heaven and earth will pass away...My words will by no means pass away," Matthew 24:34, BibleGateway.com, New King James Version (NKJV), Thomas Nelson, Inc., 1982.

"Above all...destruction of the ungodly," 2 Peter 3:3 to 7, BibleGateway.com, New King James Version (NIV), Thomas Nelson, Inc., 1982.

"Now I saw a new heaven and a new earth…these words are true and faithful," Revelation 21:1 to 5, BibleGateway.com, New King James Version (NIV), Thomas Nelson, Inc., 1982.

"This is forty times bigger than England…many square miles per person," Randy Alcorn, *Heaven* (Carol Stream: Tyndale House Publishers, Inc., 2004), 250.

"And he showed me a pure river of water of life…they shall reign forever and ever," Revelation 21:1 to 5, BibleGateway.com, New King James Version (NKJV), Thomas Nelson, Inc., 1982.

"used as a burial place…for burning garbage," Stanley N. Gundry, William Crockett, and contributors John F. Walvoord, Zachary J. Hayes, Clark H. Pinnock, *Hell* (Grand Rapids: Zondervan, 1996), 20.

"Even as Sodom…of eternal fire," "And the devil that deceived them…for ever and ever," KJV, Standard Full-Color Bible (Ohio: Standard Publishing, 2007), 452.

Chapter 9: All to the Praise and Glory of God

"The vis insita…in a straight line," Isaac Newton, *Mathematical Principles of Natural Philosophy*, translated into English by Andrew Motte (New York: First American Edition, 1846), 72.

"An object at rest…an unbalanced force," physicsclassroom.com/class/newtlaws/u2l1a.cfm.

"The only possible…self-created," "something comes into being without a cause," R. C. Sproul, *Not a Chance: The Myth of Chance in Modern Science and Cosmology* (Grand Rapids: Baker Books, 2000), 179.

"Indeed," "if it comes…its own cause," R. C. Sproul, *Not a Chance: The Myth of Chance in Modern Science and Cosmology* (Grand Rapids: Baker Books, 2000), 179–180.

"It has no cause," "it cannot be an effect," R. C. Sproul, *Not a Chance: The Myth of Chance in Modern Science and Cosmology* (Grand Rapids: Baker Books, 2000), 179.

"If there can…as God," R. C. Sproul, *Not a Chance: The Myth of Chance in Modern Science and Cosmology* (Grand Rapids: Baker Books, 2000), 174–175.

"Either the world…a first uncaused cause," Ravi Zacharias and Norman Geisler, *Who Made God, and Answers to Over 100 Other Tough Questions of Faith* (Grand Rapids: Zondervan, 2003), 25.

"Energy cannot be created nor destroyed," "running out of energy," truthnet.org/Tracts/Apologetics/God-Exist-Tract_Cosmos.pdf.

"The Second Law…a creation," truthnet.org/Tracts/Apologetics/God-Exist-Tract_Cosmos.pdf.

"Has existed eternally in a state of constant density," "space has been expanding eternally," Stephen C. Meyer, *Signature in the Cell, DNA, and the Evidence of Design* (New York: HarperCollins Publishers, 2009), 165.

"Discovery of the background…the Big Bang Theory," physicspost.com/science-article-203.html.

"Spending his time…questions like this!" Ravi Zacharias and Norman Geisler, *Who Made God, and Answers to Over 100 Other Tough Questions of Faith* (Grand Rapids: Zondervan, 2003), 28.

"Be anxious for nothing…Christ Jesus," BibleGateway.com, Philippians 4:6–7, New King James Version (NKJV), Thomas Nelson, Inc., 1982.

"Has made…in His time," biblegateway.com/passage/?search=Ecclesiastes3%3A+11&version=NKJV.

"Open your mouth wide…I will fill it," biblegateway.com/passage/?search=Psalms81%3A+10&version=NKJV.

"Neither is there…we have to do," KJV, Standard Full-Color Bible (Ohio: Standard Publishing, 2007), 1395.

"There is none good…that is, God," biblegateway.com/passage/?search=Mark10%3A+18&version=KJV.

"I am the Lord…I change not," biblegateway.com/passage/?search=Malachi3%3A+6&version=KJV.

"The same yesterday…and forever," biblegateway.com/quicksearch/?quicksearch=the+same+yesterday+&qs_version=KJV.

"Heaven and earth…shall not pass away," biblegateway.com/passage/?search=Matthew24%3A+35&version=KJV.

"Pure words…seven times," biblegateway.com/passage/?search=Psalms12%3A+6&version=KJV.

"Presence is fullness of joy…pleasure for evermore," biblegateway.com/passage/?search=Psalms16%3A11&version=KJV.

"Before the presence…exceeding joy," biblegateway.com/passage/?search=Jude24&version=KJV.

"There is…one sinner that repents," BibleGateway.com, Luke 15:10, New King James Version (NKJV), Thomas Nelson, Inc., 1982.

"Peace I leave with you," "My peace I give to you," "not as the world…I give to you," BibleGateway.com, John 14:27, New King James Version (NKJV), Thomas Nelson, Inc., 1982.

"Unresting, unhasting…of goodness and love," *Hyms* (California: Living Stream Ministry, 1980), 10.

"Peace I leave with you…my peace I give to you…not as the world…I give to you," biblegateway.com/passage/?search=john+14%3A+27&version=NKJV.

"Kind…to the evil," biblegateway.com/passage/?search=Luke6%3A+35&version=KJV.

"For God so loved the world…have everlasting life," "But God demonstrates His love…Christ died for us," "Greater love…He laid down His life for us," "By this we know love…for the brethren," "You shall love the Lord your God…and the Prophets," BibleGateway.com, John 3:16, Romans 5:8, John 15:13, 1 John 3:16, Matthew 22:37–39, New King James Version (NKJV), Thomas Nelson, Inc., 1982.

"The Spirit Himself…children of God," "Children of God…joint heirs with Christ," BibleGateway.com, Romans 8:16–17, New King James Version (NKJV), Thomas Nelson, Inc., 1982.

"But God…Christ died for us," biblegateway.com/passage/?search=Romans+5%3A+8&version=NKJV.

"Greater love…his life for his friends," BibleGateway.com, John 15:13, New King James Version (NKJV), Thomas Nelson, Inc., 1982.

"By this…His life for us…we also aught…for the brethren," biblegateway.com/quicksearch/?quicksearch=he+laid+down+his+life+for+us&qs_version=NKJV.

"You shall love…and the Prophets," biblegateway.com/passage/?search=Matthew22%3A37-40&version=NKJV.

"Children of God…joint heirs with Christ," biblegateway.com/quicksearch/?quicksearch=joint+heirs+with+Christ&qs_version=NKJV.

"Light…no darkness at all," biblegateway.com/quicksearch/?quicksearch=no+darkness+at+all&qs_version=NKJV.

"Blessed are the meek…inherit the earth," biblegateway.com/quicksearch/?quicksearch=blessed+are+the+meek&qs_version=NKJV.

"They rest day and night…and is to come," BibleGateway.com, Revelation 4:8, New King James Version (NKJV), Thomas Nelson, Inc., 1982.

"Delight themselves…of peace," biblegateway.com/passage/?search=Psalms37%3A11&version=KJV.

"Very meek…of the earth," biblegateway.com/passage/?search=numbers+12%3A+3&version=KJV.

"WHO SHALL NOT FEAR THEE O LORD…It is an attribute of attributes," A. W. Pink, *The Attributes of God*, pbministries.org/books/pink/Attributes/attrib_08.htm.

"Thorn in the flesh…to buffet [him]," "My grace…perfect in weakness," BibleGateway.com, 2 Corinthians 12:7, New King James Version (NKJV), Thomas Nelson, Inc., 1982.

"Therefore…you will know them," BibleGateway.com, Matthew 7:20, New King James Version (NKJV), Thomas Nelson, Inc., 1982.

"Nevertheless…RIGHTEOUSNESS dwells," BibleGateway.com, 2 Peter 3:13, New King James Version (NKJV), Thomas Nelson, Inc., 1982.

"Humble themselves…wicked ways," biblegateway.com/passage/?search=2+Chronicles7%3A+14&version=NKJV.

"My grace is sufficient…in weakness," biblegateway.com/passage/?search=2+Corinthians12%3A9&version=NKJV.

"In this the children of God…love his brethren," biblegateway.com/passage/?search=1+John3%3A+10&version=NKJV.

"To show His wrath and to make His power known," "endured…prepared for destruction," BibleGateway.com, Romans 9:22, New King James Version (NKJV), Thomas Nelson, Inc., 1982.

"What God has cleansed…not call common," biblegateway.com/passage/?search=Acts11%3A9&version=NKJV.

"Slack concerning His promise," "longsuffering…to repentance," BibleGateway.com, 2 Peter 3:9, New King James Version (NKJV), Thomas Nelson, Inc., 1982.

"In truth…is accepted of Him," BibleGateway.com, Acts 10:34–35, New King James Version (NKJV), Thomas Nelson, Inc., 1982.

"But I tell you…the Syrian," biblegateway.com/passage/?search=luke+4%3A+25-27&version=NKJV.

"Do not look…at the heart," biblegateway.com/passage/?search=1+Samuel16%3A+7&version=NKJV.

"Made a little lower…suffering of death," biblegateway.com/passage/?search=Hebrews2%3A+9&version=KJV.

"I will ascend into heaven…I will be like the Most High," BibleGateway.com, Isaia 14:13–14, New King James Version (NKJV), Thomas Nelson, Inc., 1982.

"And war broke out…and his angels were cast out with him," BibleGateway.com, Revelation 12:7–8, New King James Version (NKJV), Thomas Nelson, Inc., 1982.

"Whatever you want…to them," biblegateway.com/passage/?search=Matthew7%3A+12&version=NKJV.

"You shall love…as yourself," biblegateway.com/passage/?search=James2%3A+8&version=NKJV.

"We often describe…he holy provides in us," fca-devotional.blogspot.com/2011/03/holiness-of-god-rc-sproul-ch-3-fearful.html.

"There is no wisdom…against the Lord," biblegateway.com/passage/?search=Proverbs21%3A+30&version=KJV.

"High thing…knowledge of God," biblegateway.com/passage/?search=2+Corinthians10%3A5&version=KJV.

Chapter 10: The Bible Unveils God's Salvation Program for Mankind

"For God so loved the world…have everlasting life," BibleGateway.com, John 3:16, New King James Version (NKJV), Thomas Nelson, Inc., 1982.

"I have decided…a burden to bear," "A picture…a thousand words," "I you can't…out of the kitchen," "Keep your friends…enemies closer," "It wasn't raining…the Ark," 1-famous-quotes.com/top_ten_famous_quotes.htm.

"Good tidings…all people," BibleGateway.com, Luke 2:10, New King James Version (NKJV), Thomas Nelson, Inc., 1982.

"The dust…ground," "breathed…of life," "a living soul," BibleGateway.com, Genesis 2:7, Genesis 2:18, 1 Corinthians 15:45, King James Version (KJV), Thomas Nelson, Inc., 1982.

"But of the tree…thou shall surely die," biblegateway.com/passage/?search=Genesis2%3A+17&version=KJV.

"God is not…make it good," BibleGateway.com, Numbers 23:19, New King James Version (NKJV), Thomas Nelson, Inc., 1982.

"And death and hell…second death," BibleGateway.com, Revelation 20:14, King James Version (KJV), Thomas Nelson, Inc., 1982.

"The eyes…coverings," "hid themselves…of the garden," Genesis 3:7, Genesis 3:8, BibleGateway.com, New King James Version (NKJV), Thomas Nelson, Inc., 1982.

"Fearfully and wonderfully," biblegateway.com/passage/?search=psalm+139%3A+14&version=KJV.

"They ate…them all," "Let the dead…own dead," Luke 17:27–29, Luke 9:60, BibleGateway.com, New King James Version (NKJV), Thomas Nelson, Inc., 1982.

"philosophy…not after Christ," BibleGateway.com, Colossians 2:8, King James Version (KJV), Thomas Nelson, Inc., 1982.

"The life of an unregenerated…mind and will," Watchman Nee, *The Spiritual Man* (New York: Christian Fellowship Publishers, Inc., 1968), 62–63.

"heed…of demons," "able…of the truth," "to see…who seek God," "There is none…no, not one," BibleGateway.com, 1 Timothy 4:1, 2 Timothy 3:7, Psalm 14:2, Romans 3:10–12, New King James Version (NKJV), Thomas Nelson, Inc., 1982.

"So then faith…word of God," BibleGateway.com, Romans 10:17, New King James Version (NKJV), Thomas Nelson, Inc., 1982.

"According to the teaching…communion," Watchman Nee, *The Spiritual Man* (New York: Christian Fellowship Publishers, Inc., 1968), 31.

"A) The Function of Conscience...Rev. 21.10," Watchman Nee, *The Spiritual Man* (New York: Christian Fellowship Publishers, Inc., 1968), 33.

"Then Judas...and hanged himself," KJV, Standard Full-Color Bible (Ohio: Standard Publishing, 2007), 1127.

"Instructed...of the Lord," "the spirit...knowledge of [Jesus]," KJV, Standard Full-Color Bible (Ohio: Standard Publishing, 2007), 1274, 1349.

"Rejoices [not] in God," BibleGateway.com, Luke 1:47, Today's New International Version (TNIV), Thomas Nelson, Inc., 1982.

"Worship...in truth," KJV, Standard Full-Color Bible (Ohio: Standard Publishing, 2007), 1213.

"Quickened," KJV, Standard Full-Color Bible (Ohio: Standard Publishing, 2007), 1349, 1364.

"Made...alive," BibleGateway.com, Ephesians 2:1, 5; Colossians 2:13, New International Version (NIV), Thomas Nelson, Inc., 1982.

"Word...quickened me," KJV, Standard Full-Color Bible (Ohio: Standard Publishing, 2007), 734, 1395.

"Now if faith...to faith," St. Augustine, *On Grace and Free Will*, NewAdvent.org/Fathers/1510.HTM, chapter 29.

"Is not the sinner...without his assistance," Rev. C. H. Spurgeon, *Salvation Is of the Lord*, Spurgeon.org/Sermons/0131.htm.

"Author...faith," KJV, Standard Full-Color Bible (Ohio: Standard Publishing, 2007), 1402.

"Therefore God has mercy...to harden," BibleGateway.com, New International Version (NIV), Thomas Nelson, Inc., 1982.

"Again and again...we love and serve," D. James Kennedy, *Solving Bible Mysteries*, examiningcalvanism.blogspot.com/2008/07/d-james-kennedy-solving-bible-mysteries.html.

"If God chooses...receives injustice," R. C. Sproul, *What Is Reformed Theology*, ligionier.org/learn/series/what-is-reformed-theology/unconditional-election/?format=video.

"Find fault," "impossible to please Him," KJV, Standard Full-Color Bible (Ohio: Standard Publishing, 2007), 1302.

"On the contrary...back to God?" "over the clay...for common use," BibleGateway.com, Romans 9:19, Romans 9:21, New American Standard Bible (NASB), Thomas Nelson, Inc., 1982.

"Faith of the Son of God" KJV, Standard Full-Color Bible (Ohio: Standard Publishing, 2007), 1342.

"Did you receive...the hearing of faith?" BibleGateway.com, Galatians 3:2, New King James Version (NKJV), Thomas Nelson, Inc., 1982.

"But the scripture...them that believe," KJV, Standard Full-Color Bible (Ohio: Standard Publishing, 2007), 1343.

"We have boldness...the faith of him," KJV, Standard Full-Color Bible (Ohio: Standard Publishing, 2007), 1350.

"Boldly to the throne...in time of need," Hebrews 4:16, KJV, Standard Full-Color Bible (Ohio: Standard Publishing, 2007), 1395.

"Buried with Him...from the dead," Colossians 2:12, KJV, Standard Full-Color Bible (Ohio: Standard Publishing, 2007), 1364.

"Yea doubtless…God by faith," Philippians 3:8–9, KJV, Standard Full-Color Bible (Ohio: Standard Publishing, 2007), 1358.

"Common faith," "faith of the saints," "faith of God's elect," "faith of…Jesus," "faith of the gospel," KJV, Standard Full-Color Bible (Ohio: Standard Publishing, 2007), 1387, 1446, 1387, 1406, 1447, 1357.

"Remembering…our Father," "Wherefore…with power," KJV, Standard Full-Color Bible (Ohio: Standard Publishing, 2007), 1368, 1373.

"For by grace…walk in them," Ephesians 2:9–10, KJV, Standard Full-Color Bible (Ohio: Standard Publishing, 2007), 1349.

"For ye are…in Christ Jesus," Galatians 3:26, KJV, Standard Full-Color Bible (Ohio: Standard Publishing, 2007), 1343.

"Wherefore…all the saints," Ephesians 1:15, KJV, Standard Full-Color Bible (Ohio: Standard Publishing, 2007), 1349.

"We give thanks…to all the saints," Colossians 1:3–4, KJV, Standard Full-Color Bible (Ohio: Standard Publishing, 2007), 1362.

"And from a child…in Christ Jesus," 2 Timothy 3:15, KJV, Standard Full-Color Bible (Ohio: Standard Publishing, 2007), 1384.

"And after certain days…faith in Christ," Acts 24:24, KJV, Standard Full-Color Bible (Ohio: Standard Publishing, 2007), 1284.

"To open their eyes…that is in me," Acts 26; 18, KJV, Standard Full-Color Bible (Ohio: Standard Publishing, 2007), 1287.

"The promise by faith of Jesus Christ," "children…in Christ Jesus," Galatians 3:22 and 26, KJV, Standard Full-Color Bible (Ohio: Standard Publishing, 2007), 1343.

"Saints," "faithful brethren," "thanks to God…Jesus Christ," "faith in Christ Jesus," Colossians 1:1, 3, 4, KJV, Standard Full-Color Bible (Ohio: Standard Publishing, 2007), 1362.

"But continue…in Christ Jesus," 2 Timothy 3:15, KJV, Standard Full-Color Bible (Ohio: Standard Publishing, 2007), 1384.

"Concerning the faith in Christ," Acts 24:24, KJV, Standard Full-Color Bible (Ohio: Standard Publishing, 2007), 1284.

"Thy faith hath saved thee," Luke 7:50, Luke 18:42, KJV, Standard Full-Color Bible (Ohio: Standard Publishing, 2007), 1176, 1195.

"Thy faith hath made thee whole," Matthew 9:22, Mark 5:34, 10:52, Luke 8:48, 17:19, KJV, Standard Full-Color Bible (Ohio: Standard Publishing, 2007), 1099, 1140, 1150, 1178, 1192.

"Not of works…should boast," Ephesians 2:8–9, KJV, Standard Full-Color Bible (Ohio: Standard Publishing, 2007), 1349.

"The just shall live by faith," Habakkuk 2:4, Hebrews 10:38, KJV, Standard Full-Color Bible (Ohio: Standard Publishing, 2007), 1059, 1401.

"This is the Work of God…whom He sent," John 6:29, BibleGateway.com, Galatians 3:2, New King James Version (NKJV), Thomas Nelson, Inc., 1982.

"The standard of righteousness…with the cornerstone," Charles R. Swindoll, *Swindoll's New Testament Insights: Insights on Romans* (Michigan: Zondervan, 2010), 208.

"Furthermore…Christ's atonement," Charles R. Swindoll, *Swindoll's New Testament Insights: Insights on Romans* (Michigan: Zondervan, 2010), 208–209.

"The New Testament…Re. 22:12," Earl Radmacher, Ron Allen, H. Wayne House, *Compact Bible Commentary* (Nashville: Thomas Nelson, 2004), 788.

Appendix

"Let your speech always be…answer each one," Colossians 4:6, BibleGateway.com, New King James Version (NKJV), Thomas Nelson, Inc., 1982.

"But his wife looked back…a pillar of salt," Genesis 19:26, KJV, Standard Full-Color Bible (Ohio: Standard Publishing, 2007), 25.

"And every oblation of thy meat…thou shalt offer salt," Leviticus 2:13, KJV, Standard Full-Color Bible (Ohio: Standard Publishing, 2007), 127.

"All the heave offerings…to thy seed with thee," Numbers 18:9, KJV, Standard Full-Color Bible (Ohio: Standard Publishing, 2007), 196.

"Can that which is…the white of an egg," Job 6:6, KJV, Standard Full-Color Bible (Ohio: Standard Publishing, 2007), 640.

"And that which they have need…day by day without fail," Ezra 6:9, KJV, Standard Full-Color Bible (Ohio: Standard Publishing, 2007), 597.

"Ye are the salt…trodden under foot by men," Matthew 5:13, KJV, Standard Full-Color Bible (Ohio: Standard Publishing, 2007), 1092.

"Salt is good…have peace one with another," Mark 9:50, KJV, Standard Full-Color Bible (Ohio: Standard Publishing, 2007), 1147.

"Salt is good…wherewith shall it be seasoned?" Luke 14:34, KJV, Standard Full-Color Bible (Ohio: Standard Publishing, 2007), 1189.

"Let your speech be…ye ought to answer every man," Colossians 4:6, KJV, Standard Full-Color Bible (Ohio: Standard Publishing, 2007), 1365.

"For every one shall be salted…shall be salted with salt," Mark 9:49, KJV, Standard Full-Color Bible (Ohio: Standard Publishing, 2007), 1147.

Dear readers, you are encouraged to relate in the next few pages your top 100 individuals of all time! If you so desire, you may try to compare your top one thousand most influential people of all time to the author's. Please, feel free to send your list to the author's e-mail address: Piwb101@aol.com. God bless!

My Top 100 Individuals of All Time

1.
2.
3.
4.
5.
6.
7.
8.
9.
10.
11.
12.
13.
14.
15.
16.
17.
18.
19.
20.
21.
22.
23.
24.
25.
26.
27.
28.

29.
30.
31.
32.
33.
34.
35.
36.
37.
38.
39.
40.
41.
42.
43.
44.
45.
46.
47.
48.
49.
50.
51.
52.
53.
54.
55.
56.
57.
58.
59.
60.
61.
62.
63.
64.
65.
66.
67
68.
69.

A REQUIEM FOR EVOLUTION

70.
71.
72.
73.
74.
75.
76.
77.
78.
79.
80.
81.
82.
83.
84.
85.
86.
87.
88.
89.
90.
91.
92.
93.
94.
95.
96.
97.
98.
99.
100.

About the Author

Pierre W. Beausejour, the writer of *A Requiem for Evolution*, is a first-time publisher. After receiving his bachelor's degree in business administration from Baruch College, Pierre enrolled at the Alliance Theological Seminary in search of a master's degree in divinity. After completing nearly half of the ninety-four credits required for the toughest of all the master's degree programs—in fact, far more than the number of credits warranted for the Master of Theology program—Pierre left the seminary to complete a master's degree in education at Nyack College, a requirement that all New York schoolteachers should achieve within five years of their teaching career. After graduating from Nyack College, Pierre left the New York City Board of Education, where he worked for nearly two decades as a math teacher, an academy leader, a grade advisor, and a robotics coordinator.

Pierre has studied the Bible all his life under the tutelage of his dad, Jean—a pastor, writer, journalist, lawyer, translator, and a known linguist; Dr. Donald Hubbard of Bible Broadcasting Network; Pastor Daniel Mercaldo, the father of Gateway Cathedral; Pastor Jim Cymbala, the preeminent pastor of Brooklyn Tabernacle; Brother Harold of Family Stations; Brother Lee, the creator of Living Stream Ministry; Billy Graham, arguably the most influential evangelist of all time; as well as many of the most renowned televangelists of recent memory—Dr. D. James Kennedy, R. C. Sproul, Jerry Falwell, John Macarthur.